PININFARINA

PININFARINA

Antoine Prunet

Art and industry
1930-2000

Haynes Publishing

Interviews by
Luca Ciferri

Supplementary texts
Marco Makaus

Picture research
Ufficio Storico Pininfarina

Editorial supervision and production
Progetto Media

Graphic design, layout and cover design
Isabella Gianazza

Translation
Antony Shugaar

Editing
Claudia Vassallo

Editorial coordinator
Angela Grignani

Pininfarina. Art and Industry 1930-2000

*This British trade edition was published in 2000
by Haynes Publishing, Sparkford, Nr Yeovil,
Somerset BA22 7JJ.*
Tel: 01963 442030 Fax: 019630440001
Int. tel: +44 1963 442030 Fax: +44 1963
440001
E-mail: sales@haynes-manuals.co.uk
Web site: www.haynes.co.uk

ISBN 1 85960 684 9
Printed in Italy

Front cover:
'Rossa' prototype, 2000

Page 9:
A sketch by Pinin, for a vehicle with
wind-like cross section.

The dedication of the historian and author Antoine Prunet, as well as the helpful and intelligent assistance of Lorenza Pininfarina, who is in charge of public relations and advertising within the family-owned company, Francesco Pagni, who directs the company archives, and Pino Bardi of Progetto Media, who oversaw the graphic design, have all contributed to the creation of this remarkable volume, which recounts the intense and fascinating story of a workshop that, with the passage of time, grew to become a factory and finally an industry. In other words, Pininfarina.

This is a story of brilliant, forward-looking men, courageous insights, the fortunate convergence of events and the challenges posed by harrowing circumstances, and finally it is a story of notable and prestigious triumphs. This lively and captivating account will tell the story of seventy years well spent, in the pursuit of technical innovation and an unwavering adherence to impeccable taste.

The structure of this book has produced an unusual piece of editorial architecture, which can be broken down into three chief components:
—a meticulous chronological account, composed of text and image, of Pininfarina's work both in the automotive world and outside of it, showing the continuity of its corporate philosophy, consistently directed toward what is new and looking to the future;
—a sequence of images that concisely documents the successions of events in which the Pininfarina company played a leading role in this sector;
—a series of direct eyewitness accounts conveyed through so many interview/encounters (undertaken by the journalist Luca Ciferri) with both eminent personalities of the automotive world and with a number of the 2,600 employees who have worked and

continue to work for—and with—Pininfarina. What emerges is an open and non-corporate—sometimes even critical—commentary on this remarkable company and its history, as viewed from inside and outside, offering an unexpected and remarkable depiction.

This book is not mere hagiography; it adheres to a rigorous historical and documentary approach. This approach appears consistently throughout the text, covering these seventy years, and in the array of pictures, featuring over a thousand illustrations, many of them never seen before in print, which offer a gripping narrative of not only the development of Pininfarina itself, but also an overview of the larger context of culture, art, media, and society. A vivid and unusual monographic work on the way we have lived for much of the past century.

Giorgio Nada

In the year 2000, Pininfarina turns seventy, and it has been my privilege to be the president of the company for nearly half that time. This monographic work has been dedicated to the company by the publisher Giorgio Nada and I believe that it offers an unprecedented and complete vision of the reality of Pininfarina and the contribution that it has offered over the past seventy years to automotive progress in the broader context of the development of the society, culture, and history of our country. In 1966 I inherited an established company, but also a difficult task: to continue its success in creative terms and to promote its technological and industrial development. I can proudly say that I have always worked with three great ideals in mind: love for the product and a quest for aesthetic and technical excellence in that product; making proper use of human resources; the determination to operate with a 'style,' meant not only as the qualitative value of the design, but also as a consistent ethics of behaviour. This book is not meant to focus solely on the past, it is not meant as a celebration of ourselves: on the contrary, it considers the history and the strength of our tradition as a springboard from which to make a leap into the future. This is a young company, committed to a thorough-going and positive process of transformation and diversification, making a continual improvement in every sector of our activity a mission.

Sergio Pininfarina

Painting by the Maestro Ottavio Mazzonis dedicated to "The Presidents." Oil on canvas, 900 x 1,050 mm, 2000.

Art and Industry

Like so many other Italian families of modest origins, the Pininfarinas might easily have become Americans. Like other Piedmontese from the Asti area, they could easily have been farmers and winemakers. It was, however, the personality of one member of the family, Pinin, that moved things in a different direction. He followed his own instincts in 1930, laying the foundations for a success story that is still flourishing under the guidance of his heirs, 70 years later. The first and founding personage in this fascinating history was Battista Farina, the tenth child of 11 in the Farina family, hence the nickname of Pinin – meaning the youngest in the family in Piedmontese dialect. He was born in the last decade of the 19th century, coinciding with the invention of the automobile, as he himself loved to point out, notably in the title of his marvellous autobiography, *Pininfarina. Nato con l'Automobile* (Automobilia, Milan 1993). His parents and grandparents lived in Cortanze d'Asti, an area of Piedmont that produces a powerful and renowned wine, Barbera, but where labouring in the vineyards and wineries was unlikely to feed a large family. Little Pinin was just five when his family decided to leave the countryside to seek fortune in the city. The family moved to a suburb of Turin, the capital of Piedmont. Pinin had two dominant memories of his childhood: of his mother, 'the figurehead on the prow of our family ship', and the special joy that he took in shining the copper pans in the kitchen to a glistening lustre: 'The grilles of my cars, even the most modern ones, sometimes remind me, with their brilliance, of the modest trophies in our old kitchen'. From his schooldays on, he displayed a determined personality and a tendency to put himself in the forefront – a reaction, he believed, 'to his diminutive stature, a dozen centimetres shorter than his classmates'.

In Turin, the city of the kings of the House of Savoy, a guild of master craftsmen had sprung up as early as the era of horse-drawn carriages, specialising in the design, manufacture, and maintenance of vehicles of all sorts, carriages at

The Testing Centre in the Via Serrano.

The factory in the Corso Trapani in the Thirties.

first and automobiles in due time, with the foundation of the factories of Lancia and Fiat. Pinin's brother Giovanni worked as an apprentice for the coachbuilder Marcello Alessio, and this aroused Pinin's interest in cars. He would often wait for his brother at the end of the working day, and he would gaze with astonishment at the machines, so many 'monuments that gave me much greater pleasure than the many equestrian statues that filled the squares and plazas of Turin.'

Battista Farina had just turned 12 when his brother Giovanni opened his own body repair shop in Via Canova. He had secretly sketched hundreds of radiator grilles, automobile tops, and other items, clearly in the quest of ideas, but his elder brothers relegated Pinin to the seat department. The repair shop in Via Canova soon acquired a bit of a reputation in that specialty, and before long Fiat sent over a number of racers as customers. Young Pinin thus made the acquaintance of people who mattered in the automotive industry, such as Felice Nazzaro, Vincenzo Lancia, the Frenchman Louis Wagner, and other racers for Fiat. In 1910, Giovanni Farina decided to extend the activity of the workshops in Corso Tortona to include coachbuilding; also working in Corso Tortona were Giovanni's brothers Carlo and Battista, the latter now aged 17. Success came the following year, when designs submitted to Fiat by the Stabilimenti Industriali Giovanni Farina for a torpedo version of the Zero model won the approval of Fiat's president; the drawing approved by Agnelli in person was the work of little Battista, or Pinin. The Stabilimenti Farina were thus commissioned to build the bodies for that model of Fiat and Pinin was even given a violet-coloured car for his own personal use, 'like receiving a medal on the field of battle', as he later put it. Pinin soon began to dream of racing cars. He managed to persuade his openly unenthusiastic parents that the racetrack could teach him a great deal about cars, but his love of racing was cut short by obligatory military service at the age of 20.

He succeeded nonetheless in getting assigned to the Genio Automobilistico, and the remarkable fact that he possessed a driver's licence allowed him to become the personal chauffeur of a colonel who was absolutely fascinated by cars; this colonel was extremely pleased with the way the young Farina was taking care of his Itala. In reality, Farina had gone well beyond simple upkeep. He had souped up the engine, and liked to show off the powerful machine in the streets of Turin...

The First World War – Italy officially entered the conflict in May 1915 – caused Pinin to put off his racing ambitions indefinitely. Of course, events also threw the activities of the Stabilimenti Farina into complete turmoil. All cars were rationed for wartime use. The Farina factories were therefore retooled for the

The Centre for Research and Development, inaugurated in 1966.

The factory at Grugliasco in the Sixties.

manufacture of trucks, ambulances, and other vehicles for the rapidly evolving circumstances. Fiat had doubled its labour force in order to keep with the orders for weapons and for maritime and aeronautic engines, and in 1917 Agnelli himself suggested that the Farina family might venture into the field of aeronautics. Pinin, who had been an avid fan of aeroplanes ever since he was a little boy, immediately supported the idea, as enthusiastic as his brothers were diffident. Despite their hestitation, however, the suggestion was finally accepted; in time, the jury-rigged facilities of the recently founded company produced no fewer than 300 Aviatic aircraft with Gnome & Rhone engines. In 1918 the Armistice put an end to this all-too-brief excursion into a new field.

Peace coincided in Turin with a wave of strikes and an unprecedented level of revolutionary agitation. The Stabilimenti Farina returned all the same to making cars. Pinin gradually came to the conviction that craftsmanship and artistry were simply inadequate to meet the new economic challenge. 'The law of costs and competition does not take artists into account.' In other words, custom coachbuilding must necessarily give some considerable ground to mass production. Pinin had reached the decision that he needed to find a larger audience. He knew how he would fit in, too: 'If the market was going to grow, then the exceedingly precise design of prototypes would become more profitable and necessary, and manufacturing would offer various solutions in practical and economic terms.' The Farina factory in the 'Borg d'l fum' – the quarter of fog and smog in Piedmontese patois – was soon equipped with a first, pioneering stamping press, which sped up the production of hammered steel. That was a revolutionary step at the time, but for Pinin it was only the beginning. He had just announced his engagement to Rosa Copasso, but he decided all the same to take a trip to find out more about the industrial prophets in the United States. In Detroit, he succeeded in obtaining an interview with Henry Ford, who had inspired Giovanni Agnelli in the construction of his own, Italian automotive empire. Ford met with the young Italian designer and, during their conversation, the industrialist explained that coachbuilders who had failed to keep up with the new developments were doomed, without hope of reprieve. This helped to confirm Pinin's hunches about the direction of history. Intrigued by the personality of the young Farina and by the drawings that he had brought with him, the American industrialist offered him an attractive position in his company, but Pinin thanked him and declined, believing that 'it is better to be just the tail of your own fish than the head of somebody else's fish'. He returned from the United States with a few barrels of nitrocellulose paint and several shirts with tied collar, both complete novelties in the Europe of

Aerial views of the new Centre for Research and Development, built in Cambiano in 1982, and the factory at Grugliasco, built in 1958.

Facing page
Mass production: the Lancia Astura Bocca of 1937 and the Lancia Aprilia Bilux of 1946.

the time, but especially with a headful of new ideas that were to trigger tremendous and far-reaching changes. 'It was as if I had learned a new language' he later commented. The enormous popularity in America of the Ford Model T had convinced him of the vast potential of the automotive market, which was inevitably going to be a worldwide development.

In the meanwhile, Battista Farina married Rosa Copasso, on 12 March 1921, and his professional commitments in the family business continued to grow. They failed to prevent him, however, from pursuing another dream. He entered the second run of the hill-climb from Aosta to the Great St Bernard Pass, on 28 August, at the wheel of an Itala. He finished first in the touring category, but he was also pleased to renew the acquaintance of a number of famous racers that he had met, among them: Conelli and Minoia, who made the best overall time, coming in before Nazzaro. Last of all, he was pleased to see a racer to whom he had been introduced the year previous, Enzo Ferrari, about whom we shall

have more to say in other circumstances. Faced with his new responsibilities as a husband and father – Gianna was born the following year, and Sergio four years later, in 1926 – Pinin spent a limited amount of time and energy on auto racing, at least in the capacity of driver. Among the numerous manufacturers (Lancia, Fiat, Itala, Chiribiri, Isotta Fraschini, and Alfa Romeo) who commissioned the Farina brothers to build and assemble car bodies, it was Vincenzo Lancia – whom Pinin respected and admired in a particular way – who convinced him not to devote excessive time to racing. Pinin took his advice and only went to races and socialized in that setting to maintain his ties with friends and customers, rather than for racing itself.

In those years, Fiat had just 25 years of history, but the company had already acquired a

dominant position in Turin. The inauguration of the Lingotto plant, in 1920, extending for half a kilometre and boasting a test track on its roof, was one of the company's most recent visible manifestations. It was not yet common to say, as the Milanese would later do, ironically, that 'Turin is on your left, as you exit Fiat,' but it was already common knowledge that every family in Turin had at least one person who worked, directly or indirectly, for Fiat. Moreover, Giovanni Agnelli, the founder who that same year had been appointed president of Fiat, had also purchased the daily newspaper of Turin, La Stampa, in 1925, as well as founding IFI (Istituto Finanziario Industriale, literally, the Institute for Industrial Finance) in 1927. One might well wonder: is it possible to work in Turin without becoming a pawn of this mighty empire? Pinin thought that it was indeed possible to avoid Fiat's thrall, and in 1930 he decided to set up in business for himself. He commented, however: 'I worked extensively on

orders from Fiat: from the very beginning, if it had not been for Fiat, the coachbuilders of Turin would have remained little more than dilettantes, brilliant without a doubt, but nothing more than dilettantes'.

In order to achieve his goal of creating an industrial coachbuilding establishment enriched with a healthy does of fine Turinese craftsmanship, flavoured with creativity, Pinin was convinced that it was necessary to break with the tradition of carriages, the tradition that was still most popular with coachbuilders. But he was also keenly aware that the enterprise would demand a substantial redefinition of the profession, and he concluded: 'In our field, where personal initiative and temperament counted for so much, it was difficult to be so closely associated with both the successes and the failures of others'. And so he gave up his role in the Stabilimenti Farina, leaving the company to his brothers Giovanni and Carlo, and set up

for himself at number 107 in the Corso Trapani, with big signs readings 'S.A. Carrozzeria Pinin Farina', clearly distinguished from the company owned by his brothers, primarily by the nickname Pinin. The document of foundation dates from 22 May 1930. Pinin took special pains to explain that the separation was done in agreement with his family, and that it had been made possible through the generous contribution of Olimpia de Bernardi, an aunt on his mother's side. He also mentioned the encouraging words of Vincenzo Lancia: 'He was also generous with advice and assistance'.

As things turned out, the first vehicle to be registered with the new trademark of Pinin Farina – a P shaped like an F, unrelated to the stylised F of the Stabilimenti Farina – was a convertible chauffeur-driven coupé, dubbed the d'Orsay, and built on the prestigious Lancia Dilambda chassis. An advertisement dating from the same year shows a convertible Cabriolet that is slightly different, with a reference to the Paris Motor Show. Many coachbuilders had already taken on the challenge of the Dilambda chassis, foremost among them the English coachbuilders James Young, Mulliner, Vanden Plas, and Gurney Nutting, followed by the Italian coachbuilders

Viotti, Castagna, and Stabilimenti Farina, the German coachbuilders Voll und Rahrbeck, the American coachbuilders Murphy, the Belgian d'Ieteren and the French coachbuilders Kellner, Labourdette, and De Vizcaya. But Pinin Farina caught up with the competition in a hurry. His first creations on a Dilambda chassis for such renowned clients as the Principe del Drago, the Queen of Romania, the King of Iraq, or Signora Edoardo Agnelli, daughter-in-law of the all-powerful Senatore Agnelli, were all fairly conventional but nonetheless superb, much like the Isotta Fraschini 8A coupé built for the racer Carlo Felice Trossi or various spiders and cabriolets built on Fiat or Alfa Romeo chassis. In 1931, with a few extra workers, production at the plant in the Corso Trapani reached nearly 100 vehicles. In the catalogue of the special

The Alfa Romeo Giulietta Spider of 1954 and the Fiat 124 of 1966.

bodies, in the third year of the Carrozzeria Pinin Farina, 1932, there was a distinctive trend toward tilted radiator grilles and windscreens, again on Lancia chassis but also Fiat, Alfa Romeo, Hispano-Suiza, Mercedes-Benz, and even Cadillac chassis. In 1933, the tendency to tilt radiator grilles and windscreens, became more distinct, both on coupés and cabriolets, but also on sedans. The Lancia Astura Aerodinamica, a two-door coupé with a tapered tail and streamlined rear-wheel fairings, presented at the Milan Motor Show in April 1934, was spectacularly popular, and was purchased the day of the inauguration of the show by no less a name than the great racing champion Achille Varzi.

While continuing to work on custom orders, where his creative freedom was never entirely unhampered, Pinin intensified his aerodynamic research, and in 1935 developed a large sedan, without the rear volume, like the VW Golf, the Lancia Y, based on the Fiat 527 chassis, extended with a trailer for luggage, which was also streamlined. The car-and-trailer combination was quite unusual, and its owner, Madame

Jeannine Triarca, entered it in several automotive beauty contests. The same manufacturing year yielded a number of 'aerodinamico' coupés built on Alfa Romeo 6C 2300 Pescara and Lancia Astura chassis, featuring fastback rears and streamlined rear wheel arches.

In 1936, Pinin ventured further into the area of aerodynamics with the astonishing little sedan Lancia Aprilia Aerodinamica, entirely streamlined and featuring radical new pontoon wings. Three or four other versions followed, with subtle variations, as well as a cabriolet sport along the same lines, in 1938. The year 1937, however, was also marked by the unexpected death of Vincenzo Lancia, a grievous loss for Pinin. 'Their friendship was a source of exceptional technical conversation,' as Sergio explained later.

From the years just prior to the outbreak of the

Second World War, we should single out in Pinin Farina's production for special attention a sublime cabriolet (also streamlined) built in 1939 on an Alfa Romeo 8C 2900 chassis for Count Salvi del Pero. This dream cabriolet, built on a chassis that had previously been used for racing, was the star of the Concours in Nice on 27 May. Among its distinctive features was the front grille that took its inspiration from the grille of the single-seater Alfetta and the retractable front headlights, a device that had previously been seen only on the American-built Cord. Even more significant was the fact that the structure was completely made of metal, and wood had been excluded entirely: a major step forward. The workshops in the Corso Trapani built, in the same period, another Alfa Romeo 8C 2900 cabriolet on the chassis that Piero Dusio had raced with in 1937 and 1938. The design was similar, but the front end was more conventional, with an oblong radiator grille and oval headlights. We should point out that this

The Alfa Romeo 33 Giardinetta of 1984 and the Peugeot 406 Coupé of 1997.

car, thought to have been lost during the war, but rediscovered in 1989, was recently auctioned in California (USA) for a price of over $4 million. In 1939, the Carrozzeria Pinin Farina occupied a space in the Corso Trapani of 9,250 square metres. This was more or less the same floor space as in 1930, but the staff now numbered 500, and annual production had reached 800 units. War, which was declared by Italy on 10 June 1940, obviously threw everything into doubt. The workshops in the Corso Trapani were obliged to shift production from custom vehicles to the manufacture of trucks and ambulances. Later, they were asked to produce aeroplane seats. Pinin adapted to the new circumstances successfully. Then the bombing that hammered

Turin relentlessly, forced Pinin to move his operations. He chose Montechiaro d'Asti, near Cortanze, the town his family came from. Production, which by now included even a series of inexpensive wood cooking stoves, had an increasingly distant relation to cars, and when the Germans at a certain point demanded that he begin to produce boats for their army engineering corps, Pinin and his men decided to slow the workshop's pace of activity, with a sort of undeclared strike that entailed a certain level of serious risk. At the same time, they were putting the finishing touches to an understated sedan with four side windows built for the German Field Marshal Kesselring on an Alfa Romeo 6C 2500 chassis, a car that was influential over time.

By the time the war ended, Italy was on its knees. There were serious shortages of raw materials of every sort; business was at a standstill. At the Carrozzeria Pinin Farina, work started up again slowly in 1945, with the design and the limited production of the Bilux, a small

and exquisite sedan built on the long chassis of the Lancia Aprilia. It was indeed reminiscent of the Alfa Romeo built for Field Marshal Kesselring.

These Lancia Biluxes, the first example of limited-production cars, kept the core of the workshop busy. There were still very few custom orders, although a number of cabriolets were built on the same Aprilia chassis.

The last Italian Motor Show before the war had taken place in Milan in November 1938. The first after the war took place in Turin, but not until September 1948. Pinin was certainly not among the last people to sense the onset of recovery. Moreover, he had already begun to investigate the new Concours, which had started up again as early as 1946 in Turin and in San Remo, as venues in which to present his latest creations. In Paris, the Grand Palais reopened for the Motor Show in October 1946 but, as a reprisal against

The Cadillac Brougham of 1956 and the Mitsubishi Pajero Pinin of 1999.

the role of Fascist Italy in the war, Italian cars were not permitted to exhibit. That was hardly enough to discourage Pinin: 'I had a plan in mind, and I would not give it up, at any cost'. Two cars were ready at the time, and they suited his purpose perfectly. He himself took the wheel of an Alfa Romeo 2500 S cabriolet while his son Sergio – just 20 years of age – drove the Lancia Aprilia. Pinin recalled later that, as he approached Paris, for an instant he had the sensation of resembling a character out of Balzac: 'At the outskirts of the capital we cleaned and polished the two cars; then, under my breath, I spoke the trusty old words: Paris is ours...' (with apologies to Balzac's *Rastignac*). Because he had been shut out of the Grand Palais, Pinin and his son parked their cars right in front of the main entrance. It may have been just two cars parked out front, but in fact it became a counter-motor show. The press gave a great deal of attention to this happening that

had been staged by the Turinese coachbuilder, and so the spotlight was focused on the new Italian school of automotive styling. In all likelihood, the attention and results that ensued would not have been possible with a traditional presence inside the motor show.

In December 1946, a few days before Christmas, much less happy news reached the industrialist: fire broke out one night in the factory in Corso Trapani, destroying it in a few hours. Misfortune or arson? Pinin did not brood over the mishap. Instead, he set to work building a temporary structure. Even that was no easy task: there was a shortage of cement in a city that was rebuilding from the ground up, and 'the price of iron was still at black-market levels', as Pinin came to realise. He made a rapid decision: 'We shall build the industrial shed out of wood, and then we shall see'. Two months later, production began again, with triple shifts to make up for the lost time.

Pinin made an agreement with Bindo Maserati and Omer Orsi, the new owner of the Trident trademark, who wanted to introduce a new road-going Maserati. Presented in March 1947, at the Geneva Motor Show, the Maserati Sport A6 1500 offered testimony to the renewed

efficiency of the coachbuilder Pinin Farina. It was a very original grey coupé with entirely integrated wings, a small rear window set all the way back, silhouetted in three dimensions, a transparent sliding roof, and retractable headlights set in a marvellously clean-lined radiator grille. This interesting prototype was followed by a more conventional version, with normal headlights set at the extremities of the wings and a less rounded rear window. Above all, however, it marked the debut – beginning at the Turin Motor Show of 1948 – of a series of some 60 vehicles, several cabriolets and a vast majority of four-seater coupés even more rigorous than the ones that preceded them. Production continued until around 1951. Prince Bira, the Thai racer of the Maserati stable, was one of the most noted drivers of this car.

The next project, presented during the Concours of Villa d'Este, made an even greater impression:

The Testing Department (Thirties-Fifties) and the Centre for Research and Development (Sixties-Seventies).

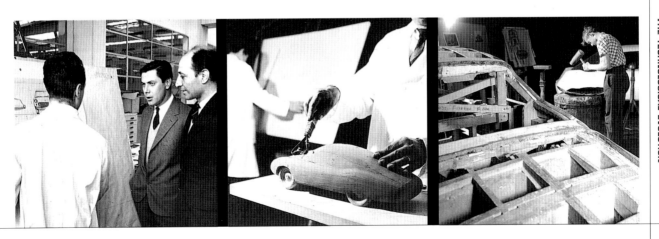

the car in question was the Cisitalia 202 that Pinin and his friend Piero Dusio – founder of Cisitalia, the one for whom Pinin had customised the Alfa Romeo 2900 in 1939 – had pursued in secret and with great enthusiasm since the darkest years of the war. Because of its remarkably sparse design, the lines of this little sedan took the entire world by storm, both consumers and critics, who wrote about the foundation of a new style, an automotive *new look*. The Italian School of styling was in the spotlight, and the planet witnessed validation of that view when the Museum of Modern Art in New York decided to acquire one of the cars for its collections as an example of sculpture in movement, as Arthur Drexler put it. Pinin Farina had introduced the automobile into the universe of art. Art and industry are two opposing shores that Pinin was cultivating with his customary virtuosity. His formula lay in the fact that he separated two apparently inseparable activities: creativity and manufacturing. The barrier between the two was permeable but strong. Since he had set up shop in the Corso Trapani, the design offices were near the workshops but

separate from them, with different addresses and entrances, at number 9 in the Via Serrano. And, as we shall have many opportunities to note, this formula was never questioned or contravened.

While continuing to execute special orders, individually or in small quantities on all sorts of chassis, often in the area of research and experimentation, Pinin Farina was constantly on a quest for what might allow him to keep his plants running on a stable, full-time basis. And so, in 1949, at the request of Jean Daninos, a French enthusiast who had worked for Citroën, and who later in the 1950s was to found the Facel line of cars, Pinin Farina came up with a coupé built on a Bentley Mark VI base, produced in a limited series in the plant in Corso Trapani, with a trademark consisting of a double F, for Farina and Facel, nicknamed the Cresta.

The Lancia Aurelia B20 was another successful project. This was a four-seater coupé whose style constituted a perfect synthesis of numerous discoveries and experiments undertaken over the years by Pinin Farina on various chassis, even though it was developed in part by Felice Mario Boano as well, who was then working at Ghia. The first embryonic version was probably the Lancia Aprilia presented at the Turin Motor Show of 1948, but many other individual vehicles built on Fiat, Alfa Romeo, and even Bentley chassis had appeared over time. This monocoque Lancia coupé, because of its many mechanical innovations, enjoyed considerable popularity beginning with its presentation, at the Turin Motor Show in 1951, and during the 18th Mille Miglia, a few weeks later. Four B20s competed in the great Italian road race to demonstrate the versatility of the new model. Its specifications evolved over the course of a production of more than 3,000 cars between 1951 and 1957. Its style, so unusual and

successful, required only a very minor touch-up. Contracts with manufacturers multiplied. The year 1951 also witnessed the presentation in the United States of a Nash-Healey spider designed by Pinin Farina. This first order from an American manufacturer to a European coachbuilder was of considerable interest. It was the outcome of a meeting between Pinin and George Romney, the president of the Nash-Kelvinator company who had come expressly to Turin for this project in 1949. The Nash roadster with an English engine made by Healey and body from Turin, along with the coupé that was soon derived from it, racked up sales of 150 in 1952, but Nash's ultimate purpose was another: it was hoped that this flower in the buttonhole would enhance the sales of their mass-market models, the Statesman and the Ambassador, by giving them a 'look by Pinin Farina, coachbuilder to kings'. Pinin was even enrolled in a far-reaching promotional campaign in the best American manner. The company styling office

had taken some liberties with the design submitted by Pinin Farina. Still, the operation worked for Nash, which was in a bit of a slump, and for Pinin Farina and his company, giving them a greater international reputation.

It was during this same period that Pinin and Enzo Ferrari first met, no longer racing in Aosta, but laying the groundwork for one of the most significant alliances in the history of cars and styling. Ferrari offered his version of events: 'My marriage with the Pinin Farina company will last. It began 15 years ago', he wrote in his memoirs, quoted in turn by Pininfarina in his own memoirs: 'I remember that Pinin was astonished at how much time I spent with him, just as I was astonished at how much time he spent with me. At a certain point, it became clear that one of us was looking for a lovely and renowned woman to dress, and the other was looking for a world-class couturier to clothe her'.

Pinin Farina recorded a few more details about the preparations for what he calls their wedding: 'This was in 1951 and Ferrari, through the intermediation of his trusted Carraroli, let me know that he wished to meet with me in

Modena. I didn't skip even a beat, and I answered: 'I am entirely willing to meet him, but I would prefer that he come first, to meet me in Turin'. Truth be told, I would not have minded letting him take a look at my factory. I was informed that Ferrari 'almost never left Modena' and that he would not be paying a call on me, and he was sorry about this because it was a major proposal'.

"Please remember', I replied, 'Turin is hardly at the ends of the Earth, and the second or third time, I will come to see him'. There was another tactical pause, as I believe is recommended in old manuals for diplomats. We reached a Solomonian solution. We decided to meet in neutral territory, in Tortona, with a very few witnesses. It was widely said that, since neither of us wished to be thrown from our horse, we

The technical centres built beginning in the Eighties.

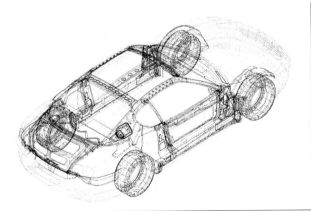

both climbed carefully down. But there was no one further than us from protocol, from the games of politics and the conquest of power; we liked unvarnished realism, the jargon of the workshop, and the background music of engines on test benches.'

In the absence of more-detailed information about the meeting, one may note as an aside that Tortona was a slightly longer trip for the car manufacturer from Maranello than for the coachbuilder from Turin. But the only restaurant in that town mentioned in the Michelin guide is named the Cavallino San Marziano, and Ferrari must have found in this reference to the Prancing Horse of Ferrari a welcome compensation... In any case, the meeting bore fruit quite soon, considering that the first Ferrari

by Pinin Farina, a 212 Inter cabriolet, was unveiled less than a month later, at the Paris Motor Show, in October 1952. The coupé on the same chassis was presented at the Brussels Motor Show in January 1953, heralding a limited series of 17 virtually identical cars. Pinin Farina and Ferrari had begun a journey together that was a spectacular as it was far-reaching, since the two names are working together, today more busily than ever.

Even more discreet, and even more significant in terms of consequences, was the meeting between Pinin and Jean-Pierre Peugeot at the end of 1950. The very first design for the 403 Berlina with the signature of Pinin Farina dates from 1951. Emerging from the overwhelming discretion was a second prototype – even closer to the mass-produced vehicle – dated 1953. Two more years would pass before the Peugeot 403 went into production in Sochaux, ultimately reaching numbers of 1,200,000 cars. As impressive as that number may seem, it is a trifle compared with what we would have if we added

up the production of all the Peugeots designed by Pinin Farina, or even those with bodies built in Turin, as is the case nowadays with the 306 cabriolet and the 406 coupé, some 50 years later!

There were certainly alliances that evaporated more quickly. The attempt at collaboration between Volkswagen and the Italian designer in 1952 is a good example. Pinin Farina explained the situation: 'I also met Professor Nordhoff, general manager of Volkswagen. I discussed with him the idea, already examined in our correspondence, of my possibly working for them. Concerning their new car, the 'bug,' I did not mince words: 'It is the opposite of my idea of a car, but it cannot have developed as it was by accident. Considering the functions it is meant to serve, it could not have a different form. I myself would not change a thing.'

The intuitive streamlining of the Lancia Aprilia (1936) and the Wind Tunnel, inaugurated in 1972. Sergio Pininfarina with Renzo Carli.

Nordhoff quickly realised that I was not just flattering him. And years later, events proved me right.'

Countless experiences with four-door luxury coupés and cabriolets built on chassis from the Rolls-Royce Silver Dawn or its sister vehicle, the Bentley Mark VI, as well as the Bentley R Type Continental, were undertaken for the gratification of some wealthy collector or other. Two interpretations on the Rover P4 chassis, far more elegant than the pompous mass-produced sedan, a cabriolet and a coupé, failed to persuade the British manufacturer in question. The same thing happened to certain models of the Jaguar XK120 and the Mark VII. British cars in that period had a very personal style that certainly had something to do with their popularity. It is easy to understand how the Turinese interpretations might strike some as alien to the style of the original manufacturer. Pinin however remembered one highly unusual customer: 'For example, there was Monsieur Perry Embiricos of Montecarlo, who brought me a Jaguar chassis, saying: 'I want to travel around Italy in a Jaguar with a body designed by you',

and who later wrote: 'I have been to Florence, Siena, and Parma with my Jaguar. What comfort, what beauty, what a wonderful car!' Depicting himself as a demigod in his Jaguar, he completely forgot to mention the beauty and wonders... of Florence, Siena, and Parma.' Other exceptions were tested and proved successful on a large scale with the English BMC group which manufactured – to Pinin Farina's design – a full range of sedans produced by Austin, Riley, and Wolseley. The best-selling models of the BMC-Pinin Farina joint venture were probably the little Austin A40, whose enormous popularity was proportional to the surprise created by its unusual design as a mini-estate car when it was first presented at the Paris Motor Show of 1958, and then the Morris 1100, with its various heirs, in 1963. The Alfa Romeo Giulietta Spider was stirring strong feelings even before its official

presentation in the definitive version, at the Turin Motor Show in April 1956. In fact, production had already begun, but the first 600 cars were set aside for the American importer Max Hoffmann who had played a crucial role in pushing Alfa Romeo to market a convertible version of the Giulietta (a role much like the one he had played in the creation of many other landmark vehicles of the post-war period, from the Jaguar XK120 to Mercedes Benz 300 SL, to mention only two). Hoffmann had even suggested that two coachbuilders be set in competition to develop the project and actually build the car. This competition for the contract involved Bertone, who had created the coupé, which had come out the year before, and Pinin Farina, whose project was finally selected, and whose factory in the Corso Trapani actually manufactured the spider. This model was so popular that it led to the construction of a new factory in Grugliasco. While waiting for this factory to be completed, the old workshops in the Corso Trapani continued to manufacture, in

The Wind Tunnel and its applications: the studies conducted by the Polytechnic of Turin; relations between Pininfarina and the CNR; the Aero-acoustic Research Centre.

diminishing order in accordance with the volumes produced, the Alfa Romeo Giulietta and Lancia B24 spiders, limited numbers of road and racing Ferraris, custom bodies for special customers, and research prototypes that might possibly result in a mass-production model. This was the case, for instance, in 1955 with two Lancia Aurelia Floridas, two prototypes whose taut lines contrasted sharply with the rounded shapes that were fashionable just then. These prototypes predated the original Flaminia Berlina presented at the Turin Motor Show of 1956 and marketed from 1957 on. Studies on the theme of the Florida were continued, carrying on with the prototype Florida II unveiled in 1957, foreshadowing the version of the four-seater coupé of the Flaminia launched in 1959.

'Where I come from, we inherit from the living, not the dead'
In 1955, with the assembly lines of the Giulietta Spider and the Lancia B24, a limited series of Ferrari Super Americas, as well as the usual

activities, the plant in the Corso Trapani was operating at full capacity, to the point that when Pinin designed a new version of the Ferrari 250GT coupé, he was forced to turn down the offer to assemble it as well. This job was, in fact, entrusted to Mario Boano, a veteran of first the Stabilimenti Farina and later the Pinin Farina company, who had gone to work for Ghia, and had finally set up in business for himself in 1953. For Pinin, this involuntary restriction became just one more of the reasons that led him to decide to build a new factory to replace the plant in the Corso Trapani, which was far too small. Sergio Farina and his brother-in-law Renzo Carli – Pinin called them 'my sons' – played a decisive role in this story. On a lot covering more than 3$^1/_2$ hectares purchased in the Via Lesna, in Grugliasco, on the western outskirts of Turin, ground was broken for the construction of a factory with an area of 28,000 square metres. The covered surface was more than triple that available in the Corso Trapani. The official inauguration took place in June 1958 and, at the end of the first year of activity of the new factory, 5,700 car bodies had

already been built. Pinin Farina had progressed from craftsmanship to industrial production. To those who offered him congratulations, Pinin would respond: 'The new factory was decided, promoted and designed by my sons. Now it is their time to run it.'
The new factory was divided into five sections: moulds and accessories, assembly of the bodies, painting, finishing and testing, and finally, research and experimentation. We should note, by the way, that the creative activity was separated from manufacturing: the old principle still applied.
The assembly line of the Ferrari 250GT coupé presented on 25 June in Milan was one of the first ones to be installed at Grugliasco. Ferrari was placing unusually high expectations on this model, since the order that was given to Pinin Farina called for no fewer than 200 cars, naturally after the construction of a number of

Research in the field of safety, which culminated in the Pininfarina Sigma of 1963 and research in the field of new techniques of construction, represented by the Peugette of 1976.

prototypes (also in the Corso Trapani), comparison of every last little detail, and tests of every sort imaginable. This was a record by the standards of Ferrari, even if the numbers were pretty modest compared with the 27,000 units of the Giulietta (and Giulia) Spider, which alone would have justified the move from Turin to Grugliasco. The working relationship with Ferrari had been strengthened: Pinin Farina had designed the entire range, including the Testa Rossa that had won the world championship that year, but he built the bodies only for the two most luxurious models: the 250GT coupé and the very exclusive 410 Super America whose third series, presented at the Paris Motor Show of 1958, was produced for a total number of just twelve cars in 1959. Also in 1959 appeared the Ferrari 250GT, a little sedan with a short chassis, and its purity of line remaining even now the absolute standard-setter. The year also witnessed the inauguration of the assembly line of the Lancia Flaminia coupé, derived from the Florida

II, whose style set the trends, with its taut lines and its rear fins continuing above the wings. At a rate of roughly three units a day, this plant would manufacture close to 5,300 cars by 1967. That was three times the rate at which the Aurelia B24 Spider had been built in the old plant. Production for the new factory in 1960, the second full year of operation, had nearly doubled, to 11,000 cars built.

The company had changed from the ground up. It was clear even when one looked at the outside of the new factory in Grugliasco. But would the arrival of the 'sons,' Sergio Farina and Renzo Carli, in place of the Founding Father – two engineers to replace a self-taught man – turn everything upside-down? Three examples chosen from among the creations of the year 1960 answer that question. The Berlina Aerodinamica X of the Turin Motor Show, with its four wheels arranged in an odd St Andrew's-cross configuration, with one wheel in the front, two on the sides, and one in the rear, and its innovative aerodynamic solutions, followed the line of Pinin Farina's first and greatest vocation, the making of prototypes which would certainly shine in the showcase settings of the Concours,

but which also suggested ideas for the future. Introduced in May 1960, the Peugeot 404 – which once again united the the Pininfarina trademark with the claws of the lion of Sochaux – is one of the most outstanding examples of co-operation between a designer and a mass-market manufacturer. Similarly, the Fiat 1500 Cabriolet offers a good example of the services that Pinin Farina could contribute in the conception and limited-series production of car models that would not be best served by large-scale automotive assembly lines. At the far end of the scale, the 'Felliniesque' special coupé built on a Ferrari 400 SA chassis, custom ordered by a private client – and not just any private client, but the 'Avvocato' himself, Gianni Agnelli – provided an excellent instance of the difficulties inherent in this sort of project.

The Audi Quartz of 1981: advanced technology and new materials.

A different example of ideas for the future was the Alfa Romeo 3500 presented in Spider Sport version in Geneva in 1959, and then the following year at the same place in a Super Sport Special version, before disappearing entirely. The only memorable element of these prototypes was their spectacular and entirely transparent roofs, but the Coupé Speciale Aerodinamico that was presented in 1962, again in Geneva, on the chassis of the Giulietta SS was certainly a direct descendant of them. And we would find that same familiar air in the 1600 Spider in 1966, again in Geneva. It was all a series of manifestations of the Duetto, whose assembly line in Grugliasco never stopped until 16 years later, in 1981, after producing nearly 30,000 convertibles.

In 1961, a decree issued by the President of the Italian Republic, Giovanni Gronchi, changed the surname Farina to Pininfarina. The official name of the family-owned company thus became Carrozzeria Pininfarina. Parallel to this semantic operation, the manufacturing business continued to grow. In 1962, the surface area of the plants in Grugliasco increased to 75,000 square metres, and production reached a high of 14,000 cars. A further leap took place in 1963 with 1,683 employees, and 19,844 cars manufactured. For Fiat, the 1600 cabriolet; for Lancia the Flavia coupé and the Flaminia coupé; for Alfa Romeo the Giulia Spider; and for Ferrari the 250GT coupé and the 400 Superamerica.

The year 1963 also witnessed the appearance of two models of Ferrari adorned with the legend design by Pininfarina, a further confirmation of the company's particular skill at developing bodies that could then be produced by third parties. In this specific case, the car was the 250 Le Mans and the coachbuilder was Scaglietti, who had for many years already been in charge of creating – under the direct supervision of Modena-based Ferrari – the bodies of the sportier models and the limited-production models.

At the Turin Motor Show the PF Sigma was presented, a sedan with sliding doors that introduced 14 technical innovations in the area of safety. Eight of those have since entered into current use. The year 1963 ended with the awarding of an honorary degree in architecture to Battista Pininfarina by the Polytechnic of Turin as the creator of the best-known and most highly regarded Italian coachbuilder on Earth. This honour would in time be augmented by the awarding of the medal of the French Légion d'Honneur, given him in 1965 by the President of the French Republic, General de Gaulle. The Paris Motor Show of 1965 was marked in particular by the presentation of the Dino Berlinetta Speciale, a research prototype focusing on form that would ultimately inspire the manufacture of both the Dino 206 and the Dino 246. Pinin would talk about this model as having been 'designed by his sons', and said that he considered it as his 'grandson'. He wrote, 'The

The attention to ecology (Ethos project, 1992-1995) and the design of a new form of ecological urban mobility: the Metrocubo, of 1999.

way the sides of the car were designed reminded me of the swept-back wings of supersonic jets. The Dino was exactly the sort of unexpected direction that I was hoping my sons would take, the best designs, the best systems are always the newest, the most recent ones, the ones that young people come up with. An edifying disproof of the words of those who say that in our field good taste lies dying'.

On 7 March 1966, the President of the Italian Republic Saragat officially inaugurated the new Centre for Research and Development, which replaced the Experimentation Division, and employed 160 in a new building occupying a surface area of 17,000 square metres, separate from the workshops themselves. Once again, the principle that Pinin had established of separating creativity and production had been respected. Battista Pininfarina died less than a month later, in Lausanne. Robert Lutz, the former chairman

of Chrysler, who placed him among the ten leading figures of the entire history of the car painted this portrait of him: 'Battista Pininfarina was not only an original, but one of the greatest industrial designers on Earth. It should be noted that he created more with his eye than with his hand, for he did nothing more than sketches: his fellow workers would take his orders to transcribe what he saw, turning them into many of the loveliest cars built before the war, especially a number of superb Alfa Romeos and Lancias. These cars clearly show that Pininfarina was also one of the first designers to establish the character of a vehicle not in terms of decoration but in terms of its functional form. His Lancia Aprilia of 1937 still tells us how far ahead of his time he was in terms of streamlining and aerodynamics. From coachbuilder to artist – the only coachbuilder whose work is exhibited in the Museum of Modern Art in New York – Pininfarina did it all'. Sergio Pininfarina thus became the president of a company, joining that title to his existing job as managing director, with his brother-in-law,

Renzo Carli. On the occasion of the inauguration of Via Pininfarina in Grugliasco, at the beginning of the year 2000, he spoke about his father again, in the words that follow: 'My father was a great industrialist and a fabulously creative designer, but I believe that his human qualities were even more exceptional than his professional gifts. What always struck me most about him was his love for young people, his will to learn, his sense of proportion and his determination – especially in his later years – to give back to his city and people what the world had given him'.

From an industrial viewpoint, the assembly lines at Grugliasco were working at full capacity on the Fiat 124 Sport Spider; this car, nicely

The Dino Berlinetta Speciale of 1965 and the BLMC 1100 'two volumes' of 1968.

designed, had just taken the place of the 1200/1500/1600 Spiders, which had been in production for seven years. The car was immediately very popular. The year 1966 also witnessed the introduction of the Alfa Romeo Duetto which – occupying though it did a market niche quite close to the 124, although Pininfarina certainly gave the two cars clearly distinct styles – was to enjoy lasting popularity, as well as a star role opposite Dustin Hoffman in the film, *The Graduate*. Alongside the Ferrari 330 GT 2+2, the GTC, and the GTS, the elegant Lancia Flavia coupé was beginning its fourth year in production. This was also the year of the introduction of the Peugeot 204, the third product (after the 403 and the 404) of a fertile collaboration with the French car manufacturer. Last of all, the surprising Ferrari 365P, a three-seater with the driver's seat in the middle, presented at the Paris Motor Show in October, and the Dino Berlinetta GT at the Turin Motor Show, a month later, both not only became desirable new additions to the remarkable collection of research-and-development

prototypes; they both pointed the way to the Dino 206 GT. Ferrari introduced the Dino 206 GT the following year, and with it set off on a new and promising adventure. Fiat had already signed an agreement to use the name Dino for a model with a V6 Ferrari engine; the cabriolet version had just gone into production in Grugliasco. Pininfarina went on to develop numerous designs for the various versions of the car, but marketing difficulties with this unusual Fiat unfortunately left those design no real hope of production.

After the inauguration of the Centre for Research and Development, the industrial complex of Grugliasco made a first step toward the computerised design of bodies, establishing a CAD centre, equipped with machinery capable of measuring the dimensions of existing parts or

prototypes and producing three-dimensional drawings on paper.

The Ferrari 365 GT 2+2 that was presented at the Paris Motor Show of 1967 replaced the 330 GT in the rarefied niche of the four-seater coupé, which had all the same become the biggest-seller in absolute terms of the entire Ferrari line. With its radically different style, the new 2+2 also replaced the 330 on the assembly lines of Grugliasco. At the Turin Motor Show a few weeks later, the Dino 206 GT appeared in its final form, with its wheelbase extended by a few centimetres to provide greater comfort. Its design – though offering no real surprises in relation to various prototypes already seen – was not uniformly popular with the public. The little Ferrari was slated to go into production in Maranello (and then to Scaglietti for the bodywork) in 1968. On the same occasion a streamlined hatchback sedan on a BMC chassis was presented, although it had no follow-up from the British manufacturer. On the other

The Ferrari Mythos of 1989 and the Fiat Sing and Fiat Song of 1996.

hand, it aroused considerable interest in others, particularly Citroën which adopted the same concept for the GS three years later, and for the CX in 1974.

Two events at the Paris Motor Show of 1968 threw the spotlight of public attention onto the coachbuilder from Turin. First, the introduction of the Peugeot 504, conceived by the designers and engineers of the two companies. Not only was this saloon became the car of the year, but, with more than three million built, the model beat every record in the annals of Peugeot. The second event was the unveiling of an entirely new Ferrari, the 365 GTB/4 Daytona. The car showed its appeal almost immediately, and the figures show it. Nearly 1,400 of the cars were sold in four years, an all-time record for Ferrari. At the Geneva Motor Show, in March 1969, the

Sigma Grand Prix was presented, a further study based on safety, but this time applied to Formula 1 (based on the Ferrari 312B). In a different sector, two new Peugeots once again attracted the attention of the numerous visitors. The cars in question were a cabriolet and a coupé built on the chassis of the 504; they were produced at Grugliasco until 1981, with changes and updatings limited to the mechanical sphere. In the list of purely experimental projects, two exercises 1969 clearly showed the versatility of Pininfarina's creativity. These were two prototypes for a little racing sedan, as spectacular as they were unexpected: one, built on the chassis of the Alfa Romeo 33, stood out for its magnificent rounded curves and gull-wing doors; the other was an incredibly low-slung car, the windscreen wrapped around to replace both the side windows and the roof. Its designation 512S Berlinetta Speciale seemed to make it a bellwether and a herald of the 512 S, which Ferrari produced in a series of 25 racing models, in 1970 – but in reality the two experimental sedans had relatively little in

common. The Modulo, presented at the Geneva Motor Show in 1970, a few months later, made extensive use of various features off the racing Berlinettas, but with no purpose other than as an exercise in purification of form to an extreme, in the tradition of the Citroën DS or the 'Barcelona' chair by Mies van der Rohe. Those comparisons were made by another great architect, Gio Ponti, in his preface to the brochure presenting this unique car, selected to represent Italy at the universal exposition at Osaka that year.

In June, the Alfa Romeo Duetto, with production at Grugliasco since 1966 reaching numbers of about 14,500 cars, underwent a major transformation. The rear section, which had previously been tapered in the shape of a cuttlebone, was now squared off. Thus the boat-tail was transformed into a truncated tail. This modification was meant to bring this spider

The Peugeot Nautilus of 1997.

closer to the rest of the product range of Alfa Romeo and, as we shall see later, it revived this car's popularity in a highly effective manner. The first event of 1971 was the inauguration in Grugliasco of the automated Centre for Calculation and Design (C.C.D), completing the CAD centre opened in 1967. At the Geneva Motor Show, there were no fewer than three worldwide debuts – the Ferrari 365 GTC/4, the Fiat 130 Coupé, and the Lancia 2000 Coupé – to raise high the banner of Pininfarina. This meant that the cars had passed – or were about to pass – from the research division to production and the recently expanded coachbuilding assembly lines. Sadly, the magnificent project for the Peugeot Riviera Estate on the chassis of the 504, presented at the Paris Motor Show, never went into production beyond the single car built, which remains in the Musée de l'Aventure Peugeot in Sochaux. Fortunately, this was not the case with the Ferrari 365 Berlinetta presented at the same show, but it would take two long years before the first Grand Touring Ferrari with a centrally mounted 12-cylinder engine went on the market. One noteworthy feature was the horizontal channel that ran

around the entire perimeter of the bodyshell, giving the impression of two stacked shells. This style feature, inherited from the Daytona, and further developed on the Modulo, was to become something of a Pininfarina factory trademark for many years to come.

The year 1972 was no less prolific. In Geneva – where the city's motor show by now ranked as the most important appointment in the European season – a sportier version of the best-selling Fiat 124 Sport Spider was presented. The bodyshell had been lightened, the interior equipment simplified, and fitted with rollbar and hard top, alloy wheels with oversize tyres and special expanded wings. This was a first project by the coachbuilder, and it would eventually lead to the Abarth version that won frequently in rallying. The same motor show witnessed the presentation of the 246 GTS, the convertible

version of the Dino, with its original removable top that could be stowed behind the seats. At the Paris Motor Show, Peugeot unveiled the 104, the smallest four-seater in European production, developed and designed in conjunction with Pininfarina. Paris was also the venue of choice for Ferrari for the introduction of the fourth-generation 2+2 coupé, the 365 GT4. Shorter, lower, and roomier, with a more spacious luggage compartment than in its predecessor, the 365 GT, it went on to become another best-seller and – under different designations but with only the slightest of stylistic retouching – it remained in production for more than 15 years on the assembly lines of Grugliasco.

The last notable event of the year 1972 was an in-house inauguration: the completion in November of the wind tunnel. The daring decision to add a wind tunnel to the equipment available at Grugliasco dated back to 1966 and, after various solutions were evaluated, work lasted for more than three years. The calibration

The Shell tanker-truck of 1937.

of that wind tunnel – one of the first on Earth and the first in Italy to use a full-size scale of 1:1 – took ten more months or so. Certainly, the farsighted nature of the decision to build the wind tunnel became increasingly evident with the looming menace of the oil crisis. One of the first concrete results of the new facility was the Abarth 2000 SE 027, a spider built for the European Championship of Manufacturers in the 2-litre category. It was first presented at the Geneva Motor Show in 1974. The wind tunnel made it possible to optimise the aerodynamic performance, but also to perfect the configuration of the interior flows of fluid and air, to cool the brakes, in the water and oil radiators, and to the engine compartment. After 16 months, the wind tunnel was working

at full capacity, not only for cars and bikes (with experiments on existing and planned vehicles, Formula 1 Ferraris, the Lancia Stratos or world-championship MV motorcycles), but in such varied areas as the equipment of the Italian national ski team, for establishing the best position to adopt during various forms of downhill descent. A further concrete automotive product of the wind tunnel was the prototype CR 25, a study of ideal aerodynamic form for a large-scale high-performance vehicle. This prototype was shown at the Turin Motor Show, bearing the Ferrari emblems, and it owed its designation to the remarkable drag coefficient of 0.256. Two more immediate projects from the year before, the Maremma Estate presented at Geneva and the Opera Berlina in Paris, both built on the chassis of the Fiat 130 Coupé, in production in Grugliasco since 1971, were fated to remain one-offs, undoubtedly victims of the first oil crisis.

Four very important presentations for Pininfarina came on the heels of one another in 1975, three of them at Geneva, in March. On the

one hand was the Peugeot 604, which was aimed at a higher market niche, while continuing a collaboration first undertaken 20 years earlier. The Rolls-Royce Camargue constituted Pininfarina's free-hand interpretation of a two-door four-seater coupé, derived from the Silver Shadow Saloon. This car of course was built in England, but it set a historic precedent: never before had the styling of a Rolls-Royce been entrusted to a non-British coachbuilder. Geneva, lastly, was the forum for the simultaneous unveiling of the Lancia Beta Montecarlo Coupé and the Spider. These cars also carried special meaning for Pininfarina, which had been commissioned for the first time to build an entire car, including the understructure. Another demonstration of the new industrial scale of the Turinese coachbuilder was further given in May, when the 100,000th

The BMC truck of 1996. The high-speed train, ETR 500, of 1987.

Fiat 124 Sport emerged from the assembly line that was regularly churning out 75 to 80 car bodies a day.

The last surprise of the year was the Ferrari 308 GTB, unveiled on the occasion of the Paris Motor Show. This two-seater version of the little Ferrari with a transverse V8 engine behind the cockpit differed from the Bertone 2+2 coupé introduced the year before by its wheelbase, 210 mm shorter, in one respect; the biggest difference, however, was the entirely different and seductive allure of its bodywork. The structure was mass-produced by Scaglietti with a tubular steel frame for a chassis, the body was made of synthetic resin instead of metal, a 'first' for a touring Ferrari.

At the Geneva Motor Show, in March 1976, two new Lancias designed by Pininfarina were presented: the Gamma Coupé and the Gamma Berlina. The coupé found its way to the production lines of the Turinese coachbuilder, while the sedan wound up on the assembly lines at Lancia. This one in any case stood out for its hatchback design which was also reminiscent of the streamlined saloon on a BMC chassis presented by Pininfarina in 1967. The design and development of the Lancia benefited, first and foremost, from the results of two years of testing in the wind tunnel. In July, the Centre for Research and Development was flanked by the Department of Numerically Controlled Machines – occupying a surface area of 300 square metres – which made it possible to streamline considerably the process of prototyping on any scale (i.e. to render in three dimensions drawings done by computer). And before 1976 was over, there was a two-fold event at the Paris Motor Show: the presentation of two new Pininfarina-Ferraris, a two-seater and a 2+2. The BB 512 was a 5-litre development of the Berlinetta Boxer, marketed since 1973 with a horizontally opposed 12-cylinder 4.4-litre engine. The lines that were established in 1971 on the prototype presented in Turin had remained unchanged save for a few minor details; production and assembly were done in Modena by Scaglietti. The 400 was, in turn, a development of the 365 GT4 2+2, presented in 1972. The bodywork had been slightly touched up, but the real news was the automatic transmission (400 Automatic), offered as an optional from the traditional mechanical equipment (400 GT). This was a revolutionary change for Ferrari, but it met with an enthusiastic welcome.

In Frankfurt, in September 1977, once again it was a Ferrari that was attracting attention to the Pininfarina stand: the 308 GTS, a convertible version of the GTB introduced two years before. This version offered a rigid removable top that was stored in a special space behind the seats. As

The G50 speedboat of 1968 and the Benéteau First 45 F5 of 1989.

with the little sedan the construction of the chassis/body structure was entrusted to Scaglietti; Ferrari had acquired a controlling interest in the company in the meantime.

In 1977 – despite the absence of the Paris Motor Show, which had become a biennial event – a new Pininfarina-Peugeot, the 305, was launched. The Sochaux-based manufacturer eventually sold more than 1.3 million of these cars.

When the Turin Motor Show debuted, in April 1978, the world of car manufacture was in the grips of malaise and confusion. The effects of the energy crisis, combined with a growing awareness of environmental and safety concerns, were exacerbated by restrictions on manufacturers that were sometimes authoritarian and in most cases harmful to the industry. In Italy, the picture was rendered even darker by staggering inflation, driving up costs and penalising manufacturers. It was in the midst of this critical juncture that Sergio Pininfarina assumed the presidency of the Association of Industrialists of Turin, a position that he held until 1983, a period that was further marked by the bloody culmination of

Italian terrorism – at least until the 'March of the 40,000,' in 1980, which put an end to the violence in Italy's factories.

This criticial situation did not catch Sergio Pininfarina unprepared, as was shown by the concept cars presented at the Italian motor show, the CNR and the Ecos. The first, developed at the suggestion of the Italian National Council for Research (the CNR), represented a study of the optimum shape to reduce fuel consumption in an average sedan, with a Cd of 0.201 as compared with an average figure of 0.460 for all European cars. The CNR won a prestigious Golden Compass design award for Pininfarina, another award that Sergio and Pinin now had in common. The Ecos on the other hand was a serious exploration of the electric-powered town car, a safe four-seater. It was the product of a

pioneering collaboration with the Fiat Research Centre.

It was during this period, in the heart of the worst crisis that Pininfarina had ever known – as was the case for the entire industrialised world at that time – that the decision was made to decentralise the Centre for Research and Development from Grugliasco to Cambiano. We shall return in due course, when discussing the inauguration of this research centre, to this enforced separation of the conceptual work and the actual manufacturing, one of the deep-rooted principles espoused by Pinin; here let us simply admire the courage of this decision, taken during a general situation that might have resulted in retrenching instead of expansion.

On the occasion of the British motor show, held for the first time that year in Birmingham, a city that was emblematic of the English car industry, in the same way that Turin was in Italy, Pininfarina presented the Jaguar XJ Spider. This design had been developed from the existing

The Pegasus of the Fincantieri (1996).

XJ-S coupé, and was meant to be built in a limited series. Its rounded shape evoked both the D-type and the E-type from the '50s and '60s, and the resemblance was only accentuated by the absence of bumpers, replaced by shock-absorbing areas that were integral to the bodywork, both front and rear. The Coventry-based manufacturer did not follow up on this project developed by Pininfarina, although the XK8 coupé and cabriolet introduced in 1996 do bear a distant family resemblance to this spider built almost 20 years earlier.

On 19 January 1979 the 150,000th body of Fiat Sport Spider emerged from the assembly lines of the Industrie Pininfarina SpA., to use the new corporate name for the Production Department. Presented in 1966 with a 1,500 cc engine, the

Fiat Sport Spider had been upgraded to 1,600 cc in 1969. From 1970 to 1975, this car was the Fiat warhorse in countless rallies. From 1974 on, it was built only for the North American market, which had already snapped up 43 per cent of total production. And this was hardly the end of the adventure.

In May, the attention of the automotive world focused on the 505, a new Pininfarina-Peugeot that was destined to become exceedingly popular. In the same spirit, Lancia had contacted Pininfarina for the restyling of the Beta four-door Berlina, presented at the IAA, the Frankfurt Motor Show. Autobianchi followed the same example for the updating of the A112, launched at the same time.

In July, Sergio Pininfarina was elected as a representative to the European Parliament, garnering 268,000 votes. He took his parliamentary seat and held it until 1988.

In March 1980, the Geneva Motor Show celebrated its 50th anniversary, just a few weeks before the 50th anniversary of the Carrozzeria

Pininfarina. The company in question was once again punctually present at the annual Swiss fair with two new creations: the restyled Lancia Montecarlo Coupé Spider and the Ferrari Mondial 8, a 2+2 coupé with a centrally mounted engine, destined to replace the 308 GT4 designed by Bertone. 'The theme that Ferrari assigned us for the development of a 2+2 seater with a centrally mounted engine was certainly a fascinating one, even though it posed considerable technical problems with the bodywork, especially with regard to the space set aside for the four passengers, the rear visibility, the usable space for luggage in connection with the distribution of weight, the behaviour of the vehicle in cross winds, the thermal and acoustic insulation of the cockpit and safety in case of impact, particularly in the front,' noted the press material, all of this while preserving a Ferrari-

The Aviatic of 1915.

Pininfarina family air. Pininfarina had accepted this challenge without fear.

The real celebration of the 50th anniversary, however, was reserved for the Turin Motor Show, which was held on a date corresponding almost perfectly with the famous date of 22 May 1930. The surprise was called Pinin and it offered, for the first time, a four-door Ferrari with a comfortable appearance, without giving up the sporty aspect that was intrinsically bound up with all the products that went under the two-fold identity of Ferrari-Pininfarina. Caught by surprise by this undertaking of his old Turinese partner, Ferrari himself carefully studied the project, and finally rejected it once and for all after deciding that a four-door sedan could never fit into his strategy. The vehicle is currently owned by Jacques Swaters, racer, manager, importer of Ferraris in Belgium, and the most important collector of Ferrari documentation on Earth. On the stand at the Turin show there was also a small collection of landmarks in the company's history, including the Lancia Astura Bocca that had recently been repurchased from an English collector, and a Ferrari 250GT SWB, newly restored with the use of the most modern equipment, which allowed the restorers to determine the distinctive dimensions of the bodies of various individual cars of this model, and thus establish a paradigmatic configuration.

The Lancia Beta Montecarlo Turbo – with body designed and built by Pininfarina – won the World Endurance Championship for 1981, and again in 1982.

An agreement with Nuova Agudio for the design and construction of a series of cableway cabins was announced in November. Although largely ignored by the media, the agreement was important all the same, and formed part of the program of diversification that Pininfarina had announced. Other products aliene to the automotive sector would follow, ranging from wristwatches to equipment for public works, and from skiboots to the interiors of aeroplanes, leading ultimately to the foundation in 1986 of Pininfarina Extra, meant to work exclusively in the field of product design.

In the context of research into the future of cars in general and into the contribution that the design of car bodies could make to fuel savings in particuliar, Pininfarina presented the Quartz in Geneva in March 1981. This coupé on an Audi 4x4 chassis, greatly lightened by the use of a startling welter of new materials that had just come on to the market or which were about to make their debut: Kevlar honeycomb, aluminium, steel-polyurethane sandwich structure, polycarbonate, carbon fibres, and so on. Presented at the same motor show was a new European version of the Fiat 2000 Spider I.E., marking the return to the European market – with a 2-litre engine with the Bosch L-Jetronic electronic injection – of the renowned spider designed and manufactured by Pininfarina (186,000 units built since 1966).

The interior of the Piaggio 808 aeroplane (1968).

At the Brussels Motor Show, in January 1982, the Talbot Samba Cabriolet was unveiled, the 15th model to emerge from the collaboration of Peugeot and Pininfarina, now entering its 27th year. For this model, which was still exploring virgin territory – that of small cabriolets derived from runabouts – Peugeot decided to make use of the Talbot trademark, and Pininfarina developed a complete programme, running from the original design to the industrialisation plan and, finally, regular production in Grugliasco. The Pininfarina stand at the Geneva Motor Show in March offered a different flavour, and presented the well-known coachbuilder in a brand-new role: that of car builder proper. The new product was the Pininfarina Spider Europa. This commitment rested on a new agreement between Fiat and Pininfarina concerning production. The first automobile to bear only the Pininfarina name, revised and modernised at various points, it was built from start to finish in Grugliasco and then marketed in the USA by Fiat Motors of North America and in Europe by a marketing network tied to Fiat. During the same

period, production began on the Peugeot 505 Estate and the Lancia Rally, a limited series derived from the Beta Montecarlo, for homologation and for rallying programme. On the eve of the opening of the Turin Motor Show, the official inauguration of the new research and study centre took place; work on the centre had begun in August 1980, and opened three months later. The centre was located in the township of Cambiano, some 20 minutes south-west of Grugliasco, and bore out Pinin's principle of always separating the conceptual work from actual production in order to manage better the various demands of designers and technicians; moreover, it was increasingly important, as Pininfarina worked more and more with different car makers, to protect the confidentiality of the creative

process. The new research centre covered 13,780 square metres, located on land covering 51,000 square metres. And this physical separation was further underscored by a legal division, with the creation of a new business entity, the Pininfarina Studi e Ricerche SpA (literally, Pininfarina Research and Development), quite distinct from Industrie Pininfarina SpA. The wind tunnel, of course, remained at Grugliasco, and so a workshop was established next to it in order to make immediate modifications on the prototypes being tested. The architecture of the main building, which was soon dubbed in common parlance, quite simply, Cambiano, took into account first and foremost the requirements of the various phases of work. Design work took place in two separate phases, with two distinct working groups: the development of models and scale drawings on the one hand, calibration of the 1:1 full-scale model and the execution of the prototype on the other. These two sectors, each of which had their own oversight facilities,

Military kitchens from the Second World War and the Ola Snaidero of 1992.

meeting rooms and facilities for making presentations to clients, were each installed on opposite sides of the main building, which also housed the reception area and a small museum. Nearly half of the land was transformed into a park, with a small lake that had also been conceived as a reservoir in case of fire – in the centre of the lake was perched, like some latter-day pagan Venus, a white Ferrari Daytona body shell – and with a restored farmhouse, now serving as accommodation for guests.

The star of the winter motor shows in Paris and Birmingham was the Lancia Gamma Olgiata, an elegant version of a two-door estate car based on the front-wheel-drive coupé presented in Geneva in 1976 and built in Grugliasco ever since. For each of the two occasions, two previous prototypes were displayed: the T-roof spider of 1978 and the Scala notchback sedan of

1980. The Spidereuropa and the Talbot Samba Cabriolet shared the remaining space on the stand.

From 1 May to 31 October Knoxville, Tennessee had hosted the international energy expo, attracting nearly 12 million visitors. Italy built a national pavilion to commemorate its own contributions to the history of science, from Galvani to Fermi. At the entrance to the pavilion the 1978 CNR stood on display; this prototype was the result of a study undertaken jointly by the Italian National Council for Research and Pininfarina.

Again in the United States, at the Miami Boat Show, the newest product of Pininfarina's diversification was presented, crowning the year: the Magnum Pininfarina, a streamlined 63ft speedboat that could reach speeds of 45 knots, powered by twin V16 Detroit Allison diesel engines, developing 1,300 hp each.

The 1983 automotive year began with the introduction of the Peugeot 205, the product of the new collaboration established with the styling office of the French car manufacturer. Peugeot's objective was to produce a compact but comfortable sedan, economic to run but

easy to develop into various versions and engine sizes. Its popularity, enhanced by its exceptionally pretty lines, was greater than anyone expected.

In Geneva in March, the new 205 was flanked, on the Pininfarina stand, by two other worldwide exclusives. One was a restyled version of the Alfa Romeo Spider with the truncated tail, production of which at Grugliasco since 1970 had passed 50,000 units. The restyling basically consisted of the adoption of American-style bumpers; a spoiler had been built into the front end, under the bumper and, and in the rear, over the boot, while the dashboard had been entirely redesigned. This third-generation car with improved streamlining perpetuated the popularity of the Alfa Romeo Spider.

The Orfina Modulo of 1983 and the model G. Cool Type of 1999 for Casio.

The second new product was the Pininfarina Spidereuropa Volumex, the latest version of the 124 Spider first built in 1966, some 200,000 of which had been built in Grugliasco. A supercharger had increased the power of the 2-litre four-cylinder engine from 105 to 135hp. More powerful brakes, recalibrated suspension and wider alloy wheels equipped with Pirelli P7 tyres completed the mechanical modifications. This was in effect the actual production of the Abarth Spidereuropa announced at the Turin Motor Show the year before.

For several years now, Sergio Pininfarina had been publicly explaining his own views on politics and business in Italy, especially during a design conference at Aspen, Colorado in June 1981. He had entitled his talk: 'An industrialist in the land of Machiavelli: a tough job'. His election in June 1983 as president of Federpiemonte, the Federation of Manufacturers of Piedmont, was another step on the path to a national role in Italian life. In the meantime, the British Royal Society of Arts conferred upon Sergio Pininfarina the title of Honorary Royal Designer for Industry, an honour that had been bestowed upon his father 30 years before, an unprecedented event in the history of that institution.

At the IAA in Frankfurt, in September, the Alfa Romeo 33 4x4 was presented, the result of a study by Pininfarina at the Turin Motor Show of 1982, based on the Alfasud chassis.

The triumph of the Lancia Beta Montecarlos designed by Pininfarina in the World Rally Championship ended 1983 on a positive note for the Italian coachbuilder.

Every other year, in January, the first European motor show was held in Brussels. In 1984, the Pininfarina stand in the Palais du Heysel served as the first motor show for the Ferrari Mondial Cabriolet, unveiled during the Ferrari Days in Modena in September and already on sale in the United States, a market for which it had primarily been designed and built. Pininfarina complied with the letter of the commission, which asked him to maintain the car's style without increasing its weight or diminishing its comfort. The cabriolet did improve the disappointing sales of the Mondial, although not enough to approach the initial objectives.

The wind tunnel came back into the story when it was made available to the cyclist Francesco Moser to help him in preparing for setting a one-hour record, and later to the mountain climber Reinold Messner, to develop the equipment needed for his climbing exploits. For Pininfarina, it was also a way of proclaiming the company's interest in competition.

One of the most important events of the Geneva Motor Show of 1984 was the presentation of the Ferrari 288 GTO, a version derived from the 308, with an engine beefed up to 400HP by the addition of two turbo chargers. The considerable increase in performance forced Pininfarina to revise the initial body design for the 308 GTB in

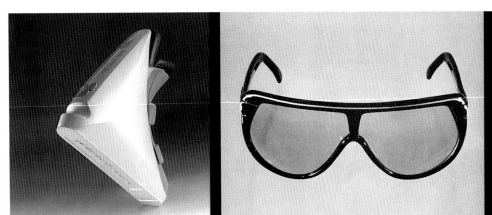

various ways. This special version enjoyed considerable acclaim and production (with the body by Scaglietti), announced as limited to 200 cars, the minimum required for homologation in Group B, was much higher... although no-one ever saw the ten racing cars that had been announced. The same Geneva Motor Show also witnessed the debut of the Alfa Romeo 33 Giardinetta estate car, with two-wheel and four-wheel drive; the mechanical side of this car had also been developed by Pininfarina.

At the Paris Motor Show, the Ferrari Testarossa had had its worldwide debut, donning the mantle of the retiring 512BBi. The decision to install the radiators in front of the rear wheels pushed Pininfarina to seek out completely new forms in a total break with the past. The Testarossa was spectacularly popular from its debut, and set a record at the Paris Salon at the Porte de Versailles, with 26 confirmed sales, at a

price of nearly 900,000 francs each. The success of this new collaboration between Ferrari and Pininfarina (who also manufactured the body at Grugliasco) was not ephemeral: the Testarossa and its derived versions, the 512 TR and the 512M, remain to this day the 'best sellers' of the 12-cylinder vehicles built in Maranello.

The year 1984 also witnessed the development of the relationship with two other major manufacturers, Honda and Cadillac. These contacts offered enormous potential, to the degree that it was decided to build a new factory covering more than ten hectares of land, at San Giorgio Canavese, near the airport of Caselle, some 26 kilometres to the north of Turin, with an investment of about 50 billion Italian lire over a three-year period.

At the Geneva Motor Show of 1985, Pininfarina presented two new developments that were slightly more restrained than those of the year before. The Ferrari 412 represented a slight restyling for the final version of the 400. The prototype of the Peugeot Griffe 4, a sporty coupé endowed with a particularly luminous top,

had two goals. In the first place it was meant to celebrate the 30th anniversay of collaboration with the French car maker, which had begun with the 1955 Peugeot 403. But it was also meant to shake up the coupé sector which, after the boom of the 1950s and '60s, was beginning to vanish from the showrooms. There were two other models on the stand: the Alfa Romeo 33 Giardinetta, for which Pininfarina had overseen various phases of production right up to complete assembly, including mechanical parts, and a revised Pininfarina Spidereuropa, with some technical innovations, while a new series of 300 examples of Spider Volumex was to follow the 200 that had been programmed initially. It was then announced that the Cadillac convertible would be launched, to be

On this page and on the following pages Advertising communication from the Thirties to the present.

Facing page
The Garmont ski boot of 1974, Ratti eyeglasses of 1982, and eyeglasses for the Ferdinand Menrad Group of 1991.

manufactured in the new factory in San Giorgio Canavese, planned for the second half of 1986 and dubbed the Allanté.

In July, the 200,000th Fiat Spider, which had become in the meanwhile the Pininfarina Spidereuropa, emerged from the factory of Grugliasco where, in the context of a vast programme of investments, a new painting facility was going into operation.

Pininfarina was present at the Frankfurt Motor Show with three worldwide premieres: two Ferraris and one Lancia. On the Ferrari 328 GTB and 328 GTS – replacing the 308 GTB and the 308 GTS after ten years of popularity – a slight restyling accompanied the new transverse V8 engine, beefed up from 3 litres to 3.2 litres. The same mechanical evolution and a few details and improvements transformed the 2+2 coupé and cabriolet into the Mondial 3.2. In contrast with the two Ferraris, which would have their

bodies mounted by Scaglietti, the Lancia Thema estate car – which embodied various new ideas by Pininfarina – was scheduled for production in Grugliasco beginning in the second half of 1986, not for bodywork alone, but also for the assembly of various mechanical components. The introduction of the Peugeot 205 cabriolet, at the Geneva Motor Show in March 1986, confirmed that collaboration between Peugeot and Pininfarina was as solid as ever, following the commemoration of 30 years working together. The objective of adapting the cabriolet to the original silhouette of the three-door version had been attained successfully. Pininfarina had been commissioned to manufacture complete car bodies at a rate of 50 per day; the finished bodies were then shipped to the Peugeot plant in Mulhouse.

In Geneva as well, the Alfa Romeo Spider (more than 83,000 of wich had been built in three body versions since it was introduced in 1966) made way for a fourth version, dubbed the Quadrifoglio Verde.

The first presentation of the Cadillac Allanté, took place at Palm Beach, Florida, in March, and

was reserved for the Cadillac sales network of America, while the preparation of the factory in San Giorgio Canavese, where the bodywork was to be assembled, was not yet complete. Numerous events would take place in the United States, while the European launch was not scheduled until the Paris Motor Show, in October.

Next came the Turin Motor Show, in April. Without wasting time, Pininfarina had developed two studies for a Vivace spider and a coupé, and they were exhibited alongside the Quadrifoglio Verde Spider. Some influence of these two prototypes based on lightness, streamlining, compactness, and the traditional image of Alfa

Romeo, could be seen in the new models presented in Paris in 1994.

In April 1986, Pininfarina Extra was founded; this company was to focus on the development of sectors of activity outside of the field transport. Among the first products was a line of luggage, presented at the Mipel in September. As the company grew, it developed varied products: telephone sets for Telecom Italia, percolators for Lavazza, watches for Casio, furniture for Poltrona Frau, electric home appliances for Riello, stoves for Snaidero, interactive helmets for Computer Union, architectural complexes for the island nation of Malta, and even one order for a building that would house a scientific base in the Antarctic.

Before summer, a light-grey Ferrari Testarossa Spider with a white roof was delivered to 'l'Avvocato', Giovanni Agnelli: a one-off that had been kept absolutely secret for many months.

Aside from the identity of its new owner, this unique Testarossa was interesting because it indicated a continual, although not excessively showy activity on the part of Pininfarina in the construction of one-off vehicles for special customers. In effect, this activity was to grow considerably in the years that followed.

In October, at the Paris Motor Show, the Pininfarina stand displayed the Alfa Romeo Quadrifoglio Verde, the Ferrari Testarossa, the Lancia Thema estate car, the Peugeot 205 Cabriolet and, of course, the Cadillac Allanté, which was making its official debut in Europe. Production had begun in Detroit, where components were manufactured and then shipped to Turin, where they were assembled in Grugliasco and San Giorgio Canavese. Several Alitalia and Lufthansa Boeing 747 cargo planes shuttled finished bodies back and forth between Caselle and Detroit. More than 22,000 Allantés were thus shipped to the United States throughout 1993.

These sizeable investments led to a capital increase – from 10 to 13.2 billion lire – covered by a corresponding float of 25 per cent more shares. Pininfarina was by now quoted in the Milan stock market.

Another event of the year 1986 was the announcement by Breda Ferroviaria of an exclusive collaboration with Pininfarina in the design of the Italian high-speed train, the ETR 500, the aerodynamic research, styling, and interior decoration. For once, in Geneva in March 1987, Pininfarina had nothing new to present at the motor show. On the other hand, the first 1:5 scale models of the ETR 500 were presented at the first Transpublic Motor Show, in April.

In May 1987, Peugeot launched the 405, a notchback sedan designed by Pininfarina and positioned in the upper-middle market segment.

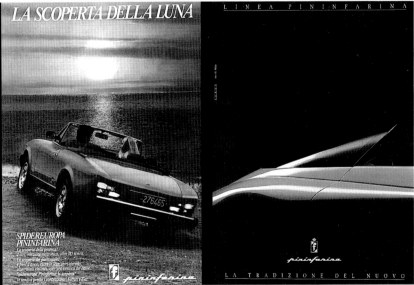

The 405 won the enviable recognition of Car of the Year for 1988, heralding an enormous popularity. Two more worldwide innovations, whose design was developed by Pininfarina Studi e Ricerche, were presented in September at the enormous IAA car show in Frankfurt. First and foremost, the Alfa Romeo 164, a sporty notchback sedan with the mission of reinforcing the worldwide image of the company. Also, the Ferrari F40, designed with the collaboration of Cambiano; the designation referred to the 40th anniversary of Ferrari, the 'Casa di Maranello'. This extreme two-seater little sedan, equipped with a V8 twin-turbo 478hp engine, was to enjoy astounding popularity, with more than 1,300 cars sold at the peak of the speculative supercar boom. In the sector of public transport, the Bredabus 2001, presented in the same period, attracted notice for the comfort it provided to passengers. The exterior and interior design of industrial and touring vehicles for Breda was developed by Pininfarina, which continued to expand its activity in that field as well.

During the course of the year 1987, the plants of the Industrie Pininfarina, whose assembly lines were producing the Ferrari Testarossa and the Ferrari 412, the Lancia Thema estate car, the Peugeot 205 Cabriolet, the Alfa Romeo Spider, and the Cadillac Allanté, were the subject of a three-year programme of renovation and updating, at a cost of some 80 billion Italian lire. An increase in production from 21,000 to 22,000 vehicles was planned for 1988, chiefly through the addition of a special series of the Peugeot 205 Cabriolet alongside the CT and CTI versions already in production: the Peugeot 205 Cabriolet Junior, presented in Geneva, was an even lower-priced convertible, targeting a younger consumer.

The Turin Motor Show in April 1988, saw the presentation of the Hit concept car, a 2+2 coupé wedding the mechanical side of the Lancia Delta Integrale with a chassis and body made of carbonfibre. The purpose of this vehicle was to explore a new area of use with a compact and light coupé, sporty in terms of transmission and engine, and attractive in terms of silhouette and its mild-mannered personality.

On 26 May, Sergio Pininfarina was elected by a wide majority as the president of Confindustria, the Association of Italian Manufacturers. That allowed him right up to 1992 to play a leading role in the abolition of the wage-price index, in favour of a payment and salary system based more on efficiency than on automatic wage-hike mechanisms.

In the wake of the popularity of the Peugeot 405 in its difficult market segment, the estate version was presented at the Paris Motor Show, clearly showing the 'fingerprints' of Pininfarina. The result of a study by Pininfarina, an electric convertible roof mechanism, was also presented for the Peugeot 205 Cabriolet on that occasion,

and was rapidly installed on production vehicles manufactured at Grugliasco.

In March 1989, the big news at the Geneva Motor Show was the Cadillac Allanté in its European version. The Cadillac convertible, hitherto restricted to the North American market, was presented with a more powerful engine and with several improvements in function and appearance, and meant to make the car meet more closely with European expectations.

In Frankfurt in September, Ferrari presented the latest model to emerge from the company's collaboration with Pininfarina, the 348. Offered simultaneously in sedan and open-top versions, it was replacing – with its V8 engine now placed longitudinally in front of the rear train – the 328, which had sold quite well.

The Tokyo Motor Show, a huge automotive showcase for the Far East, witnessed Pininfarina's first presentation in 1989, a demonstration of his intent to become a global player. A surprise for that occasion was the Mythos. This prototype concealed the mechanical structure of the Testarossa beneath an extreme version of a spider, a reaction against the monotony of bio-design. The Mythos fitted into the lineage of the 250 P5 of 1968, the 512 S of 1969, and the Modulo of 1970, in the wake of a nine-year drought of 'dream cars', which many were beginning to find excessively long, beginning with Lorenzo Ramaciotti, general manager of Pininfarina Studi e Ricerche. The Mythos was the first non-Japanese concept car to win the readership poll organised by the Japanese magazine, *Car Styling*. It was also named Concept Car of the Year by the international jury of the Car Design Award. The year 1989 ended with the Boat Show of Paris, where Bénéteau presented the F45, a yacht designed by Pininfarina, a collaboration that would produce many more yachts and powerboats. The NAIAS (North American International Auto Show) opened a few days later in Detroit. Pininfarina took part for the first time, presenting the Mythos, the Cadillac Allanté, as well as a new version of the Alfa Romeo Spider. This fourth restyling of the Duetto, of which more than 100,000 had been produced since its introduction in 1966, was pretty thorough-going, especially on the rear of the car, with a small integral spoiler on the boot in place of the black plastic spoiler applied to the previous model. Beginning in 1968, Pininfarina had taken over the entire construction process of the Alfa Romeo Spider, right up to delivery to the sales network.

In March 1990, in Geneva, the Mythos and the Alfa Romeo Spider were given their European premiere, while the Peugeot 205 Cabriolet 'Roland Garros', a special series inspired by the renowned French tennis tournament, was inaugurating the electric convertible roof motor conceived by Pininfarina. In total, the production of the 205 Cabriolet went well over 72,000 cars. Eleven years after the design of an ideal aerodynamic shape was presented at the Turin Motor Show of 1978 by the CNR, Pininfarina

The Automotive Beauty Contest of Como of 1934 and the Paris Motor Show of 1946.

designed and built, in collaboration with Fiat Auto and again for the same agency, a new prototype exploring the theme of energy conservation. The result was a project for a mid-sized European sedan with a plastic body and Fiat mechanical component, designated the CNR E2, maintaining the established standards of production and safety, while remaining under a Cd of 0.193. It was presented at the Turin Motor Show, where it revealed a shape that was radically different from its predecessor.

On the breathtaking terrace of the Forte Belvedere, high above Florence, the magnificent exhibition Idea Ferrari (which celebrated the creative ideas of the renowned manufacturer, who had died two years before) also paid indirect homage to Pininfarina for his unflagging contribution from 1952 to Ferrari designs.

In 1991, when the car market was undergoing another worldwide crisis, Pininfarina continued its unbroken growth with a production of 35,000 vehicles and a labour force of 2,100. A new

company had just been founded in Germany, alongside the Italian operating companies, in order to increase the level of flexibility and competitiveness and to better serve the needs of car manufacturers in the areas of models, equipment, and prototypes. That year, in August, the Peugeot 106 was also launched, a new product of the collaboration between Turin and La Garenne.

Pininfarina returned to Detroit in January 1991 with the Chronos, a study in forms and materials for a sporty and original compact coupé built on the chassis of the entirely new Opel Lotus Omega saloon. For the second participation in the Motor City motor show, Pininfarina chose to render homage to General Motors. Leaving aside the Allanté, relations between the Turinese industrialist and the largest car builder on Earth actually dated back to the Cadillac V-16 roadster of 1936, and included not only a long series of

prototypes built on Cadillac chassis but also on Buick and Chevrolet chassis.

For the third participation in the Detroit Motor Show, in January 1992, Pininfarina presented a Cadillac and a Ferrari. The Allanté was entering its seventh year on the market with a new 290hp 32-valve engine, designated Northstar, with numerous technical and stylistic improvements. The Ferrari 512 TR, which had replaced the Testarossa on the assembly lines of Grugliasco (where only the body was built with final assembly taking place in Maranello), had been given the difficult challenge of taking the place of a car that held the record in Ferrari history, with more than 7,200 units sold since its presentation in 1984, of which 3,800 were in Europe and 2,160 in the United States.

Things were entirely different at the Turin Motor Show in April, with the Ethos, a prototype of a racing 'barchetta' that was also ecological, ultralight and recyclable, stuffed with innovations with its two-stroke three-cylinder 95hp Orbital engine approaching the amazing threshold of zero emission, its extruded aluminium understructure and its bodywork in aluminium and plastic. The Fiat Cinquecento

42

The Paris Motor Show of 1952 and the Brussels Motor Show of 1972.

Facing page
The Detroit Motor Show of 1991 and the Frankfurt Motor Show of 1999.

Pick-up 4x4 targeted a younger consumer on the other hand.

Paris, in October 1992, was the first motor show for the Ferrari 456 GT, a 2+2 coupé replacing the 412 on the assembly lines after two years' absence from both the market and Grugliasco. The rounded shapes of its aluminium body made a sharp contrast with the earlier 2+2s. The 456 was also surprising in its perfect synthesis between sportiness and comfort for four persons. It was named the Most Beautiful Car in the World of 1993 in the category of two-door Grand Touring cars, with a special mention for its contribution to the figurative culture of modern times. Its body shell would be built in Grugliasco at a rate of three units a day, and then would be transferred to Maranello for the assembly of the mechanical components. Between 1992 and 1994, the range of vehicles produced by Pininfarina had been revamped

entirely, and at the Geneva Motor Show four models were presented: the Ferrari 456 GT, the Fiat Coupé, the Peugeot 205 Cabriolet Junior and the Peugeot 306 Cabriolet, which had had its worldwide debut at Frankfurt in September 1993. This was a four-seater convertible with a two-layer roof that could be folded away entirely under a rigid cover. This car was introduced in early 1994 at Industrie Pininfarina, when it was named the Most Beautiful Cabriolet of the Year by an international jury, and is still in production in 2000. For this model, Peugeot had commissioned Pininfarina to design, engineer, and produce the bodywork. The case of the Fiat Coupé, on the market from Spring 1994, is different: the silhouette was designed by the Fiat styling centre, while Pininfarina Studi e Ricerche undertook the design of the interior, and Industrie Pininfarina oversaw the bodywork and manufactured the entire vehicle, applying a new system of integrated factory production. This front-wheel-drive coupé with a transversally mounted engine, marked Fiat's successful return to a market segment from which it had been absent for more than 20 years. The Spunto, a styling prototype shown at the following Turin

Motor Show, was an entirely new vehicle built on the chassis of the Fiat Punto: a hatchback, two-door car with considerable clearance beneath and special understructure shielding to allow off-road use.

The Ferrari F355 with a 3.5-litre V8 engine and a six-speed gearbox, introduced in May 1994 in GTB and GTS versions to replace the 348, was another particularly successful design by Pininfarina. The design was then further developed into a cabriolet (355 Spider) in Spring 1995, and then beginning in Summer 1997, it became available with an electro-hydraulic steeringwheel-mounted gear change (the 355 F1). At the Mondial de l'Automobile, the new name of the motor show in Paris, Ferrari presented, in 1994, the F512M, a temporary restyling of the 512 TR, before the new 12-cylinder two-seater berlinetta from Maranello was introduced. In the Design Space, a specific area of the motor show, Pininfarina displayed its three Ethos prototypes, the fruit of research on the subject of the 'eco-

compatible' car begun in 1991 with various partner companies. After the first Ethos spider with a two-cycle Orbital engine, presented at the Turin Motor Show of 1992, the Ethos 2 was a quest for the same objective of maximum energy efficiency but with a coupé body, while two years later, in Turin, the Ethos 3 was a proposal for a small urban, five-seater sedan, only 3.36 metres in length. Nine months later, the Ethos 3 EV was presented at the Los Angeles Motor Show in California, a state that is particularly committed to the fight against pollution. This was a version adapted to American standards and requirements, and driven by electric power, EV standing for electric vehicle. Each of these prototypes carried within it seeds of vehicles that we shall see in the future.

The year 1994 also witnessed the presentation of two Alfa Romeos with front-wheel drive and a transverse engine a coupé and a convertible designed by Pininfarina the GTV and the Spider. On 15 February 1995, between the motor shows of Los Angeles and Geneva, Sergio Pininfarina found the time to travel to New Delhi to make a detailed presentation of the capacities of his multifaceted group to an association of Indian industrialists, turning his attention once again to the future.

In March, the Geneva Motor Show was the venue for the greatly discussed debut of the Ferrari F50. Less than ten years after the F40, this reply from Ferrari-design by Pininfarina Studi e Ricerche left the other 'supercars' standing still . . . And the 349 cars planned were almost all sold on the spot. This presentation preceded by a few weeks the award by the Italian Association for Industrial Design of the *Compasso d'Oro* to Sergio Pininfarina. This award was particularly welcome since his father had received the same honour in 1957.
The Bentley Azure, another revelation at the same Geneva Motor Show, threw a spotlight on another little publicised collaboration with Pininfarina, which had been primarily responsible for the design and production of the convertible roof, as well as the work required on the bodyshell to accommodate the power unit required to fold and stow the top under a rigid cover: a demanding job in both technical and aesthetic terms. Moreover, Pininfarina had received the job of assembling and painting the body, a responsibility entrusted to a non-British supplier for the first time, as well as the installation of the top and the finishing elements linked to it. In effect, aside from all the normal creations of the designer-coachbuilder that experts in the field and the general public are aware of, there are other jobs that are not at all well known, especially in the field of components. Thanks to its extensive experience with convertibles for instance, Pininfarina designed and developed the cabriolet version of the Rover 200 and the MGF, as well as manufacturing the mechanisms for the top at a

The exhibition of Italian Coachbuilders at the Milan Triennale (1947).

rate of 100 a day. The experience acquired in more than 25 years of work in the Grugliasco wind tunnel was put to use by creating the *Centro di ricerche aerodinamiche e Aeroacustiche Pininfarina*, (Pininfarina Centre for Aerodynamic and Aero-acoustic Research), which has established interesting relationships with the leading European car makers including Audi, BMW, Fiat, and Peugeot.

The presentation of the Honda Argento Vivo at the Tokyo Motor Show of 1995 underscored on the other hand, the ties of collaboration on a purely creative level that existed with the Japanese manufacturer. This collaboration, begun in 1978, did not become public until the HPX project in 1984 and the little Honda City cabriolet marketed in Japan that same year. The aluminium, wood, and resin visible in the

Argento Vivo invented a timeless aesthetic equilibrium. It broke so sharply with everyday monotony that the American car magazine *AutoWeek* named it as the Best of the Show as the best car presented at the Tokyo Motor Show, defining it as an automotive jewel, an instant classic. For its part, the Japanese car magazine *Car Styling*, which had already given special mention to the Mythos in 1989, awarded it the Golden Marker Trophy 1995 as the best concept car of the year.

For the Turin Motor Show, in April 1996, Fiat Auto had asked the most important Italian designers to exhibit their interpretations of the Bravo and Brava. Pininfarina certainly pulled no punches, and proposed two different designs, one for each model, on the same theme as the minivan, making an effort to avoid the clichés of simplified parallel-piped architecture that seemed to characterise the European projects in this market segment, and trying to preserve a certain family air with the basic models. Exhibited on the collective coachbuilders' stand, the Song was designed for off-road, sporty use; the Sing, presented on the Pininfarina stand, was

on the other hand, conceived for regular road use. We are all familiar with the subsequent popularity of this formula.

Pininfarina was also present at the Lingotto in 1996 with a research vehicle that explored the theme of the minivan in different dimensional terms. The CNR Eta Beta was a cunning 'Minivan', with hybrid gas-electric propulsion. It had gullwing doors and a telescopic body that could shorten the overall length by 200 mm by means of retractable rear door.

On 25 July 1996, in Seoul, the capital of South Korea, a month-long exhibition opened in which Pininfarina had taken an active part. Under the title, Civilization, City, and Car – Pininfarina: from Leonardo to the Future, the exhibition treated five themes linked to Italy and Pininfarina, with a parallel focus on Leonardo da Vinci, history, the present, research, diversification, and myth.

In Paris, at the Mondial of 1996, the three new developments presented at the Pininfarina stand

represented the various forms of collaboration that the coachbuilders found by Pinin had succeeded in creating in conjunction with car makers. For the Ferrari 550 Maranello, Pininfarina had participated in the design of both the body and the interior. This new cutting edge of the Ferrari line explored the theme of the sporty 12-cylinder berlinetta, taking the place of the Testarossa/512, in an entirely different way since the engine, a 5.5 litre V12, was set in the front while the six-speed gearbox formed a single-block with the rear axle. In the case of the much-admired Peugeot 406 Coupé, collaboration with the French manufacturer continued a three-level development. In fact, aside from the design, Pininfarina had been commissioned, for the first time, with the complete production of this car, including the engineering phase, since all that it had in common with the saloon was the platform. Following the presentation, the Peugeot coupé received some of the most prestigious awards available, such as the Most Beautiful Car in the World, 1997 in its category, the Car Design Award for the best production vehicle, and the

title of the Most Beautiful Car of the Year, 1998. The Lancia Kappa estate car, which was unveiled in Turin, in May, was also produced from start to finish by Pininfarina, but based on a bodyshell that was prepared by Lancia, its design having been established in collaboration with the Lancia Style Centre.

The agreement signed a few weeks later at the Chinese Embassy in Rome with the Hafei Motor Company for production in China of a vehicle designed and conceived in Italy, inaugurated for Pininfarina, a new foothold on the future in a market whose potential is recognised by the entire world of industry.

Aside from upgraded version of the Peugeot 306 Cabriolet, which had entered its third year of production, the Pininfarina stand at the Geneva Motor Show in March 1997, presented the

Nautilus, a new and fascinating product of the research done at Cambiano. At the same time it was pointed out that this formal study, which bore the Peugeot trademark, may have been alluring but was not destined to have any further manufacturing development. It was limited to offering a purely stylistic interpretation – although it was a totally functional prototype – on the theme of large sporty sedans. The idea of a body formed by two areas which seemed to slide plastically one inside the other had previously been tested with the Mythos spider of 1989, but the four-door configuration gave it an entirely new power. The reference to the mythical submarine created by the inexhaustible imagination of Jules Verne was certainly not an idle one, considering the prominence of the glass surfaces and the many innovations, interior and exterior, not to mention the numerous stylistic references.

On 15 July 1997, it was once again the assembly lines of Turin that attracted attention with the production of the 50,000th Fiat Coupé, proof of an incontestable success of that remarkable Fiat,

The exhibition of the Ethos Project, held in Milan in the Department of Architecture at the Polytechnic, the exhibition entitled 'Beauté Mobile' (Montreal, 1995), and the exhibition entitled 'Civilization, City, and Car. Pininfarina, from Leonardo to the Future' (Seoul, 1996).

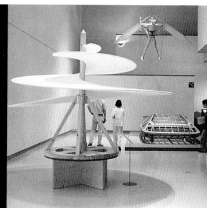

marketed since February 1994.

On 11 September in Rome, the French ambassador awarded Sergio Pininfarina the Officer's Cross of the Légion d'Honneur in recognition of more than 40 years of collaboration with the French car industry as well as his commitment in favour of the development of a high-speed railway line between Italy and France.

The year 1998 witnessed the development of new ideas in various directions. The Dardo constituted an updated concept for a Alfa Romeo Spider, in the finest tradition of the Milanese car maker. On the other hand, a few minor improvements had been applied to the Ferrari 456, renamed the 456M for the occasion in recognition of an intelligent evolution of this 2+2, still widely admired even after five years. In Geneva, in March 1999, it was once again a Ferrari monopolising the attention with the 360

Modena. The first Ferrari with an extruded-aluminium triangulated body shell was presented as a world premiere on the Ferrari and Pininfarina stands, as joint creators. The car that replaced the F355 was the 163rd Ferrari designed by the Turin coachbuilder; indeed there are some winks at the past in a form that was first and foremost functional and innovative. Thus the air intakes on the rear wings are evocative of the 250 LM that won the Le Mans 24 Hours in 1965, and the double radiator grille which, while echoing the 1961 Formula 1 World Champion, featured the new installation of the radiators and lowslung aerodynamic function. In 1999, this superb pureblood Ferrari received the award of the Most Beautiful Car of the Year in the category of sporty sedans.

Geneva also witnessed the debut of the EUROC, a single-seater roadster conceived at the initiative of the company of the same name, founded to organise the European Roadster Championship, a new formula of track racing. Pininfarina had designed the external lines of this racing car, which was displayed on the Karmann stand, which had designed the frame. Production was programmed for Dallara, while

the choice of the front-mounted engine was left to customers and racers.

The 69th Swiss motor show had also been chosen by Peugeot to present the second version of the 406, with restyling by Pininfarina. Also on display at Palexpo were two stylistic interpretations that were forerunners of the Pinin Pajero, an urban off-road vehicle destined for the market niche, then at its most popular, of sport utility vehicles. Mitsubishi Motors commissioned Pininfarina to design and build the European version. The decision of the Japanese manufacturer was the latest recognition of the new standing of Pininfarina in the world of car manufacturing, both as an overall partner for production and as a provider of specific service skills at all stages, from design to technological development to industrialisation. The production lines for the Pinin Pajero were set in motion at the end of the summer. The process was distributed between Grugliasco, where the assembly of the bodyshell took place,

Pinin and his son Sergio.

followed by painting in a specially renovated plant, and the new factory at Bairo, inaugurated in July, for the assembly, the interior finishing, and final check over followed by testing on a special track. 'The inauguration of a manufacturing plant is always a signal of vitality and faith in the future, but also a sign of economic growth and increased employment,' said Sergio Pininfarina at the opening of this fourth factory.

Two months later, Pininfarina had returned to the Far East for the presentation of the Songhuaj iang Zhongyi, a minivan on a Suzuki base that seated seven in a 3+2+3 configuration, just 3.57 metres long, with an engine – either 970 or 1,051 cc – arranged under the front seats. Pininfarina's role in this promising project was the design, development of prototypes, and the establishment of industrialisation. Production of the first Italo-Chinese vehicle began in August, in the Hafei group Factory, in Harbin, with a short-term objective of 100,000 cars a year. Even though it is a city in Manchuria, unknown to

many Westerners, Harbin constitutes an indication of the absolute global status attained by Pininfarina over its 70 years of history. Harbin was in fact the birthplace of Louis Klemantaski, a great motor racing photographer who took some of the best-known photographs of racing cars designed by Pininfarina in the 1950s, including shots of Peter Collins taken from the navigator's seat of the Ferrari 335S in the 1957 Mille Miglia.

In Frankfurt, the major European motor show in September, Pininfarina unveiled his design of an urban car, a theme that seemed at the time to be a leading concern for many manufacturers. The idea of the Metrocubo (or M^3, meaning cubic metre) was triggered at Pininfarina by the vertically mounted puncture-proof tyres of the Pax System from Michelin. The absence of a spare tyre and the possibility of mounting different size wheels on front and back, containing brakes and suspension, allowed the development of an ideal flat platform and, therefore, a modular cockpit that could accommodate five people while remaining only 2.58 metres long. Environmental concerns, an omnipresent theme, dictates a hybrid power plant for this city project teeming with ideas.

In the month of October, at the Tokyo Motor Show, the Metrocubo took three prestigious Concept Car of the Year Awards, announced during the Automotive Designer's Night. The Concept Car of the Year Awards, organized by the magazine *Automotive News International*, were assigned in four categories – Interior Concept, Safety Concept, Environmental Concept, and, quite simply, Concept of the Year – in accordance with criteria of technology, feasibility, potential cost of production, actual consumer benefits, and level of innovation. Metrocubo took first place in the category of Interior Concept for the best interior design of the year, second place in the category of Environmental Concept as the second-best prototype of the year in the context of environmental research, and third place in the category of Safety Concept for successfully reconciling safety issues with the design of an extreme minicar.

Sergio Pininfarina and his brother-in-law Renzo Carli.

Upon his return to the IAA in Frankfurt, which opened a few weeks after the centenary of Fiat, Pininfarina decided to commemorate this anniversary of its historic car making partner, by presenting the surprise prototype of the Wish, a cabriolet-coupé built on the chassis of the Fiat Punto, which had been introduced a few months earlier. In this study, which joined the rationality of technical qualities with the charm and gaiety of youth, there is clearly an evocation of numerous collaborations between the two Turin-based companies, from the 525 SS 'False Cabriolet' presented at the Concours of Rome in 1931 to the Fiat Coupé which is still in production at Grugliasco.

With the production of the 50,000th Peugeot 406 Coupé from the plant in San Giorgio Canavese, on 16 November, the last page of the 70 years had been turned. Pininfarina was entering the third millennium in great form, as could be seen once again from its presence at the Geneva Motor Show of 2000.

At the 70th Geneva Motor Show, Pininfarina was also commemorating its own 70th anniversary, and it had assembled a collection of cars that summarised the various associations with the automotive industry.

The Peugeot 406 Coupé represented the complete array of possibile collaborations: design, conception, development, industrialisation, and production.

The mission of design focused on the Ferrari 360 Spider and the Daewoo Tacuma. The composite services of design, engineering, and development were expressed by the Songhuaj iang Zhongyi, currently in production in China, while the activities of industrialisation and production were illustrated by the Mitsubishi Pajero Pinin. At the Turin Motor Show in June 2000, Pininfarina officially celebrated its 70th year of activity with a new 'dream car' based on Ferrari mechanical components, confirming – if it had been necessary – that Pininfarina and the car still constituted an ongoing dream.

Nowadays, the group – quoted on the stock exchange since 1986 – is firmly held by the family, whose third generation, already in positions of influence, is ready to take over the new shift, as was confirmed recently by Gianni Agnelli, the 'patron' of Fiat and the grandson of the Giovanni Agnelli who had – as we may remember – given a first opportunity to the very young Pinin: 'Pininfarina? That is the Italian coachbuilder that we feel closest to. I know him, I knew his father, I know the new generation. They are the best around, and I don't say this just because of our ties of friendship, but because I really think that it is true.'

The third generation: Andrea, Lorenza, and Paolo Pininfarina.

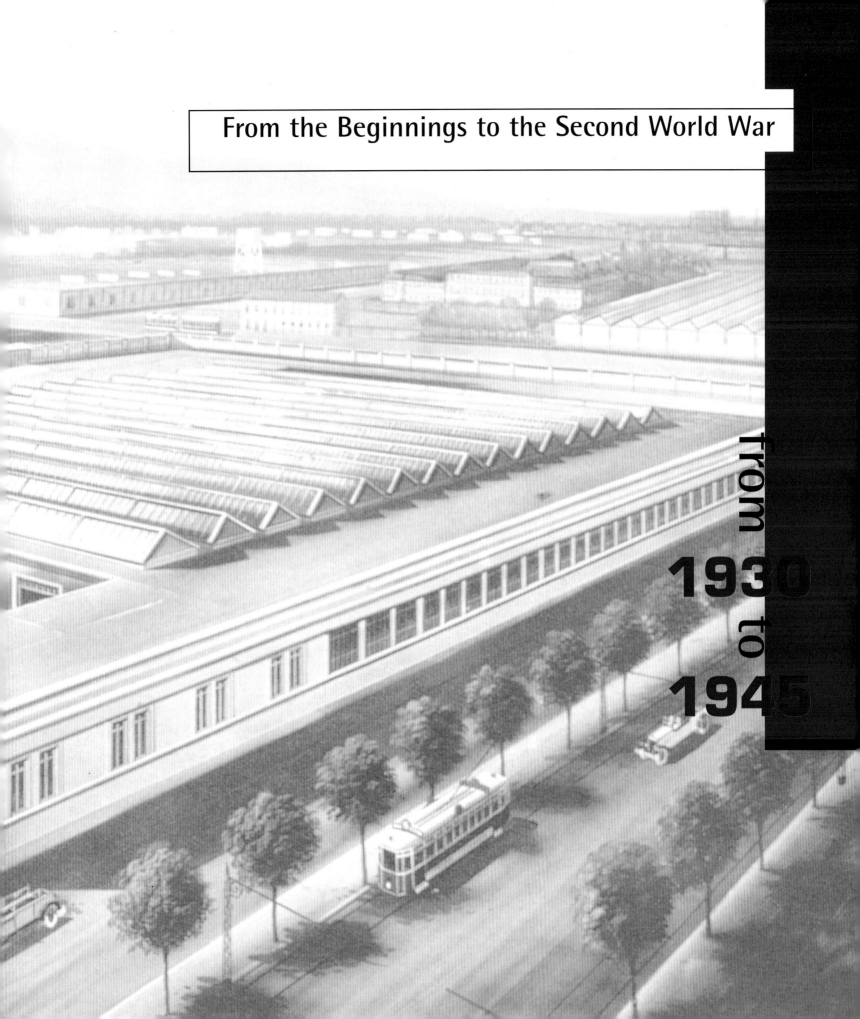

From the Beginnings to the Second World War

from
1930
to
1945

Battista 'Pinin' Farina in 1920.

Pinin's origins: his mother Giacinta Vigna Farina.

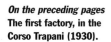

On the preceding pages
The first factory, in the Corso Trapani (1930).

Pinin, middle, with his brother Giovanni, left, talking with a customer.

Pinin Farina, in 1910, driving a vehicle of the period.

Pinin Farina testing a Fiat 501 in 1921.

Pinin, with a little Temperino, competed in many mountain car races.

Pinin in an Aviatic, mass produced during the First World War.

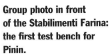

Group photo in front of the Stabilimenti Farina: the first test bench for Pinin.

The visit of a group of American technicians to the Stabilimenti Farina.

Pinin, right, enlisted in the Corps of Railway Engineers.

Pinin photographed in 1963
in Verona in a Fiat Zero, his
first creation.

Left
Senator Giovanni Agnelli,
founder of Fiat.

Pinin with his wife Rosa on their honeymoon, in Rome in March 1921.

Rosa and Pinin Farina in 1929, with their children Gianna and Sergio.

Traveling to America in 1920.

Quite early, Pinin felt a need to travel to the unutes States to learn more about its automobile industry.

In 1921 in an Itala, at the starting line of the Aosta-Grand Saint Bernard race: Pinin set a record for the category during that race, a record that stood unbeaten for eleven years.

The finish line of the Aosta-Grand Saint Bernard race.

"I have said it before, but I am happy to repeat it: Pininfarina is the Italian coachbuilder we feel closest to. They are the best, and I am not saying this just because we are friends, but because I really do think so. I know Sergio, I knew his father, I know the new generation," recalls Gianni Agnelli, honorary president of Fiat S.p.A.

LC What do you remember about Pinin?

GA "Lots of things, because I would go frequently to his shop in Corso Trapani 107 in Turin. Often I would see his son there, Sergio, at the time just a boy, and we would all look at those spectacular cars with admiration. I remember the men who worked on the bodies, and it was a pleasure to watch Pinin as he designed the wings, the lines, and then we would select the materials, the Marshall Plan headlights or those made in Italy, and many other details. These were custom-made cars, personalised to the tastes of the customer, made-to-order, with a remarkable attention to every detail: the quality of the convertible roof or the leather, the design of the headlights, the materials for the instrument panel, the chrome plating; of course I paid special attention and interest to the automobiles that were being made for my mother, my family, or people I knew. In short, a client of Pinin's could watch the preparation of the car they had ordered step by step, week after week, something like watching the construction of a house in which you are going to live. More than a coachbuilder's shop, that was an atelier, a jeweller's, with an artistic genius overseeing it all. It was not until later, in the late-Fifties and the Sixties, that Pininfarina progressed from the dimension of a 'boutique' to a more industrial scale, and the watershed was the Giulietta Spider, which represented the first major industrial production of the company. Nowadays, Pininfarina is a major industrial operation, capable of undertaking the entire cycle of production for a car, from design to final assembly, for the leading car makers of the world, such as General Motors, Peugeot, Mitsubishi, Ferrari, and the Fiat Group."

LC Do you remember any of these cars in particular?

GA "Perhaps the most remarkable ones—and I am speaking of the years before the war, the late Thirties—were the cabriolet versions of the Lancia Astura and Dilambda, also known as the "Bocca types," because of a certain Signor Bocca who sold Pininfarina cars in Biella to that special clientele, enthusiastic and of course rather well-to-do, especially fond of those rather special models."

LC Did Pininfarina build any 'special' vehicles for you?

GA "Yes, and they were all beauties. In 1955 he made me a Ferrari 375 America, in 1959 a Ferrari 410 Super America, and then in 1967 a three-seater Ferrari, with a centrally mounted steering wheel, the 365 P, with a glass roof that allowed total visibility, and then a Testarossa Spider; later—I think at the turn of the Seventies—a 130 estate car, dubbed the Maremma."

LC Do you think that there were any special reasons that Pininfarina was founded in Turin, near Fiat?

GA "In Turin, the air was full of mechanics and cars, not unlike in Wolfsburg or Detroit: in brief, here was an ideal environment and culture. Perhaps only in Milan could there have been anything similar in those years, with Alfa Romeo and great coachbuilders such as Touring, Zagato, and others. But in particular the Farina family was close to cars and the world of cars. A cousin of theirs, Nino Farina, was the first world champion of Formula One in 1950 with Alfa Romeo. That same Nino Farina, was an officer in the cavalry, Nizza Cavalleria, and an instructor at the cavalry officers' academy in Pinerolo when the Corps moved from horses to armoured vehicles. It was as if nowadays we had as an instructor a world champion like Schumacher or Lauda."

LC What resemblance is there between Pinin and his son Sergio?

GA "They are similar in many ways: Pinin—as I have said—was a remarkable factory man, and I remember later that he was enthusiastically involved in a series of public initiatives undertaken on the occasion of Italia '61 for the centenary of the unification of our country. I want to say that I met and grew to appreciate Pinin in a more social context. In his son, Sergio, this characteristic has become even more pronounced, and I have always noted in him a strong leaning toward public and civic service, as a member of the Italian parliament, as the president of the manufacturers' assocation, Confindustria, and in other important public offices."

LC And in terms of the Pininfarina 'style', what are the differences?

GA "It seems to me that they have one characteristic in common: a sense of aesthetics, in the sense of classic and balanced line. It is sort of like talking about Cimabue and Giotto."

LC And what about young Andrea?

GA "He strikes me as a worthy descendent, because he unites the strong social and public commitment with considerable professional skills in preserving the success and prestige of the company name. As president of Federmeccanica he is admired by industrialists and respected by his trade union counterparts. As an entrepreneur he is respected by his colleagues."

LC Could you give us a short definition of the Pininfarina art of designing and building an automobile?

GA "Nowadays, all car makers, even those which have an in-house Styling Centre, such as Fiat, often make use of external designers. In Turin, for instance, there are skilful designers such as Giugiaro or Bertone. But the Pininfarina family were certainly trendsetters, the first to transform the style of an automobile into an important industrial component, and I would say that they are the founders of the Italian style of car design. Pininfarina contributed to making the world aware of the car design of our country."

LC What is the true story of the famous radiator chosen by your grandfather when, at the turn of the twentieth century, Fiat was a young company?

GA "This episode dated back to 1911 and took place in the Fiat plant in Corso Dante. This is what happened: my grandfather saw a pair of radiators—they had been selected from an initial series of twenty—intended for the Fiat Zero. And so he turned to Pinin Farina, who was a 17-year-old boy, and asked him: 'Which one would you recommend?' and Pinin responded: 'That one; I built it myself.' Let us say that relations between Fiat and Pininfarina began right then and there."

The Fiat Zero of 1912, Pinin Farina's first creation.

The cover of the first book of the 'Minutes of the Assemblies' of the Carrozzeria Pinin Farina.

The founding document of the Società Anonima 'Carrozzeria Pinin Farina,' 22 May 1930.

The first factory, in the Corso Trapani.

Pinin's mother, Giacinta, with her daughter-in-law Margherita Farina, wife of Carlo Farina, and a friend, in the Corso Trapani. Behind them, a 'faux cabriolet,' Fiat 521C.

Berlina a coda su chassis LANCIA "Dilambda„ corto: Grand Prix per le guide interne al XXIV Concorso d'Eleganza di Montecarlo

CARROZZERIA
PININ FARINA S.A.
vetture di lusso e di gran lusso

CORSO TRAPANI, 107 · TELEFONI 32.745 - 32.356 · TORINO

The first advertisements clearly indicated the type of clientele that Pinin Farina was targeting.

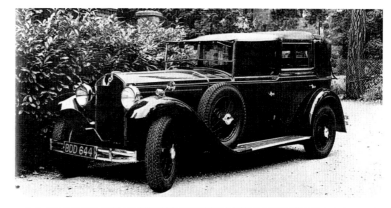

CARROZZERIA
PININ FARINA
Esecuzioni di gran lusso

Guida Interna 4 posti su chassis Dilamda mod. 232 esposta all'Olympia di Londra

TORINO
CORSO TRAPANI, 107

Vincenzo Lancia, a great racer, car builder, and a founding partner in the Carrozzeria Pinin Farina, in his Fiat 100 HP racing car, used in 1905-06 in the Gordon Bennett Cup and in the Coppa Florio.

One of the first Lancias with body by Pinin Farina, a Dilambda 'cabriolet d'Orsay,' owned by the noted English journalist Ronald 'Steady' Barker in the Seventies and Eighties.

The Lancia Dilambda chassis served as a foundation for many splendid custom cars.

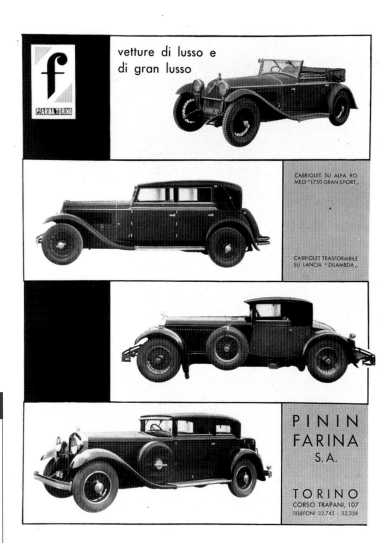

60

The construction of one-offs
made it possible to make
a broad and diverse array
of bodies on the chassis
of many different models
of car.

In the layout of advertising
pages, one can see
a considerable level
of elegance and graphic
research.

As early as 1930, Farina
was seeking out innovative
solutions and successfully
marketing them.

On the following page
Heraldic crests for
customers in an
advertisement from 1931.

Prince Alighiero Giovannelli
won the first prize in 1931

with his splendid Fiat 525 SS
Pinin Farina at the
Automotive Beauty Contest
of Rome.

"LUMINOSA"

S.A.R.
il Duca d'Aosta

S. A. R.
il Principe di Piemonte

S. A. R.
il Duca di Genova

S. E.
la Principessa di Ratibor

S. A. R.
la Principessa Elena di Romania

S. A. R.
il Principe Conrad di Baviera

S. A. S.
la Principessa di Monaco

S. A. R.
il Principe Axel di Danimarca

FROM THE GOLDEN
BOOK OF

PININ FARINA BODY
TURIN

Count Trossi at the wheel of the Mercedes Benz SS in Corso Vittorio in Turin, on the occasion of the Automotive Beauty Contest.

62

COUPÉ A DUE POSTI SU ISPA-NO SUIZA "GRAN SPORT"

A Gran Sport Coupé, built in 1931 on a Hispano Suiza chassis for Count Carlo Felice Trossi, an outstanding gentleman racer.

The year was 1931: a super-sporty Mercedes Benz SS built for Count Carlo Felice Trossi, on the occasion of the Automotive Beauty Contest of Monte Carlo.

The Fiat 518 A Ardita
'double phaeton' of 1932.

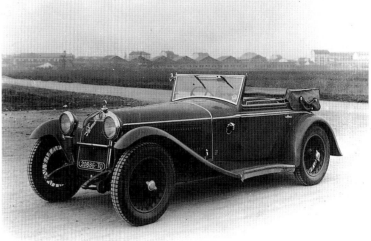

An Alfa Romeo 6C 1750
GTC of 1931.

The celebrated Cadillac V16
Spider 2+2 of 1931, built
for the Maharaja
of Orcha in a photo of
the period.

An Itala 65 Cabriolet
of 1932.

An Alfa Romeo 8C 2300
Cabriolet built in 1933
for Baroness Maud von
Thyssen: it took part
in the Automotive Beauty
Contests of Monte Carlo,
Cannes, and Villa d'Este.

A streamlined 'internal
guide' on a Lancia Astura
chassis, built in 1934
for Achille Varzi. When the
client allowed him to do so,
Pinin Farina always sought
out innovative solutions.

A handsome sedan from 1934 on a Packard chassis, built for Germano Bonetti, a businessman from the Ticino.

Sergio Farina, son of Pinin, in 1933.

Another Alfa Romeo 8C 2300 Cabriolet, at the Automotive Beauty Contest of Villa d'Este in 1934.

One of the two Rolls-Royce Phantom IIs built by Pinin Farina, constructed on the chassis no. 20 SK for the Marquis Demetrio Imperiali, here at the Automotive Beauty Contest of 1935.

The Fiat Ardita owned
by Jeanine Triaca at the
Automotive Beauty Contest
of Montecarlo in 1935.

With the Fiat for Jeanine
Triaca the level of formal
research had gone so far as
to create a special luggage
rack, also silhouetted like
the tail of the vehicle.

A Lancia Astura Berlina
at the Automotive Beauty
Contest of Montreux
in 1936.

At the Automotive Beauty
Contest of Sestrière, this
sumptuous Lancia Astura
Cabriolet distinguished
itself. Characterized by its
tapering shape, the two-part
movable windscreen, the
braided-leather upholstery,
and above all one of the
first powered convertible
roofs, this car was so well
liked by the Bocca brothers,
representatives for Lancia in
the areas of Vercelli,
Novara, and Biella, as well
as personal friends of both
Lancia and Farina, that they
ordered a small series of
cars. That is why it is known
as the 'Astura Bocca';
Pininfarina purchased one
for his own collection in the
Eighties.

OTTOBRE 1936   17

PININ FARINA / S. A. / TORINO

Carrozzerie di Lusso e di Gran Lusso

Le nuove Carrozzerie sono munite di cristalli di sicurezza "VIS" e "SECURIT"

GUIDA INTERNA A 2 POSTI "AERODINAMICA" SU ALFA ROMEO TIPO "PESCARA"

CORSO TRAPANI 107 / TELEFONI 32.356 / 32.745

68

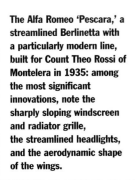

The Alfa Romeo 'Pescara,' a streamlined Berlinetta with a particularly modern line, built for Count Theo Rossi of Montelera in 1935: among the most significant innovations, note the sharply sloping windscreen and radiator grille, the streamlined headlights, and the aerodynamic shape of the wings.

The 6C 2300, built on chassis no. 700522, was presented at the Milan Motor Show.

The Lancia Aprilia
Aerodinamica in action
during the uphill race
of Sassi-Superga.

The Lancia Aprilia
Aerodinamica, a racing
Berlinetta of 1936, was
a revolutionary vehicle
in terms of both technology
and appearance: it featured
a coefficient of 0.40,
an astounding achievement
if we consider that it was
attained strictly by
an intuitive and empirical
approach, without the
possibility of any scientific
control of the design
process.

Panoramic view of the Milan Motor Show of 1937, one of the most important ones of the time.

The Alfa Romeo 8C 2900 B 'Corto,' probably owned by Piero Dusio, who was to found Cisitalia after the war.

One of the first Lancia Aprilia chassis was given this cabriolet body, photographed at Villa Olmo.

The second Rolls-Royce Phantom II (the first had been built for Marquis Demetrio Imperiali), characterized by a sloping radiator grille. It was built in 1937 for Signor Wax of Milan, whose family still represents Connolly. It apparently still exists, and is in the garage of a wealthy Milanese family.

73

THE IMMORTAL 2.9

SUNDAY, 29 AUGUST 1999

CHRISTIE'S
INTERNATIONAL
MOTOR CARS

The Alfa Romeo 8C 2900 B
was the most remarkable
sports car of the late
Thirties.

A streamlined coupé on an Astura chassis, shown here at the Automotive Beauty Contest of Villa d'Este of 1937.

A 'Bocca type' Astura.

The front assembly of the coupé built on an Astura chassis.

An Astura with a radiator grille that is less classical than that of the 'Bocca type.' Note the mechanism of the separate windscreen and the braided treatment of the leather upholstery.

A 'Bocca type' Astura was discovered, in poor condition, by an English collector, and was restored by Pininfarina in the Sixties. After many years in England, it was repurchased by Pininfarina. Its first official appearance was on the 'stand of the 50th anniversary' at the Turin Motor Show of 1980.

The 'Bocca type' Astura in the Pininfarina collection.

In 1938, Mr. Coal, of General Motors, met Pinin Farina and toured his factory.

At the 'Exhibition of Autarky' of 1938, a convertible on an Alfa Romeo 6C 2300 chassis.

An interesting Mercedes Benz 500, or, more probably, 540 K. At first sight, it seems like a production 'Sindelfingen,' with the same front assembly, bonnet, and curve of the wings. What stands out as different, on the other hand, is the one-piece windscreen and the convertible top.

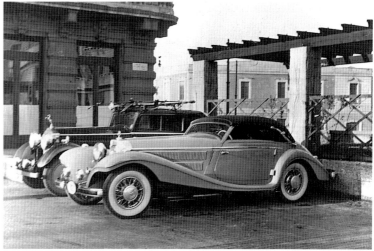

NEL 1940 . . . . .

Al mio piccolo grande amico Ottavio Massonis
Pinin Farina

Caro Ottavio,
Il disegno che mi hai gentilmente mandato è una meraviglia, ha veramente della realtà: una macchina che si avanza! Bisogna essere un artista per fare un disegno così bene. Il vedere i tuoi disegni mi sprona a fare ogni sforzo per fare bene. Vorrei avere io questa fortuna, ciò che mio papà desidera tanto. Arrivederci presto.
Sergio
28-10-XVI

Sig. Ottavio Massonis
V. San Domenico 11

Torino

Postcard written by Sergio Farina, then twelve, to the painter Ottavio Massonis, then sixteen, to thank him for a sketch that he had sent him (photo above).

A sketch from 1938 dedicated by Pinin to his friend the painter Ottavio Massonis, a foreshadowing of the automobiles of the years to come.

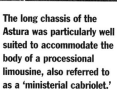

At the Berlin Motor Show of 1938, among the spectators admiring the Lancia Astura was Adolf Hitler.

The long chassis of the Astura was particularly well suited to accommodate the body of a processional limousine, also referred to as a 'ministerial cabriolet.'

A sportier Alfa Romeo was used in the visit of the King of Italy to Tripoli, shown here with the governor of the colony of Libya, Italo Balbo.

The Alfa Romeo 8C 2900 Spider built for Count Del Pero, with retractable headlights and a radiator grille reminiscent of that of the 158 Grand Prix.

Sergio Farina, about thirteen, in a Fiat 508 C Speciale. The car, also known as the 'Nuova Balilla,' must have been modified in its mechanical part as well, to judge from the lowered height of the bonnet.

Pinin, shown here in 1939, never forgot his favourite childhood pastime, bocce ball.

A Lancia Aprilia with a sedan body, and sunroof, from 1939, produced in a limited series, in front of the factory of the Corso Trapani.

An Alfa Romeo 6C 2500
Turismo Berlina, not very
different from the
production version.

This Spider on an Alfa
Romeo 6C 2500 Super
Sport chassis, of which two
models were built, certainly
in the postwar period—one
of them for the racer Franco
Cortese—represented
a phase in the process
of experimentation that was
to lead to the elimination
of the archaic bumpers.

Modello AUTOAMBULANZA 1100/L **Studio**

Costo Materiali forniti da ditte esterne comprese le lavorazioni e . . . . L.
Materiali di consumo (stagno, elettrodi, stracci, abrasivi, pasta, benzina, ecc.) . »
TOTALE L.
Costo Mano d'Opera interna . . . . L.
Spese generali sulla M. O. 200% . . . . »
TOTALE L.
Costo sui materiali per scarti d'officina e per modifiche 15% . . . . L.
» attrezzature in conto ditte esterne, compless. . . . . diviso per vett. . . . L.
» » costruite internamente » . . . . L.
(compresa M. O. materiale e spese generali)
Totale L.
TOTALE COMPLESSIVO L.
Peso autotelaio Kg. . . . . Peso Carrozzeria Kg. . . . . Totale Kg. . . . .
Produzione progressiva da inizio modello N. . . . 40

(Senza portaruote (compreso copertone)

Modello AUTOCARRO MILITARE 3 RO LANCIA **Studio** 1° (1-500)

Costo Materiali forniti da ditte esterne comprese le lavorazioni e . . . . L.
Materiali di consumo (stagno, elettrodi, stracci, abrasivi, pasta, benzina, ecc.) . »
TOTALE L.
Costo Mano d'Opera interna . . . . L.
Spese generali sulla M. O. 20.0% . . . . »
TOTALE L.
Costo sui materiali per scarti d'officina e per modifiche 15% . . . . L.
» attrezzature in conto ditte esterne, compless. . . . . diviso per vett. . . . L.
» » costruite internamente » . . . . L.
(compresa M. O. materiale e spese generali)
Totale L.
TOTALE COMPLESSIVO L.
Peso autotelaio Kg. 4470 Peso Carrozzeria Kg. 1170 Totale Kg. 5640 8350,=
Produzione progressiva da inizio modello N. . . . .

Modello ARMATURA CUFFIA PER FUCILE MITRAGL. **Studio**

Costo Materiali forniti da ditte esterne comprese le lavorazioni e . . . . L. 162 08
Materiali di consumo (stagno, elettrodi, stracci, abrasivi, pasta, benzina, ecc.) . » 162 08
TOTALE L.
Costo Mano d'Opera interna . . . . L. 11 70
Spese generali sulla M. O. 200% . . . . » 23 50
TOTALE L. 35 23
Costo sui materiali per scarti d'officina e per modifiche 15% . . . . L. 23 20
» attrezzature in conto ditte esterne, compless. . . . . diviso per vett. . . . L.
» » costruite internamente » 5094,21 . . . . L. 1 01
(compresa M. O. materiale e spese generali)
Totale L. 24 21
TOTALE COMPLESSIVO L. 222 10
Peso autotelaio Kg. . . . . Peso Carrozzeria Kg. . . . . Totale Kg. 193,20
Produzione progressiva da inizio modello N. 2500

Modello COMMESSA D.U.L.G. MARMITTE

Costo Materiali forniti da ditte esterne comprese le lavorazioni e . . . . L. 75 03
Materiali di consumo (stagno, elettrodi, stracci, abrasivi, pasta, benzina, ecc.) . » 75 03
TOTALE L.
Costo Mano d'Opera interna . . . . L.
Spese generali sulla M. O. 200% . . . . »
TOTALE L.
Costo sui materiali per scarti d'officina e per modifiche 15% . . . . L.
» attrezzature in conto ditte esterne, compless. . . . . diviso per vett. . . . L.
» » costruite internamente » 404,50 . . . . L.
(compresa M. O. materiale e spese generali)
Totale L.
TOTALE COMPLESSIVO L.
Peso autotelaio Kg. . . . . Peso Carrozzeria Kg. . . . . Totale Kg. . . . .
Produzione progressiva da inizio modello N. 303

The file for the estimates requested by the government ministry for the purchase of a series of ambulances on Fiat 1100 L chassis, of which 40 were built.

The sketch for these trucks on a Lancia 3 Ro chassis date back to the war, and 500 of them were actually built.

On the other hand, during the war Pinin Farina was forced to manufacture 2,500 pieces of headgear for machine gunners.

A commission from the war: the 303 mufflers that went with the soldiers to the front.

"We Pininfarina veterans are young and tough. Young because 50 per cent of the membership, some 700 out of 1,200, are still on the job. Tough because we are united and joined by solidarity: more than 99.9 per cent of those who have a right to join, those who have been in the company for more than 20 years, actually do enlist in the Gruppo Anziani, or veterans group," Ugo Bassino proudly explains; he joined Pininfarina as a sheetmetal-pounder, or 'battilastra,' in 1941 and retired in 1978, when he was a department foreman. Since 1972 he has been the director of the Gruppo Anziani Pininfarina and since 1987 he has been the president of the local chapter of ANLA, the national labour association of his division.

LC There are six glittering stones on your Pininfarina badge: what do they mean?

UB "Let's take this one thing at a time. At the end of your twentieth year of work at Pininfarina you qualify as a 'veteran,' or an 'elder'—an anziano. And this badge is awarded every year in May, in our company event, which always begins at 8 in the morning with 600-800 persons meeting at Pinin's grave, to remember a person who—if

he had never existed—we would have had to invent him, because the world needs men like him, who serve their families, young people, society at large. Then, during the ceremony proper, Engineer Sergio Pininfarina assigns this badge to the 'new' veterans. The little diamonds are added afterwards: one every five years thereafter. Along with the glittering stone, if you are still working, you are also given a loyalty bonus: the previous month's pay is doubled. So that is what these six little glittering stones represent: I remained faithful to Pininfarina for thirty years after I had become a veteran, after my first twenty years."

LC What if one of your members leaves the company before retirement?

UB "They are expelled, because they are no longer one of us."

LC So Bassino is still a tough guy, just like back in the factory...

UB "I am not hard-natured, but if you want to be a director, you have to know how to command respect. When I joined Pininfarina I was just a kid, I was fourteen and I was so skinny I had to stand on a wooden box to operate my vice. In those days there were 36 of us in

my department. When I retired, I was running a workshop with 500 people. And there was considerable turnover: in 35 years at Pininfarina we must have trained about three or four thousand kids, teaching them and sending them on their way. I didn't give them what are called in Piedmontese dialect "turcet," the way that Pinin had done with me, but I had my hands full with them, that is for sure."

LC How long did Piedmontese dialect remain the official language of the plant?

UB "Until 1958, and then when we moved to the new factory in Grugliasco we shifted to Italian because by that point there were only about forty Piedmontese out of 450."

LC What was it like working with Pinin?

UB "Fascinating, but difficult. There were no blueprints, he had the car in his head, and we had to make it with hammers and tongs. Everything was an ongoing discussion, in dialect, 'lí la voglio 'na frisa più piena, lí 'na frisa più secca...' here I want it milled a little less, and there I want it milled a little more, he would say, and you would just pray that you had understood. And until you really had understood, you would just have to do it over and over again. When he really did get angry, for real, he might even pick up a sledge hammer and started demolishing a finished car: for us that meant another night's work in the workshop. Pinin was a guy who was demanding, that is certainly true, but he would also allow you to be creative. Sometimes, the combination of his ideas with

our manual interpretation, would lead to the creation of something better than what he had had in mind at the outset."

LC And what about Sergio?

UB "I met him when I was 15 and he was 16. I never thought of him as my boss, but just as a friend. For that matter, for us workers Pininfarina was never 'their' factory, it was always 'our' factory. Sergio would come to the factory after school, and we would play pranks on him, which he always accepted gracefully."

LC In 1946, part of Pininfarina caught fire and burned. You were there that day: what really happened?

UB "There were Resistance weapons hidden in an attic, and so an isolated little fire, coming into contact with gunpowder, grew quickly into a major fire. The entire seat-making division and part of the photographic archives went up in flames."

LC During wartime, there were Resistance weapons in Pininfarina, but also passive resistance...

UB "Certainly. When the German commandant would come to the factory to check that the gasometers that they had ordered us to build were working properly, it was a pleasure to show him that they all worked like Swiss watches, the famous quality of Pininfarina. But may God strike me dead right here and now if we ever forgot to remove one single valve before shipping off the gasometers to Germany...."

Pinin Farina in 1945.

The year was 1944: Sergio Farina at age 17 in the Red Cross.

Portrait of Marshall Badoglio, with a dedication to Pinin Farina.

The fire of 1946 that destroyed the Finishing Department in the factory and part of the photographic archives.

Pinin Farina

designs the world's most beautiful car

Nash

Golden Airflyte

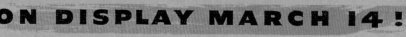 ON DISPLAY MARCH 14!

Rebirth: Italian Style Around the World

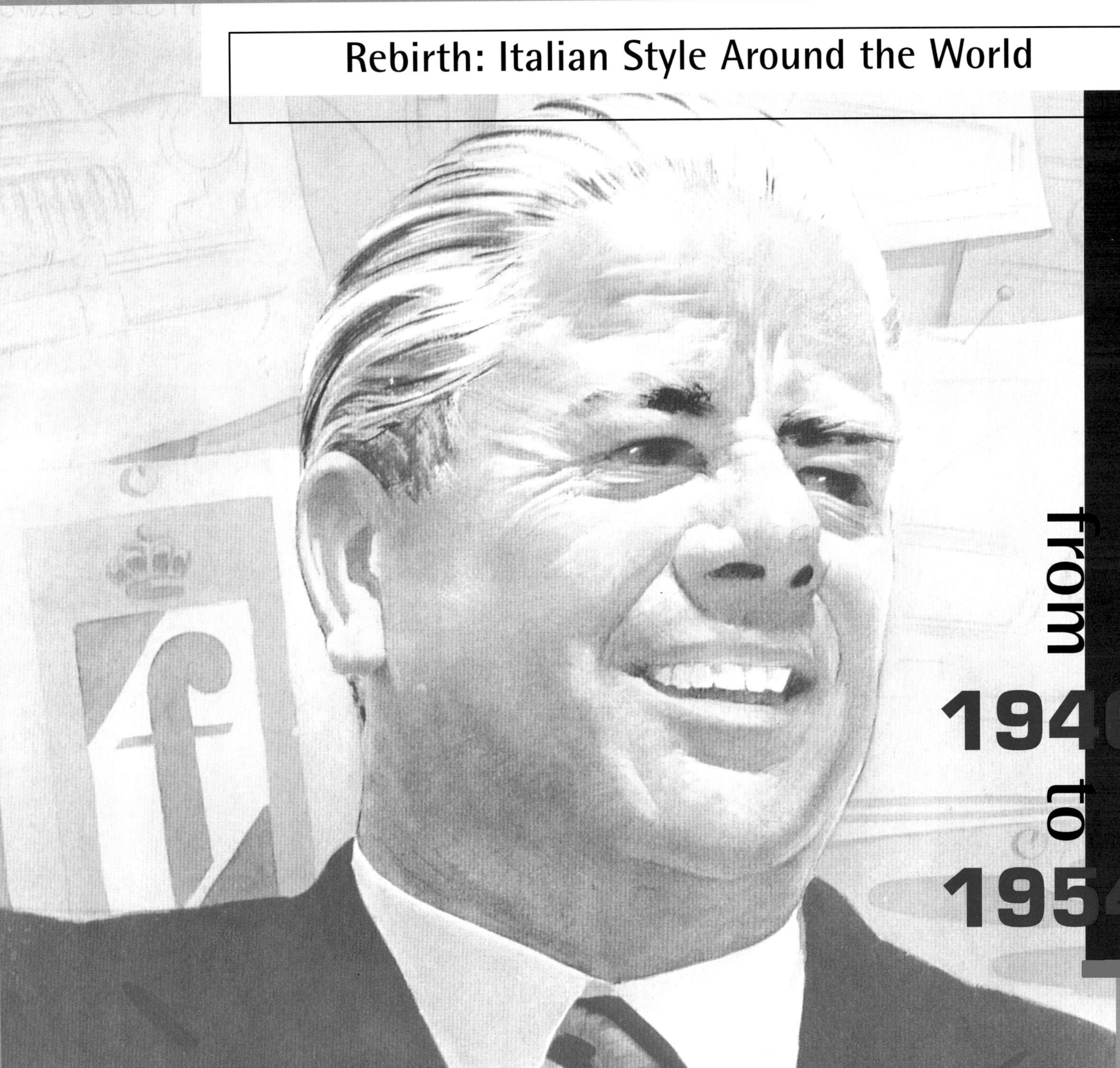

from 1946 to 1954

An Alfa Romeo 6C 2500
Sport Cabriolet (chassis
no. 915,169), with a one-
piece flank, which took part
in the Automotive Beauty
Contest concomitant with
the Italian Fashion Show
in Lausanne, in October of
1946. The proud owner was
Giuliana Ciuccioli Tortoli
of Milan.

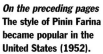

On the preceding pages
The style of Pinin Farina
became popular in the
United States (1952).

An 'old' Lancia Astura
refashioned in 1946 with
a bizarre roadster body for
a Mr. Huriburn. The
enlargement on the bonnet
was a stratagem to lower
the line of the bodywork.
Michael Frostick in his book

'Pinin Farina Master
Coachbuilder' (Dalton
Watson, 1977) compared
it to the Bugatti Royale
by M. Esders.

Sergio with a Lancia Aprilia Cabriolet travelling from Turin to the Paris 'Anti-Salon.' His father was driving an Alfa Romeo 2500 S.

Pinin and his wife Rosa with their children Gianna and Sergio on holiday at Santa Margherita Ligure in 1946.

Pinin and Sergio at the famous 'Anti-Salon' of Paris, in 1946. All Italian carmakers were excluded from the first Paris Motor Show after the war. Pininfarina, accompanied by his son Sergio, exhibited two cars in front of the Grand Palais, site of the motor show. The French press touted the success of the 'Anti-Salon' of the Turinese coachbuilder.

"The Pininfarinas? Good folks. And honest competitors." Nuccio Bertone, in a long and wide-ranging conversation in September 1988, spoke with a blend of respect and envy. *"One thing I always envied was their relationship with Ferrari, which they had consolidated over time, and which led to reciprocal benefits. We established a similar relationship with Lamborghini, but we were not so fortunate: that factory was always in trouble, and so we never had the same consistency in our relationships—there were brief highs and lows that just seemed to go on for too long."*

LC And yet, in the history of neighbourliness between Bertone and Pininfarina, there is one car that triggered discord: a Ferrari, in fact, the 250GT of 1962...

NB "In effect, that car created a few problems, especially because a few pretty daffy journalists wrote that it represented the cause of a feud between Enzo Ferrari and Pinin Farina. But that was absolutely not the case."

LC Tell us exactly what happened...

NB "Gladly. Enzo Ferrari liked me very much. When we would talk about product, he would say to me quite frankly: 'Bertone, I like the way you see automobiles, these are the sort of designs that I am looking for.' On one of my visits to Maranello, after we were done with our chat, he walked me to the door and saw the car I had arrived in, an Iso Grifo. Grinning, he quietly said to me: 'Bertone, it is time you had a car.'

I immediately understood, and I shot back at him: 'Listen, don't talk to me about cars, because I want a Ferrari, but I don't want to invade Pinin's territory, considering that he is your trusted coachbuilder as well as an officer of your company." Ferrari said very tersely: 'So ask me for a chassis.' Well I did. This 250GT was going to be my own personal car and so, in making it, I asked my stylist of the period, Giorgetto Giugiaro, to follow my ideas one hundred per cent. After I built this car, I could not resist presenting it in one or two motor shows, just for the personal satisfaction. As a result, rumours started, including the fable of a feud. So I picked up the phone and I called Sergio and told him: 'Sorry, I presented the car because it is a nice car, people like to see it, but it is my own personal car. Believe me: Ferrari gave me the chassis for my own personal use, that was the understanding.' Sergio wasn't angry, but I could tell he was uneasy."

LC Do you envy Pininfarina for anything beside having had the greater good luck of crossing paths with Enzo Ferrari instead of Ferruccio Lamborghini?

NB "Bertone was not in the same position as Pininfarina were already now (1988) as there are two sons and a daughter working in the company, and therefore a strong family inheritance. Instead, I have two daughters, and I have to guide them and explain things to them. My hope for the future is that everything will go all right, that they will not marry the wrong men: when you fall head over heels in love, it is hard to change your mind."

The Alfa Romeo 6C 2500 owned by Giuliana Ciuccioli, after being awarded the Grand Prix d'Honneur at the Automotive Beauty Contest of Monte Carlo in March 1947. The front assembly shows that at times Pinin Farina sought out innovative solutions without being limited by the characteristic motifs of the Company.

Sergio Farina driving an Aprilia Cabriolet at the Automotive Beauty Contest of Turin (1947).

The Maserati A6 1500 Pinin Farina in front of the factory of the Corso Trapani. This bodywork is exceptionally handsome. Elegant proportions, one-piece "pontoon" flanks, a lovely front assembly with retractable headlights, a long low bonnet, an opening Plexiglas top, and a Plexiglas rear window.

Prince Ranier of Monaco, third from the left, with the Belgian journalist and author Paul Frère and the Maserati A6 1500 at the Automotive Beauty Contest of Monte Carlo of 1947.

An award given to Alfieri Maserati for the A6 1500 Pinin Farina.

Pinin Farina in 1951 at the Museum of Modern Art (MoMA) with his most successful creation, the Cisitalia 202 (1947); with a tubular chassis, Pinin built and manufactured on a limited basis a Berlinetta with aluminium frame welded to a skeleton of fine sheet steel, whose formal appearance marked a decisive turning point in the development of automotive style.

Among the '8 Automobiles' exhibited at the Museum of Modern Art in New York in 1951, there was a Cisitalia 202. Forefather of the new look in cars, described by Arthur Drexler as "sculpture in motion," it was later the first car in the world to be acquired as part of the museum's permanent collection.

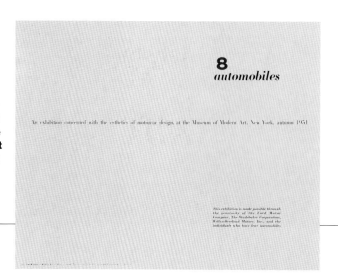

8
automobiles

An exhibition concerned with the esthetics of motorcar design, at the Museum of Modern Art, New York, autumn 1951

This exhibition is made possible through the generosity of the Ford Motor Company, The Studebaker Corporation, Willys-Overland Motors, Inc., and the individuals who have lent automobiles.

The Cisitalia 202 was
presented in 1947 at the
Exhibition of Coachbuilders
at the Milan Triennale.

The Cisitalia 202 shown
on the occasion of a Grand
Prix, probably at the track
known as the Circuito
del Valentino on 12 October
1947. This car, more than
any other, changed
the world of automobiles
in the postwar period.

The Cisitalia 202 in Seoul
in 1996 for the exhibition
'Civilization, City and Car.
Pininfarina, from Leonardo
to the Future.'

In the Corso Trapani
limited series of cars were
produced, as shown here
by the Alfa Romeo 6C 2500
and the Aprilia Bilux.

In the immediate postwar
period, Pinin's creativity was
at its highest levels. This
is demonstrated by these
three Aprilias of 1948:
the first is being admired
by Gino Bartali.

The second one was
a forerunner of the Aurelia
B20.

The third, on the other
hand, the Aprilia Bilux, was
a bellwether of the Aurelia
Berlina which was produced
two years later.

A model similar to the Bentley Mark VI, also with a modified radiator grille, but in a more orthodox style, which was to give rise to the limited series of the Cresta.

A Bentley Mark VI two-door sedan, built in 1949 as a one-off and presented at Paris.

The Cresta series was characterised by this heraldic emblem with a double-F, one for Farina and one for Facel, the French company that had commissioned the cars.

A Berlinetta on a Fiat 1100 S chassis. It also enjoyed enormous popularity at Villa d'Este: another step forward in the evolution that was to lead to the Aurelia B20.

Another 2500 Cabriolet, this time on an 'S' chassis, much closer to the production version.

The Alfa Romeo 6C 2500 chassis, and especially the Super Sport version, allowed Pinin to try out new lines and solutions. Here a two-seater convertible which won first place among the Italian cars at Villa d'Este, in September 1949. A nearly identical model was shown at the Paris Motor Show.

At the Geneva Motor Show in 1951: a limousine version and the production convertible lancia Aurelia —here, however, enriched with chrome-plated ornamentations—built on the B50 platform.

"The first Pininfarinas that I can remember were family cars in the late Forties: a splendid silver convertible Aprilia with a dark-blue interior owned by my uncle, my mother's brother, one of the first convertible Aurelia V6 1750s with body by Pininfarina, owned by the father of the girl who was to become my wife. The legendary Cisitalia, on the other hand, I had first seen it on the street; typical, since everything beautiful in Italy always and inevitably winds up in Switzerland," recalls Bob Lutz, now president of the Exide Corporation after a lifetime spent in the executive suites of General Motors, Opel, BMW, Ford, and Chrysler.

LC Later on you met Pinin in person. What did you say to each other?

BL "Unfortunately, nothing at all. It happened at a Frankfurt Motor Show at the beginning of the Sixties. I was part of a delegation from General Motors and, since I was very young, I did not have the necessary seniority to actually speak. Moreover, I was ashamed of my Italian, which I had taught myself from signs on trains (trilingual in Switzerland). And so I spoke not a word, though I was proud to be in the presence of a man who was already a legend."

LC What is the origin of what you call the 'Pininfarina legend'?

BL "They have always had a style all their own, a perfect equilibrium between exquisite elegance and simplicity. The Lancia Florida II was quite simply spectacular, it truly marked a new era in terms of styling. The one thing about the Pininfarina style that always struck me was the magnificent simplicity of the beauty. Never any optical illusions or exoticism to attract attention. To make a comparison, while I have always admired Bertone, I am convinced that Pininfarina could never have designed the BATs,

10 & 11 September, 1987
FRANKFURT

Robert Lutz

because it has always eschewed excessive forms. For that matter, for a designer, the most difficult thing to attain is, in fact, harmony."

LC Many believe that the work done by Pininfarina has profoundly influenced the entire world automotive industry. And yet, in seventy years of work, you can count the Pininfarinas 'Made in the USA' on the fingers of one hand...

BL "True, but America is a very strange country. For decades everybody here thought that the epitome of elegance was a Cadillac with tailfins, and so of course there was not the kind of sensibility that was needed to understand Italian style. Then again, perhaps, Pininfarina was unlucky. With Nash they had some impact, but only limited impact because Nash was one of the 'small four,' not one of the 'big three.' Last of all, the usual syndrome that afflicts Detroit, known as NIH (not invented here). Everything that comes from 'outside,' is looked at with hostility. More than once I have tried to convince my superiors to ask Italian designers to submit proposals as well, first Frua, and later Pininfarina, but to no good purpose. I remember once at GM, I thought I had made some headway, but with photographs of a few mediocre products from British Leyland they responded that Pininfarina just wasn't up to the job of designing a successful production vehicle. Personally I disagreed, even though I have to admit that often they don't do their absolute best work on production cars. I think, for instance, of many Peugeots that are a little too 'bland.' On the other hand, on limited series, where there was more freedom, they have

created magnificent cars, from the Giulietta Sprint to the Fiat 124 Spider."

LC When we talk about Pininfarina, we always wind up talking about Ferraris. Which Ferrari do you consider the most beautiful?

BL "It is easier for me to choose immediately what I liked least: the 1984 Testarossa, with those awful side grilles. For me, Pininfarina is a champion of simplicity and that Testarossa represents the exception that proved the rule. In absolute terms, the loveliest one is perhaps the 250 SWB, the essence of a modern Ferrari, a car that in fact defined the image of the trademark. Also particularly handsome were all of the Dinos, despite the fact that they were relatively small cars. Among the most recent cars, the 456 GT seemed to me the most successful interpretation of the Ferrari spirit."

LC Three research prototypes of the last few years, each of them light-years away from the other: Argento Vivo, Nautilus, and Metrocubo. Which do you prefer?

BL "Well, in a corporate spirit, I ought to say the Metrocubo, because it has Exide batteries! Jokes aside, it is a truly interesting vehicle, full of contents. As for the Argento Vivo, there is no question at all: it is beautiful. The Nautilus is simply fabulous: one of the best four-door hatchback saloons that I have ever seen."

Production in the Pinin
Farina factory of the Corso
Trapani, in the Forties.

Manual work and equipment for the start of limited production at the Pinin Farina factory of the Corso Trapani.

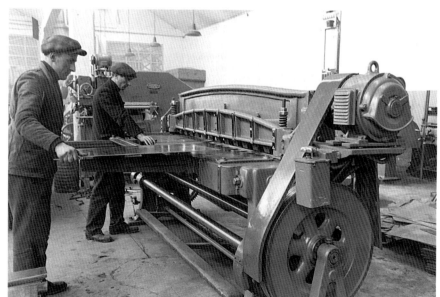

Department for sheet metal
work in the Corso Trapani,
in the Forties.

"I began repairing wings when I was 13 years old. I stopped building Ferraris when I was 75. We have produced—they tell me—about twenty thousand of them. Almost all of them designed by Pininfarina. Enzo Ferrari made my fortune, and Pinin always loved me. I certainly couldn't have asked for anything more," recalls Sergio Scaglietti, founder of the coachbuilders Carrozzeria Scaglietti, finally absorbed by Ferrari in 1970.

LC How and when did you become what they call in Modena the trusted 'carrozzaio' or coachbuilder for Enzo Ferrari?

SS "In 1938 I was working in a body repair shop in Modena, in the Via Trento e Trieste, across from the offices of the Scuderia Ferrari, or Ferrari racing team, which in those days was racing Alfa Romeos. What we mostly did was to repair the wings of Alfa 1750s and 2300s; the vibrations wound up snapping the clamps. The first real jobs arrived in 1950, when we had to repair Ferraris with bodies by Touring and Vignale. One day Cacciari, a Modenese gentleman driver, brought us his 2-litre V12 in terrible shape, really ready for the dump. 'Instead of fixing this one, I will make you a new one,' I suggested. Ferrari himself saw our barchetta, liked it, and gave us the first real commission: preparing three 4500s for the Carrera Mexicana."

LC In the mid-Fifties Ferrari began working with Pinin Farina: how did this triangle function?

SS "Spectacularly well. On our own we did only three Ferraris: the 250 Testarossa in 1958, the 250 GTO in 1964, and the California, even though there were a couple of 'corrections' on this last one suggested by Pinin, which we were perfectly happy to implement. For that matter, we have never thought of Pininfarina as a rival: we worked as one for Ferrari. In terms of relationships, they were never three-way meetings. Ferrari would decide on the style with his stylist, Pinin. Then Pininfarina would send us an approved model, generally on a scale of 1:10, and from that we would build the life-size form, 1:1 in wire. On this basis, the dialogue between us and Pininfarina, that is, between 'carrozzai,' or body makers."

LC There were never drawings or plans of form or shapes to adhere to: how would you respect the spirit of the Pininfarina design?

SS "We worked by rule of thumb. Often modifying as we went, because when you pass from a little scale model to life size, there are always details to be worked out. Sometimes we understood perfectly and some of our 'interpretations' were actually approved by the stylists at Pininfarina. Other times, we made gross mistakes: we really got yelled at when the tail of the BB came out a full centimetre too low! Other times we just invented as we went: the Dino Coupé originated in Pininfarina, while we 'designed' the Spider by sawing a Coupé in half. In any case, those were heroic years: we didn't bother with scientific time-to-market studies. It would take us five months to go from a scale model to the first car delivered

to the customer! Nobody would design hinges, they were just made as we went along... In any case, we always got along fine with Pinin and his people, because we all basically wanted the same thing: beautiful cars."

LC What was it like to work with Pinin?

SS "He was pretty gruff. Even with Ferrari he was anything but pliable. Both of them had pretty similar characters: they went straight to the point. And they always had plenty to talk about: Ferrari wanted a new car every day, but he was always behind in his payments!"

LC What are the loveliest Ferraris by Pininfarina?

SS "All of them. To me, perhaps, the 275 is still the absolute top. The Le Mans, too, was spectacular. And then there was the first 250 2+2: just marvellous."

LC You think they were all beautiful? In Modena the 365 GTC/4 of 1971 was dubbed 'the hunchback': and certainly not as a compliment...

SS "Careful, even the 'hunchback' was aesthetically successful. It had a different problem: because it was too heavy, it didn't ride all that well."

Pinin with his 'two sons,' Renzo Carli and Sergio, in 1950.

At the Testing Department in the Via Serrano, a building separate from the factory of the Corso Trapani where production took place, as early as the late Forties design was being done for industrial clients as well.

The Testing Department
in the Via Serrano.

At the Turin Motor Show of 1950, Pinin Farina shows the Bentley Mark VI Cresta to the President of the Italian Republic Luigi Einaudi.

Silvana Pampanini in her Alfa Romeo 1900 Cabriolet, a version of which only 88 were built.

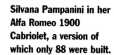

A Lancia Aprilia Cabriolet Speciale at the Automotive Beauty Contest at Monte Carlo in 1950.

The Alfa Romeo 6C 2500 S (chassis no. 915,365), for which Pinin had completely abandoned any vestiges of the typical Alfa 'scudetto.' The car, now the property of a Milanese collector, is yet another variation on the theme of the two-door 'fastback' Berlinetta, and it is shown here at the Automotive Beauty Contest at Nervi in 1950, a few months after its successful participation at the Geneva Motor Show.

Pinin, with Sergio Farina
and Renzo Carli, on 'Queen
Mary', in the summer
of 1950.

Boarding cards
for the 'Queen Mary'
and the 'Queen Elizabeth.'

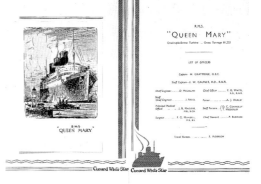

At the end of the Fifties,
Pinin with Aristotele
Onassis, left, and John
Perona.

Sergio and Giorgia Farina
on their honeymoon,
in 1951.

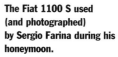

The Fiat 1100 S used
(and photographed)
by Sergio Farina during his
honeymoon.

At the Turin Motor Show of 1951, the Lancia Aurelia was present on the stands of many coachbuilders, due to the fact that Lancia supplied a chassis-complete platform that was perfect for the creation of special bodywork. The convertible on the right—whose simplified version appeared in the Lancia catalogue—was instead embellished with many refinements: chrome additions, inset handles, high-powered headlights set in the front assembly, bumpers and chrome hubcaps, fine-finish leather interiors, and even a hydraulic power convertible roof. Probably this is the car that was sold to the Pandozy family of Milan.

The factory of the Corso Trapani in 1951, with the line dedicated to the production of the B20.

One of the first models of the Aurelia B20, the fruit of much study and experimentation, starting with the Cisitalia and continuing through various Alfa Romeos, Fiats, Maseratis, and even Bentleys.

Nino Farina, son of Giovanni
and nephew of Pinin,
is shown at the wheel of the
Alfa Romeo 8C single-seater.
He became World Champion
in Formula 1 in 1951
in an Alfa Romeo 159.

Bottom
A special coupé,
very elegant, on the chassis
of an Aurelia B50, later
produced in a very few
models on B52 chassis.

A two-door sedan with
an unusual line was built
in 1951 for Commendator
Luigi Bressani on a Rolls-
Royce Silver Wraith chassis.
The car was exhibited at the
Turin Motor Show.

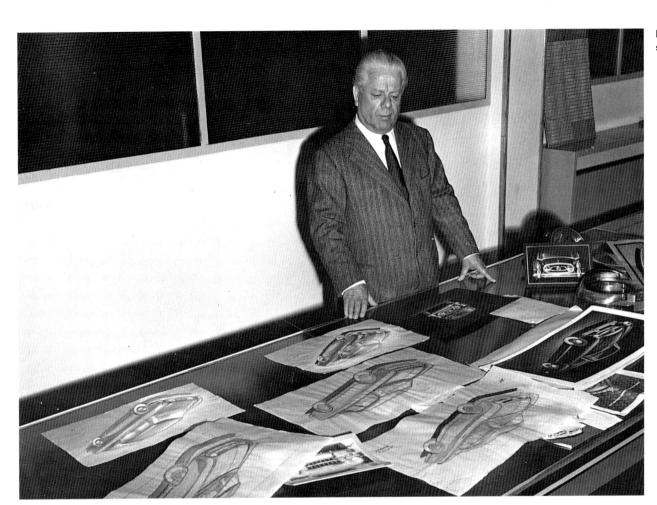

Pinin in 1952 as he studies several sketches.

AMERICAN CHAMBER OF COMMERCE FOR TRADE WITH ITALY, INC.

ESTABLISHED 1887

CERTIFICATE OF MERIT

Pinin Farina

IS AWARDED THIS CITATION FOR HIS WORLD-FAMOUS ACHIEVEMENTS IN CREATIVE AUTOMOTIVE DESIGN AND FOR HIS CONSTANT EFFORT TO FURTHER TRADE RELATIONS BETWEEN THE UNITED STATES AND ITALY.

_____
DATE

_____
PRESIDENT

The 'Certificate of Merit' awarded by the Italian-American Chamber of Commerce.

The cars of Pinin Farina were described as 'Rolling Sculptures' by the respected weekly 'The New Yorker' (1952).

The photo of Pinin in the press release from the Nash-Kelvinator Corporation.

From: Public Relations Department
Nash Motors Division
Nash Kelvinator Corporation
Detroit 32, Michigan

FOR RELEASE FEB. 13, 1952, AND THEREAFTER

FAMED AUTO STYLIST

Pinin Farina, stylist of the 1952 Nash-Healey sportscar.

An advertisement for Nash, focusing on the headline 'The difference that is Farina!'

The advertising campaign for the introduction of the Nash-Healey in the United States, 1952.

A poster for the launch of the Nash Golden Airflyte.

Pour son 50ème ANNIVERSAIRE,

NASH vous invite à admirer les plus somptueuses voitures de l'époque.

New York, 1952: Pinin Farina and Renzo Carli with Kate Norris on the occasion of one of her shows.

Nous vous présentons les Nash Golden Airflytes 1952 — les premières voitures américaines dessinées par PININ FARINA, le plus célèbre constructeur de carrosseries de luxe. — Nouveau moteur Super Jetfire. — Nouvelle boîte Hydra-Matic à double étagement. — Nouvelle suspension Airflex. — Vision totale. — Compartiments ultra-spacieux. — Sécurité accrue. — Intérieur de haut luxe.

On the set of the film 'Sabrina' (1955) with Audrey Hepburn, Humphrey Bogart, and William Holden, who drove a Nash-Healey Spider.

Sergio, Pinin, and Walt Disney in the United States (1952).

In 1955 Pinin shows one of his creations to Prince Leopold of Belgium, a great car fan.

Pinin and George Mason,
president of Nash-Kelvinator.

The first Ferrari designed and with body built by Pinin Farina: the 212 Inter, chassis no. 0177E, owned by Georges Filippinetti, finished in dark bordeau with interior in natural leather, completed on 23 June 1952.

The line of the car was very simple, but embellished with a few skilful touches such as the chrome silhouette, the inset handles, and the luxurious interior.

1952, Grand Prix of Monte Carlo: among the others, Pinin and Sergio Farina.

Early Fifties: Pinin with his son Sergio.

Pinin accepts a prize at the Automotive Beauty Contest of Rome in 1952.

On a Maserati A6 2000 chassis, yet another variation on the theme of the notchback Berlinetta.

The PF200 of 1953, on a B 52 chassis. The car body is characterized by its streamlined silhouette, tapered toward the tail, the smooth sides, the raised circular front air intake, which generates the central part of the hood, also circular in cross section. Evidently there is the influence of the aeronautics of the era.

The attempt to develop an alternative line for Volkswagen, 1952.

Renato Rascel—shown here with Sergio Farina at the Turin Motor Show—loved fine cars and purchased the PF 200. An evolution of the same design on a Cadillac chassis was built in 1954 for the American jazz impresario Norman Grantz.

The glorious Lancia D24 of 1953. Now only one survives in private ownership, but a few replicas were built in the Eighties and Nineties.

A 2+2 coupé on a Fiat 1100 TV chassis (1953).

A Berlina Speciale on a Fiat 1900 chassis.

The elegant convertible on a
Rover 75 chassis, of 1953.
The two-door sedan
of 1954. Both of them are
now in Great Britain.

"In the 50s and 60s, when I was a young designer in Detroit, the creativity and flair of post war Italian automobile design was in its prime. In those days "Mecca" for automobile designers was the hall at the Turin Motor Show where Italian coachbuilders exhibited their latest creations – a collection of wild and wonderful expressions of the coachbuilder's art. In this design maze, one coachbuilder stood head and shoulders above the rest. It was Pininfarina" recalls Chuck Jordan, vice president of design at General Motors, now retired.

LC What made Pininfarina cars so special in those years?

CJ "Pininfarina's cars were elegant, distinctive and refined. They had style and vitality. They were not flashy faddish designs like some of the others. Pininfarina's work exuded a feeling of honesty, sincerity and consistency. Their cleanly rounded body shapes had a voluptuous quality that made you want to run your hand over the surfaces. Pininfarina designs faithfully respected the heritage of the marque but, at the same time, always had something new to say designwise to move that heritage forward. Even the details were perfectly executed. I had never seen cars quite as exciting and beautiful. These qualities in Pininfarina designs continue to this day and I know why".

LC During your long tenure at GM, you developed a close relationship with Sergio Pininfarina ...

CJ "Correct. I first met Sergio during those exciting Turin show days. Over the years we have become personal friends and even worked together on several design projects. Knowing Sergio is to understand why Pininfarina designs have integrity, style and sincerity. Like the conductor of a great orchestra, Sergio sets the tempo, the mood and the direction. His philosophy and his personality are reflected in every design Pininfarina creates – and it shows in the consistent quality of Pininfarina designs".

LC If, in an hypothetical Noah's ark of automotive design, you had to choose a Pininfarina's car to be saved from the Flood, which one would it be?

CJ "A Ferrari, of course. From 1952 Sergio – and the talented Pininfarina organisation –

have created virtually every Ferrari design, including some of the racing cars. What an amazing accomplishment! I can't think of any relationship in automotive history that has resulted in such a long and rich heritage of outstanding design. My favourite Pininfarina design is the Ferrari 250GT Lusso (1962). Like many other Pininfarina designs, it looks as good today as it did the day it was born. Sergio often said 'good design is timeless'. He is absolutely right and his company has produced many beautiful examples that verify this truth. Pininfarina cars age, but they never get old".

Enzo Ferrari and Pinin Farina in 1954. The car is probably a 340 Le Mans, perhaps no. 0320, used to race by Nino Farina, (nephew of Pinin), and Mike Hawthorn.

Ferrari gives Pinin Farina a prize. Behind Ferrari, Nello Ugolini, racing director for the Ferrari team and, with the cigar, Giovanni Canestrini, the leading motoring journalist of the time.

The chassis for the Ferrari 375 MM entered Pinin Farina in July 1954, and the coachbuilding shop was painted baby blue.

The Ferrari 375 MM (chassis no. 0456AM), purchased by Roberto Rossellini for Ingrid Bergman. Not only because of the celebrity of the client, this car was significant inasmuch as it featured a series of style elements that were to influence automotive design for at least twenty years. In particular, the retractable headlights, the side air exhausts, later seen on the 250 GTO and the 275 GTB, and the treatment of the rear window and the tail, reappearing on the Dino and even the Jaguar XJS.

A Pinin Farina con la riconoscenza per la preziosa collaborazione
Luc. Ciolfi

Campionato Italiano 1954

The gentleman racer Luciano Ciolfi, who with his Fiat 1100 TV Farina participated, among other things, in the Giro di Sicilia of 1954.

The letter in which Luciano Ciolfi wrote about his participation in the Giro di Sicilia of 1954.

VIA LOCRI, 1

ROMA 7 aprile 1954
TEL. 71839

Caro Sergio,

ti invio per espresso le foto del Giro di Sici
lia in cui mi hanno ripreso sia alla partenza che in corsa. Spero che
siano di tuo gradimento e fanne l'uso che ritieni più opportuno.Inol
tre ti accludo un foglio in cui sono riportate le classifiche genera
li di detta corsa. Essendomi state richieste delle fotografie sia dal
la Marelli che dalla Pirelli, ti sarei grato se ne facessi fare qual
che copia e me la inviassi.

Domenica correrò a Firenze ma non credo che po
trò fare bella figura come nel Giro di Sicilia in quanto l'ultima cor
sa é stata massacrante e Giannini non sa se riuscirà;a fare in tempo
a rimettere perfettamente a posto la vettura.

Ti prego gradire i miei più cordiali ed affettuo
si saluti.

P.S. Tieni presente che ho migliorato
il record sul giro di ben 6 Km. orari!!   Ciolfi

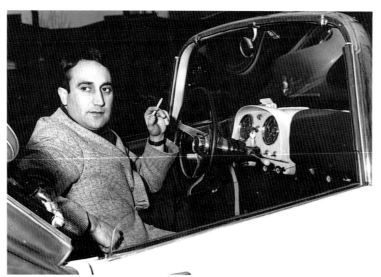

Pinin Farina was a passionate lover of the game of golf. Here we see him with the golf pro and teacher Lillo Angelini.

A caricature of Pinin Farina signed by the members of the Circolo degli Artisti, a club of which he was president, in January 1954.

Pinin and Sergio with De Dubé.

On the preceding page
On the left the journalist Emilio Fede in his Fiat 1100 Spider.

On the right Ciolfi's 1100 TV at the starting line of the Giro di Sicilia. This type of car ran in other races, including the Mille Miglia. In 1955, three of them started.

Nino Farina with the Ferrari 375 Plus at the starting line of the Mille Miglia of 1954, with his co-driver Luigi Parenti.

At the Giro di Sicilia on 4 April 1954, Piero Taruffi won with the Lancia D24 with an average speed of 103.743 kph. The same vehicle was restored in the Eighties by Count Vittorio Zanon.

The Bentley R Type Continental was the fastest production four-seater on Earth, and it had become the most sought-after of all the Bentleys built by Rolls-Royce after 1931. This vehicle, chassis no. BC49C, is literally unique: of the other 207 R Continentals, in fact, 193 had bodies by Mulliner, six by Park Ward, five by Franay, and three by Graber. It was delivered by Pinin Farina in the summer of 1954 to Charles Attwood, who actually only kept it for a year. It was painted beige, with a red-leather interior, and fortunately it still exists.

Sergio Farina at the Automotive Beauty Contest of the Pincio, in Rome, with a Ferrari 250 Europa.

Sergio Farina receiving an award from Michele Favia of the Core, founder of the magazine 'Motor' which had organized the Automotive Beauty Contest, one of the 'founding fathers' of Italian automotive journalism.

Pinin Farina at work on
a sketch for the Lancia
Aurelia B24.

The B24 S, also called
'America,' at the Automotive
Beauty Contest of Turin
in 1954.

Finishing line in the Corso Trapani: the Fiat 1100 TV Coupé, the Aurelia B24, and the Aurelia B20.

Bottom
Assembly of a B24 in the Corso Trapani (1954).

The Aurelia B24 Spider was characterized by a more distinctly shaped flank, by a wrap-around windscreen, and by the absence of roll-down windows. Driving it is Signora Chiantelassa.

In June 1955 a USIS documentary was filmed in the factory of the Corso Trapani. In the foreground, two Lancia Aurelia B24s.

132

The B24 was greatly appreciated by the celebrities of the period. Raf Vallone began a tradition that was to be emulated by his daughter.

2ª rallye automobilistico del cinema
ANNA MARIA SANDRI-RAF VALLONE

Françoise Sagan was also captivated by the allure of the B24, shown here in the successive version, known as the 'Convertible' (1956).

From Craftsmanship to Factory

from 1955 to 1966

Pinin and Sergio Farina with
Count Oddone
di Camerana watching
a Fiat 600 with a new body
at the Geneva Motor Show
of 1955.

On the same occasion, with
Engineer Minola
of Fiat, Count Biscaretti
di Ruffia and Count
Giovannino Lurani, journalist
and already an outstanding
gentleman racer.

Pinin and Sergio Farina
with Heinz Nordhoff, the
mastermind of the rebirth
of Volkswagen.

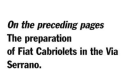

On the preceding pages
The preparation
of Fiat Cabriolets in the Via
Serrano.

At the Turin Motor Show
in April 1955, Gina
Lollobrigida admires the
body of the Ferrari 375
America built for Gianni
Agnelli (chassis
no. 0355AL).

A renowned photograph of Pinin with the head of the Testing Department, Musso, and Olivero, chief of the Painting Department, emblematic of his ' tactile' relationship with cars.

A sketch done by Pinin in 1959.

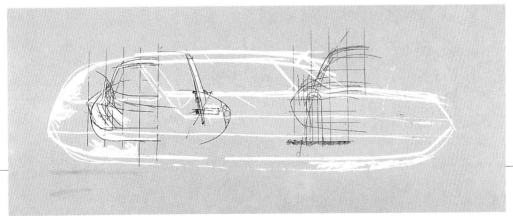

Pinin with Giuseppe Luraghi, president of Alfa, on his right, and Ugo Zagato with his son Elio (Balocco, 1962).

On the Alfa Romeo track at Balocco, on the occasion of the presentation of the Giulia Spider on 27 June 1962, Pinin Farina relied on the expertise of his test driver G.B. Guidotti.

The Alfa Romeo Giulietta Spider, a car that marked—with the 27000 units produced—the definitive transition of Pinin Farina from the crafts dimension to true industrial status.

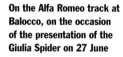

139

Top
The assembly lines of the
Corso Trapani. In the
foreground, a Fiat 1100 TV
Convertible, nearby a
number of Giulietta Spiders.

Centre
Check at the Painting
Department.

Assembly Department: the
Fiat 1100 TV Convertible,
the Alfa Romeo Giulietta
spider and the Lancia
Aurelia B20.

A car transporter has loaded
the transformable Fiat 1100
TVs, while the Giuliettas wait
their turn. The cars are
moved on special carts,
since they are without
wheels until the mechanical
components were mounted
at the car maker's factory.

A Monsieur Pinin Farina

26 Février 1955

Léopold

140

A Monsieur Pinin Farina,

En souvenir de deux de ses plus beaux enfants

Léopold

Turin, le 8 Octobre 1955

A calling card of Leopold of Belgium: relations with the Royal House were close and frequent.

A photograph dedicated to Pinin Farina 'in commemoration of two of his loveliest daughters' by Prince Leopold of Belgium. These 'daughters' were the Ferrari 342 America no. 0234 AL of 1953, and the 375 Plus no. 0488 AM of 1955.

In 1955, the Pinin Farina preview of the estate car concept, on a Fiat 1100 TV chassis.

The first Peugeot designed by Pinin Farina, the 403 Berlina (sedan), dated back to 1955; this was the first big hit for the French car maker, and more than 1.2 million were sold.

A 403 at the exhibition in Seoul 'Civilization, City, and Car. Pininfarina, from Leonardo to the Future' of 1996.

The Fiat 8V with body built for Giovanni Nasi, vice president of Fiat. Very similar to the Ferrari 375 MM of his cousin Gianni Agnelli.

The Jaguar XK120 presented at the Geneva Motor Show. The only one built, in 1955, it may have been constructed for a private client. The treatment of the front bumpers is reminiscent of the Lancia Aurelia B24S.

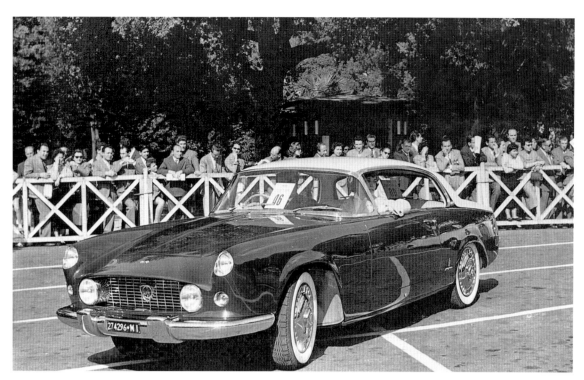

In October of 1955 the formal research prototype Florida I, with two doors, registered in Milan, took part in the Automotive Beauty Contest of Rome. The car is still extant, in Milan.

Facing page
Lorenza, Andrea, Paolo and Sergio Pininfarina pictured in 1998 in a Lancia Florida II.

The Florida II, presented at the Geneva Motor Show of 1957, was Pinin Farina's personal vehicle until his death. Horizontal radiator grille, low bonnet and high wings, revolutionary layout of the rear roof, dihedral treatment of the flanks, absence of a central upright element and a brilliant patented solution for the opening of the doors: all stylistic features that continued to influence world car production for many years.

Again on a Lancia Aurelia B56 chassis, the Florida I four-door was built in 1956, with book-style opening and without an upright element. It was presented at the Brussels Motor Show.

Bottom
Heir to the Florida, the Flaminia represented for Lancia entry to the modern era, symbolized by the elimination of the archaic vertical radiator grille. It was presented in Turin in 1956.

One of the first Flaminia coupés, designed and produced by Pinin Farina, inspired by the Florida II, delivered by Sergio Farina and Renzo Carli to the actress Marisa del Frate.

At the Geneva Motor Show of 1956, Pinin Farina greeted the president of the Helvetic Confederation, Markus Feldmann.

At the Turin Motor Show of 1956 with the Italian President Gronchi and the future President Leone.

Pinin Farina with Le Marichal and Paul Panhard.

Sergio Farina and the Alfa Romeo 3500 'Super Flow,' forerunner of the Duetto, at the Turin Motor Show of 1956.

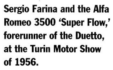

Sergio Farina at the Paris Motor Show with some journalists.

The coupé, on a Jaguar Mark VII chassis, built for the Greek ship builder Embiricos (1956) who, before the war, had ordered a Bentley from the Parisian coachbuilder Van Vooren, inspired by the streamlined Alfa Romeo 'Pescara' by Pinin Farina and the 'Super Flow II.'

Sergio Farina at the Automotive Beauty Contest of Venice, in June 1956, with a Jaguar 'Embiricos.'

Pinin Farina contributed to the great project (1960-68) of salvaging the Egyptian temples of Abu Simbel, about to be submerged by the huge reservoir created by the greater Aswan dam. In 1967 the Temple of Ellessiya was donated by the Egyptian government to the people of Italy in gratitude, and rebuilt at the Museo Egizio of Turin with the technical assistance of Pininfarina.

Pinin and Sergio with the Fiat 600 Multipla 'Eden Roc,' destined for two very special clients, Henry Ford II and Gianni Agnelli.

Prince Pignatelli, Sergio Farina, Henry Ford II, and Gianni Agnelli in 1956 at Pinin Farina to view the 'Eden Roc.'

Sergio Farina watches Franco Martinengo, director of the Styling Centre, as he presents the 'Eden Roc' model.

An 'Eden Roc' being loaded on to a ship bound for America.

The 'Eden Roc' in Cannes in 1957.

At the Brussels Motor Show of January 1956, Sergio with King Baudouin of Belgium. In the foreground, the Ferrari 410 SA.

The Ferrari 410 SA. At Brussels the first of the 16 built was exhibited— no. 0423SA—and then purchased by Count Fritz Somski.

The Cadillac Cabriolet of 1958 at the Paris Motor Show, with Sergio, Pinin Farina and the president of General Motors, Harlow Curtice.

On the same occasion, the president of General Motors tries out the driver's seat of the Cadillac Cabriolet. The roof would rise when the door was opened, to facilitate entry.

The assembly lines of the
Lancia Appia coupé.

In the mid-Fifties, in the
factory of the Corso
Trapani, the Lancia Appia
coupé was already being
produced in a numerically
distinct series.

The actress Sylva Koscina
with 'her' Lancia Appia
coupé.

In 1956 Pinin left it up to his sons to decide on making an investment in a new and larger factory in Grugliasco.

At the Motor Show of Geneva of 1957, Pinin Farina showed two speed-record-setting Abarths, one with an 1100 engine, derived from Alfa Romeo, the other with a 750 engine derived from Fiat.

Farina, father and son, and between them, the Italian President Gronchi.

Pinin Farina in 1957 with Gianni Lancia, son of the great Vincenzo Lancia.

In 1956 construction
began on the new plant
at Grugliasco.

Bottom
On 30 October of 1957 the
plans for the new plant at
Grugliasco were presented
to the press.

Right
The press touring the new
plant at Grugliasco
in 1957.

The factory at Grugliasco
in 1958, almost finished.

Pinin on the roof
of the new plant and inside
the building.

"In the mid-Fifties I was little more than a kid, I wasn't even an industrial designer, I was just a model-maker, or 'figurinista,' at the Centro Stile Fiat, or styling centre. When the Lancia Aurelia B24 Spider was presented, I was astounded, and I finally really understood who Pinin Farina was: it all come down to the capacity of one individual to attract the attention of those who had the taste and the means to select and purchase custom-made products," explained Giorgetto Giugiaro, cofounder and president of Italdesign.

LC   Of the 70 years of activity of Pininfarina, you lived for more than 40 as a direct competitor. How did you see Pinin and how do you see Pininfarina today?

GG   "Certainly, he represents the apex of model-making. His forte has always been his consistency, for that matter a creative like me manages to understand when he has made his mark. What remains is the school, a family style, but you can see the difference. As long as Pinin was 'on track,' he was the unrivalled king, all of the others—including me—were nothing but an alternative, a corollary. Pininfarina remains, in any case, a landmark for Italian design. When in the Sixties and Seventies the Turin Motor Show was attended by crowds of executives from car makers around the world, the real reason that they would come was to see what Pininfarina was presenting, which in fact made our sector more important and particularly well known to the ends of the Earth."

LC   Aside from the Aurelia B24, what other vehicles particularly impressed you?

GG   "Lots of them, beginning with the Cisitalia which, with the integration of the wings, marked a moment of transition for the entire automotive industry. Then the Ferrari 250 LM, for its capacity to give a certain kind of style even to an exceedingly technical product, such as a racing car. Even though it is absolutely functional, with a technical imprint, it manages to be lovely and refined, while renouncing however any uselessly coy and flirtatious treatment. The Ferrari 275 GTB represented a major turning point in the design of racing cars: it gave a strong impression of power, even in its synthesis with good taste. The hint of a spoiler on the tail was, in those years, a shocking element."

LC   Only production cars? Many people venerate the Modulo as a fetish of the larger world of Italian industrial design...

GG   "I disagree, and there are two reasons. First of all, I am more impressed with the mass-production vehicles than the research prototypes produced by Pininfarina. Second, the Modulo can certainly claim to be an avant-garde vision of the automobile, but it is also relatively sterile because it is obviously impossible to actually produce. In terms of the experimental vehicles of that period, I was most impressed with the Alfa 33 and the Ferrari 512 S which, however advanced they may have been, were in any case feasible in technical terms."

LC   In the couple Ferrari-Pininfarina, at a certain point, another personality intrudes, your own Italdesign. When and with what results?

GG   "Only twice. At the time of the 348 and more recently with Montezemolo for the 360 Modena. My personal sensation? More than a Ferrari by Giugiaro, it seemed to me that in Maranello they especially wanted a powerful stimulus for Pininfarina."

LC   Always and only praise for Pininfarina. Chivalry is a very nice thing, but they must have made mistakes at some point...

GG   "Certainly, but creative workers are the least appropriate people to criticise the uncertainty of others. We have all indulged in excess, overdesigned things, often you let your client take you down a path that you never would have taken if you had followed your own taste and sensibility. For instance, the Allanté: too much Cadillac and too little Pininfarina. Another case was the Lancia Gamma, saloon and coupé, a rare occasion in which they too—as can happen sooner or later to everyone—gave in too much to the fashion reigning in those years."

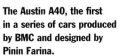

The Austin A40, the first in a series of cars produced by BMC and designed by Pinin Farina.

Pinin and Sergio Farina with Sir Leonard Lord, president of BMC, and Sir George Harriman, vice president, in 1959, with the Austin A40 designed by Pinin Farina.

Pinin with his daughter-in-law Giorgia, in a picture snapped by Sergio.

Pinin in 1958 with his grandchildren (from left to right) Elisabetta, Lorenza, Andrea, Paolo, and Umberta.

The Nash 'Palm Beach,'
(1956) stylistically an
offshoot of the Lancia
Aurelia PF200; on the right,
Renzo Carli and Franco
Martinengo, director of the
Styling Centre.

Bottom
In October of 1958, the
'joint chiefs of staff' of Fiat
touring Grugliasco
(from left): Engineer Bono,
Engineer Nasi, Gianni
Agnelli, and Vittorio Valletta.

Paris Motor Show of 1958:
the Farinas with Mario del
Monaco and the Cadillac
Cabriolet.

Pinin, in 1958, with his 'two sons': Sergio and his son-in-law Renzo Carli.

The Ferrari 410SA (no. 1015SA), at first painted white and later painted 'gentian blue.' Built in the summer of 1958, it was exhibited at the Turin Motor Show the following November.

The assembly line for the Ferrari 250GT.

The Ferrari 250GT, produced in limited series by Pinin Farina. The car no. 0851 GT, built in May 1958 and later sent to Chinetti in America.

The first Ferrari 250
Testarossa (no. 0766),
presented in late February
1959.

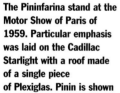

Giorgio Albertazzi and Anna
Proclemer, visiting Pinin
Farina, observe a Ferrari
250GT.

At the Turin Motor Show,
Sergio Farina with the
Ferrari 400 SA
(no. 1517SA) built for
Gianni Agnelli, here in the
first version with air intakes.

The Pininfarina stand at the
Motor Show of Paris of
1959. Particular emphasis
was laid on the Cadillac
Starlight with a roof made
of a single piece
of Plexiglas. Pinin is shown

welcoming (centre
photograph) French
President Charles de Gaulle.
A few weeks later, the
Starlight was also shown
at the Motor Show of Turin
(photograph on the right);

Renzo Carli and Sergio
Farina were justifiably
proud.

February 18, 1959: the actor James Stewart with Prince von Fürstenberg touring Pinin Farina.

Signorina Ciucci, an expert on automobiles and the champion of the television quiz show 'Lascia o Raddoppia,' in her Alfa Romeo 3500 Super Sport, in May 1959.

One of the most successful Ferrari, the 250 GT Sedan 'SWB,' named because of its short wheelbase, with respect to the preceding 'Tour de France' versions. Here a model from the street series 'Lusso,' probably dating from 1961.

Bottom
A recent photo of the 250 GT Sedan 'SWB' (1959) from the Pininfarina Collection, restored for the fiftieth anniversary in 1980.

Left
On 22 March 1959 Pinin, along with the journalist Giovanni Canestrini, set out for a journey around the world: here they are in a street in Tokyo.

Right
Pinin in Washington with the ambassador Manlio Brosio.

Bottom
Pinin Farina, a man of acute intelligence. Traveling for him always meant "learning."

The journey continues: here they are in Auckland.

Pinin in Polynesia.

A phase of manufacturing: the wooden template was used in pounding out by hand the sheet-metal panels that were to be used in the body.

The record-setting Abarth in a studio at the Testing Department.

"I wanted to become a designer, but in Turin I only had contact with the Carrozzeria Ghia, where I had worked as an intern for two summers. And so, in the summer of 1957, I applied to Pininfarina. I had a meeting with Sergio: it was a very interesting talk, and he gave me some very useful advice," remembers Bruno Sacco who then, for more than twenty-five years, went on to oversee design at Mercedes Benz. "Sergio admitted that the profession of designer and stylist was an attractive one, but that I should not kid myself: it would never make me rich. 'You won't have a yacht or a house in the mountains,' he said to me, and now, at the end of my career, I can say that he was absolutely right."

LC Was it only a courtesy meeting or was that day in 1957 a genuine test?

BS "Sergio asked me to do an 'exercise' on the chassis of the new Fiat 500. A few weeks later I went back to show it to him, he really liked one of my sketches, and he asked me to develop it. Well, I did, and I was even paid for it."

LC And then?

BS "I was already negotiating with Mercedes Benz, which hired me in December of 1957. I went back to Pininfarina to tell them that I would be going to Germany, but Sergio wasn't there, so I told one of his coworkers to say goodbye for me."

LC If a university were to invite you tomorrow to talk about coachbuilders, how would you present Pininfarina?

BS "As the mother of Italian coachbuilders, where the trade is handed down from father to son. We are now on the third generation in the company, while the fourth generation is still in school."

LC Some speak of Pininfarina as the "royal family" of Italian industrial design...

BS "Royalty can mean many things; what counts most is people. From this point of view, I think that Sergio is a complex and unique individual. He is an outstanding technician, a superlative entrepreneur, and also a creative who knows the profession of styling like the back of his hand. In addition, he has performed social services: he has been the president of various business associations. Note, moreover, that he did so during years when terrorism was raging, and therefore faced considerable personal risks."

LC Let's go back to the imaginary lecture hall. What five emblematic vehicles would you show your audience in order to explain Pininfarina design to them?

BS "I would begin with the Cisitalia, agreed universally to be a masterpiece, and in fact it is

part of the permanent collection of the Museum of Modern Art in New York, even though I personally never really liked it much. Then come two lovely Lancias, the Aurelia B24 Spider and the Florida II, upon which—a titbit of information that is not widely known—the doors operated with Mercedes Benz locking mechanisms. Then a classic Ferrari, the 250 SWB of 1960, while among the more recent vehicles I would mention the Peugeot 406 Coupé. Last of all, among the pure research prototypes, I would certainly mention the Modulo."

LC How could it be that in their long histories, the destinies of Pininfarina and Mercedes Benz have never managed to intertwine?

BS "Honestly, I can't come up with an answer. And yet we have met countless times over the past forty years. I clearly remember the first time, at the end of the Sixties. They came to us—invited by Karl Wilfert, my direct superior at the time—Sergio and his brother-in-law Renzo Carli, a great technician. It was an exploratory meeting, and my job was really that of onlooker. Other contacts followed but, for one reason or another, they all petered out into nothing. The most recent was not long ago: for the design and production of the CLK Cabriolet, I had suggested Pininfarina and I know that Sergio really wanted the job. Instead, in the end, they decided to go with Karmann. I hope that they will be more fortunate in the new millennium."

One of the models
for the Fiat X aerodynamic
research prototype,
developed with
the Polytechnic of Turin
(1960).

The Fiat X aerodynamic
research prototype, with
rhomboidal configuration
of the wheels, being tested
by with Sergio and Renzo
Carli.

Top
**Pinin and Enzo Ferrari
in the Sixties.**

**Pinin and Juan Manuel
Fangio in the Sixties
in Buenos Aires.**

**Pinin Farina with Maria
Beatrice di Savoia,
at the Circolo degli Artisti
in Turin.**

**Pinin with the opera singer
Renata Tebaldi.**

Sergio Pininfarina in the Sixties.

Sergio Pininfarina and Renzo Carli with the template for pounding sheet metal for the Ferrari 400 SA.

Sergio and Pinin in front of the entrance to the factory of Grugliasco.

Between September
and October 1960, on the
"raised track" of Monza,
the Abarth Special with
body by Pinin Farina took
eight world records, with
engine displacements
of 750 cc and 1000 cc,
with the racers Baghetti,
Maglioli, Cattini, Rigamonti,
Manfredini, Bassi, Thiele,
Castellina, and Leto di
Priolo, as well as the future
journalist Mario Poltronieri.

The Peugeot 404 of 1960,
the second great success of
the Franco-Italian
partnership.

"France had a wonderful school of automotive design right up to the Second World War, when it vanished. From the post war period to the present day, the Italian school has been dominant, with the most remarkable period in the Fifties and Sixties. And so the Italians, and especially Pininfarina, have always been the point of reference for the modern automobile," maintains Gérard Welter, who has worked at the Peugeot Styling Centre since 1960; he has been its director since 1998. "In the adventure with Ferrari, Pininfarina did some fantastic things. From the "barchettas" of the Sixties, which served as inspiration for all sorts of things, including the celebrated AC Cobra, to the long series of MMs, a point of reference for all of us designers, like the 250 GTO for that matter. With these Ferraris, Pininfarina gave the whole world of design the imagination and the foundations to develop true modern automobiles."

LC And Pininfarina for Peugeot?

GW "By now it would be too difficult to separate the history of the modern Peugeot company from that of Pininfarina. The collaboration dates all the way back to the 403; they brought to our trademark a skill, a mastery that we lacked. Pinin Farina was more than a coachbuilder, he was also an industrialist and, from the 404 on, we produced the cars together as well. The work with Peugeot then was more than just a consultation on styling, it was a true global collaboration."

LC What has changed in the last nearly 50 years of working together?

GW "When we began to work with Pininfarina, we had to learn the craft of coachbuilding from them. Now we have mastered that skill, we are competitive and in competition, not only with Pininfarina, but also with other outside designers. Nowadays the Styling Centres of the manufacturers are more integrated into the activities of the manufacturer, but we at Peugeot always want to feel the "heat" of the outside world, and in this aspect Pininfarina is our institutional and privileged counterpart."

LC In times like these, of increasingly strong and integrated in-house Styling Centres, does a small "external" studio like Pininfarina run the risk of becoming a fragile vase set between large cast-iron urns?

GW "Of course, for an external studio, it will be increasingly difficult to put one's name on a mass-produced vehicle, even if there will always be exceptions to the rule, especially in the world of creativity, where it is precisely the creative who makes even the impossible possible. I would say that in the future the coachbuilder will offer primarily a contribution to the overall thinking on a new model, not the complete solution to the problem. In biblical terms, perhaps I might say that the in-house Styling Centres are now so many giants like Goliath, but the world nowadays is too competitive to look only at what we do, and so we will always need little Davids who force us to broaden our vision."

LC In so many years of collaboration, what Pininfarina project was the most stirring and exciting for you?

GW "Without a doubt, the 504 Coupé. At the time, our Styling Centre was still embryonic, and even the floor was just plain asphalt. When they unloaded the model from the forklift and pushed it into the presentation room, we were all left breathless. I looked at it, and to myself I said: 'Superb!' We studied it at length and then,

without needing to talk it over, we decided to industrialise it without any modifications. It was—and still is—a really beautiful car."

LC Those were the days when Davids could still beat Goliaths.

GW "That's not what I would say. In those days, our Styling Centre was the little David!"

LC Among the many designs done by Pininfarina for other clients in nearly fifty years, is there one that you wish could have been a Peugeot?

GW "The only 'other' Pininfarinas that interested me were Ferraris, but Peugeot doesn't produce cars of that sort. In general, I would like to say that Pininfarina is even more 'specialised' in Ferraris than in Peugeots. But that doesn't bother us: we are more than happy to be forced to 'cohabit' with Ferrari in the heart of Pininfarina."

165

Workshops for painting
the cars, at the end of
the Fifties.

Finishing Department.

166

On the finishing line
it is possible to see several
Fiat 1500 Cabriolets,
two Fiat 1500 GTs, and
a Peugeot 404 Cabriolet.

The Fiat 1500 Cabriolet
of 1959-60, with twin-shaft
engine of OSCA derivation
and a body identical to that
of the 1200.

Gianni Agnelli's Ferrari 410 SA, no. 1517SA, after the modifications of May 1960: elimination of the front side air intakes, new bumpers in sheet metal and a new chrome silhouette along the flank.

Sergio Farina with Sir Alec Issigonis, the brilliant designer of the Mini.

Pinin Farina with the Ferrari 250 GT 'Lusso' (1962).

Left
Pinin with Sofia Loren
at the exhibition curated by
him, 'Moda Stile
e Costume,' inaugurated
in June 1961 in Turin for
the centennial of
the unification of Italy.

Top right
On the same occasion
with Herbert Von Karajan,
a great lover of fine
automobiles.

Arturo Benedetti
Michelangeli admiring the
Ferrari 400 SA 'Superfast
II' of 1960 (chassis
no. 2207SA).

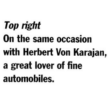

Queen Elizabeth II on an
official visit to Turin for
the centennial celebration
of the unification of Italy.

On the occasion
of the Queen's tour, three
processional vehicles were
built with Flaminia
mechanical parts, one of
which is still used by Italy's
Quirinale, or presidential
palace, on official
occasions. The vehicle
shown belongs to the British
Royal House.

In 1963 Pininfarina built this one-off coupé with the mechanical components of a Lancia Flaminia 2.8, shown here at the Automotive Beauty Contest of Alassio in 1965.

The silhouette of the Lancia Flaminia Coupé by Pininfarina (1958-69).

The elegant Lancia Flavia Coupé 2+2 of 1961, offered in 1500 and 1800 versions.

AUTOMOBILE CLUB FIRENZE   AZIENDA AUTONOMA TURISMO DI FIRENZE

Concorso internazionale di eleganza per autovetture
FIRENZE • GIARDINO DI BOBOLI • 20-21 MAGGIO 1961

Gran Premio d'Onore

ALLA FABBRICA DI CARROZZERIE

S.p.A. Pininfarina

AUTOMOBILE CLUB FIRENZE
IL PRESIDENTE
Dr. Ing. P. Barracci

AZIENDA AUTONOMA TURISMO
DI FIRENZE
IL PRESIDENTE
Prof. Ing. A. Tuccini

2999 - A PAGAMENTO
ESTRATTO
Si dà atto che con decreto del Presidente della Repubblica in data 6 Giugno 1961 - trascritto nei registri di nascita del Comune di Torino - Anno 1961 - n. 666 - 1 - 2 - B, i signori - Cav. del Lavoro Farina Battista, nato a Torino il 2. 11. 1893 ed ivi residente in Corso Stati Uniti n. 61; e ingegner Farina Sergio, nato a Torino il 8/9/1926 e residente a Torino, Corso Matteotti n. 42, B, quali Presidenti del Consiglio di Amministrazione il primo ed Amministratore Delegato il secondo della Società per Azioni CARROZZERIA PININFARINA, con sede in Torino e col capitale sociale di LIRE 8.000.000 versato; vennero autorizzati a cambiare il cognome: "Farina" in quello di: "PININFARINA" e pertanto i sopradetti Signori potranno fare uso per l'avvenire, in tutti gli atti ed in ogni circostanza, di quest'ultimo cognome.
Torino, li 26/10/1961 -
Manacorda Umberto Not.
Tribunale di Torino Ufficio Società Depositato il 27 Ottobre 1961 Numero 14641 Registro d'Ordine N. -- Trascrizione N. 186 Società N. 2099/950 Fascicolo.
Pagata tassa in L. 2005
Il Cancelliere
Manfredi

A relaxed and casual scene: Sergio chased by Renzo Carli and the journalists Bernard Cahier and Paul Frère at the Geneva Motor Show of 1961.

Harley Earl, styling director for General Motors, between Sergio Pininfarina and Renzo Carli, in September 1961.

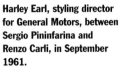

Two years after their first meeting, Pinin and De Gaulle meet again.

In December 1961 Pininfarina with the unfortunate racer Lorenzo Bandini, third from the right.

Offshoot of the 'X,' but with a more conventional chassis, the Fiat 'Y,' shown here at the Automotive Beauty Contest of Cortina d'Ampezzo in July 1962.

Bottom
Pininfarina also wished to try water-skiing.

Pinin at Grugliasco with his Ferrari 250GT; on the bonnet, a little globe to commemorate his round-the-world voyage.

DUE MAGHI A SANREMO

SANREMO — Il mago della carrozzeria d'auto Pinin Farina apprende le « malizie » dello sci nautico dal mago Hans Nöbl
(Foto Moreschi)

Gino Paoli in an Alfa Romeo
2600 Convertible (1962).

173

At the Turin Motor Show
of 1962 Pinin and Sergio
with President of the Italian
Republic Antonio Segni.

A special convertible, with
a particularly successful
appearance, on an Alfa
Romeo 2600 chassis.

"I first met Pinin Farina in the early Sixties. At the time I was fifteen years old and knew nothing about cars: I just went around with my father," recalls Piero Ferrari, vice president of the Ferrari Motor Company. *"Of that first meeting, I remember that we went to the plant in Grugliasco, which had just been finished. My father was taking Pinin plans for self-bearing frames based on a front-mounted V8 engine derived from a rear-mounted Sport V8 engine. That vehicle was never made, but the mechanical structure with the rear gearbox, survived, and was later used on the GTC, the GTS, and the Daytona.*

What was meeting in those years was not just two companies but two generations of two families: on the one hand, Pinin and my father, who were carrying on the real discussion, and on the other, Sergio and myself, and mostly we listened. Generally the meetings went on until quite late and my father used to cap off these long days of work with sparkling and convivial dinners, of which I have lovely memories."

LC How long did you have to wait before you gained the 'right to speak' in the meetings with the Pininfarinas?

PF "Quite a few years. I began to work at Ferrari at the end of 1965, but mainly focusing on racing until 1987. My meetings with Pininfarina therefore were only occasional, and I had direct contacts only for the Sigma F1. That vehicle was never really understood: many looked at it as a pure exercise in style for motor shows, but in fact it contained many extremely valid concepts, especially in the area of safety. From when I began to work with product, in 1988, I worked more closely with them, also because now I am a member of the committee that oversees style."

LC Pinin Farina and Enzo Ferrari may have had thousands of great qualities, but certainly not a nice character. What fights must have developed out of the contract between two such strong personalities.

PF "I never saw them really fight. My father would grumble about the costs, never about the quality of the work of Pininfarina. It never happened that a car was entirely rejected. Instead, often, my father would fail to understand 100 per cent the spirit of certain motor show prototypes, such as the Modulo and the 512 S,

but he let them go on anyway. He never saw the Mythos, which was instead much closer to his sensibility, to his way of 'feeling' street Ferraris."

LC And yet, in the long history of Ferrari and Pininfarina, there was more than one 'betrayal' in the area of design.

PF "Attempts, yes, but in the end Pininfarina always won out."

LC And the Dino 308 GT4 by Bertone?

PF "The decision was not based on a choice of style; it was industrially based. In order to understand it, we must however first take a step back in time. Fiat was producing in the Rivalta plant the V6 Dino engine, which we used for our Dinos and for two Fiat vehicles, the two-seater Spider built by Pininfarina and the 2+2 Coupé, built by Bertone. In the transition from the V6 Dino to the V8, Fiat was to halt production of vehicles with Ferrari engines, while we believed

that the most logical choice was to carry on with our partners of the type: two-seater coupés with Pininfarina, 2+2s with Bertone. And so it was not a stylistic betrayal, as much as a choice in favour of industrial continuity."

LC Can we ask a Ferrari to choose the best-looking Ferrari in history?

PF "Certainly, but the answer cannot be a simple one, because every era has its favourite. And, in any case, all the Pininfarinas age well, like those lovely older women who were clearly beautiful girls in their youth. So here is my list: for the Sixties, the 330 GTC/GTS, extremely elegant and superbly balanced. For the Seventies, unquestionably, the BB. For the Eighties, the Testarossa: nowadays it seems a little flashy, but when it was introduced, it made everyone's heart beat a little faster."

LC One car that is missing from your gallery is the mythical—for many—Daytona. Why is that?

PF "Because stylistically it is not consistent between front and back. There was a prototype made during development with a different front headlight assembly. We saw it again on Rodeo Drive during the presentation in the US of the 550 Maranello and, in perfect agreement with Sergio, we had the very same thought: that time we did not choose the best one."

Gianni Mazzocchi, founder of the publishing house Editoriale Domus.

The PF 'Sigma,' prototype of a safe car, was presented in New York in 1963. This was a bodywork study with 14 innovative technical solutions in the field of safety, undertaken at the behest of Gianni Mazzocchi—the father of Italian automotive journalism, founder of the publishing house Editoriale Domus in 1929, and director of the magazine 'Quattroruote'—and Pininfarina, to offer a concrete contribution to the issue of safety.

Right
The PF 'Sigma' at the exhibition 'La Sicurezza del Traffico' (Safety in Traffic) held in Munich in June 1965. In 1966 it was also presented to the American Senate, which had passed the most advanced legislation in the field of safety. From 1969 on, the car has been part of the permanent collection of the Transportation Museum in Lucerne.

Pinin once again in Brazil,
at the waterfall of Iguaçù
in 1963.

Bottom
Pinin at Saõ Paulo in Brazil
in November of the same
year.

Another stop on the same
trip: Chile.

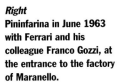

Ferrari, Pininfarina, and his
Ferrari 250 GT Lusso
(no. 4335GT).

Right
**Pininfarina in June 1963
with Ferrari and his
colleague Franco Gozzi, at
the entrance to the factory
of Maranello.**

**In the Ferrari Racing
Division.**

**Pininfarina with Enzo
Ferrari.**

In Paris, in May 1963, with the wooden buck of the Ferrari 250 GT California.

Pinin with his 250 GT, on 27 June 1963.

Renzo Carli, Ferruccio Bernabò, Sir Alec Issigonis, Athos Evangelisti, Sergio Pininfarina, Gino Rancati: industry and the press.

Pinin's personal Ferrari 250 GT 'Lusso' (no. 4335GT). Like other cars used by Pinin, there was no quarter-light on the left side.

"I first visited Pininfarina 35 years ago although the real attraction came in 1996 at the FISITA Congress in Prague, when I met Sergio Pininfarina", explains Hirokazu Nakamura, then Chairman of Mitsubishi Motors Corporation and who is to date its Executive Counsellor. "Sergio started talking about the future of design, and I the future of the engine, as my dream as a young engineer was a direct injection petrol engine, which with the GDI finally became a reality. We just had far too much to talk about so we decided to have dinner together. He told me of his father's wish to work with us and this, to be honest, I found rather touching. On my way back from Prague, I stopped off in Turin to visit Pininfarina and there I decided that very soon we would have been working together".

LC In the past, however, I believe that there had already been some talk of production at the Pininfarina plant...

HN "Well, we had actually examined this possibility for the second generation of the Pajero. At one point we were even thinking of manufacturing it in Europe and Italy, being the Continental market which took in the most, seemed to be the ideal country and Pininfarina the most suitable place to produce it. This however, remained a more theoretical project than realistic operative plan: we were already

working on the new plant in Holland, now known as NedCar BV, and it would have been far too difficult for us to manage two production lines in Europe".

LC Italy did, however, see the production of a new Pajero, but only in 1999...

HN "Pajero Pinin. Everyone wanted to call it Pajero Farina, perhaps because it sounded more similar to the name Pininfarina. I, however, insisted on Pinin and was assisted by Lorenza Pininfarina, who reminded all my colleagues that in the Torinese dialect 'Pinin' means 'little one'. A name which perfectly suited the new, smaller version Pajero".

LC So from partners to friends: what do Hirokazu Nakamura and Sergio Pininfarina have in common?

HN "Age, love for cars and flight, as we are both aeronautical engineers. Then of course our passion for golf. In this area Sergio is better than I am but being such a gentleman he lets me drive from the ladies tee, making the game an open challenge".

Right
Pinin on the day he was awarded a degree in architecture 'ad honoris causam' (1963).

The Austin Morris 1100, engineered by Alec Issigonis and designed by Pininfarina.

The diploma in architecture 'ad honoris causam' for Battista Farina.

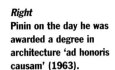

IN NOME DELLA LEGGE
Noi Prof. Dott. Ing. ANTONIO CAPETTI
Rettore del Politecnico di Torino

Visto l'art. 169 del Testo Unico delle Leggi sulla Istruzione Superiore, approvato con R. D. 31 Agosto 1933. n. 1592; vista la deliberazione in data 20 Marzo 1963 con la quale il Consiglio della Facoltà di Architettura ha proposto all'unanimità il conferimento della LAUREA AD HONOREM IN ARCHITETTURA al Cavaliere del Lavoro BATTISTA PININFARINA. nato a Torino il 2 Novembre 1895. in riconoscimento della meritata fama di singolare perizia da lui raggiunta nelle discipline architettoniche quale creatore della più nota ed apprezzata carrozzeria del nostro Paese. industria che seppe far assurgere a glorie mondiali. imponendo anche all'estero lo stile architettonico italiano;

vista la lettera in data 11 Aprile 1963 n. 1886. con la quale il Ministero della Pubblica Istruzione ha approvato la deliberazione predetta;

conferiamo a

BATTISTA PININFARINA
LA LAUREA AD HONOREM IN ARCHITETTURA

Il presente diploma di laurea viene rilasciato a tutti gli effetti di legge.

DATO A TORINO IL 6 NOVEMBRE 1963

IL DIRETTORE AMMINISTRATIVO   IL RETTORE   IL PRESIDE DELLA FACOLTÀ

One of the last Ferrari 400 SA, in a photo from 1963.

The actor Raf Vallone at the wheel of a Ferrari 400 SA at the Turin Motor Show of 1963.

26 June 1963: Agnelli
and Pininfarina in Verona
during the Raid
Internazionale '1899.'

The Fiat 2300 'Lausanne,'
a one-off (1963).

At the Turin Motor Show
of 1963, Sergio shows the
'Lausanne' to the soccer
player Omar Sivori.

Pininfarina in Grugliasco in 1964.

Sergio with his sister Gianna Pininfarina Carli.

Renzo Carli and Sergio Pininfarina.

Bernard of the Netherlands with Enzo Ferrari, Pinin and Sergio touring Grugliasco, in June 1964.

In June of 1964 in Maranello with G.B. Loudon, president of Shell, and Enzo Ferrari. In the background, a first-series 330 GT 2+2.

"For years I would see Pinin Farina every morning, but I never met him. While I was on my way to my high school, the Liceo Scientifico Galileo Ferraris, I would see him leaving home for the plant, in his Lancia Florida II, which was black with a turquoise interior, a colour combination of considerable elegance. I knew perfectly well who he was, because in order to get in free to the motor show, in those years, I would work as an 'usher,' or more modestly, a 'ticket-taker,'" recalled Paolo Cantarella, managing director of Fiat S.p.A. and president of Fiat Auto.

LC When did you first work professionally with Pininfarina?

PC "As a supplier, around 1984-85, when I was in charge of the Comau. Pininfarina, on behalf of General Motors, was overseeing the engineering of the GM-200 project, which was to engender the trio of the Chevrolet Lumina APV, Oldsmobile Silhouette, and Pontiac Trans Sport minivans. We, as Comau USA, were participating as a partner in the development and in the production technologies. As a client I would see them again at the beginning of the Nineties, when in Fiat Auto we laid the foundations for the production of the Coupé. And then, starting with the 360 Modena, I finally entered what had seemed to me, ever since I was a boy, a magical world, the Nirvana of every car fan: the creation of new Ferraris."

LC In your vision of Pininfarina, which aspect is predominant: the creative or the productive?

PC "In fact I see them as interconnected, inasmuch as I consider Pininfarina the natural candidate for limited production or sports cars."

LC Say that you met a foreign colleague who had never heard of Pininfarina. How would you describe it in a few words?

PC "Impossible: anyone who works in this sector, anywhere on Earth, would know perfectly well who Pininfarina is and what it does. Only a Martian could be entirely ignorant, and then I would say simply, they design Ferraris."

LC Can we try to talk about Pininfarina for a minute without talking about Ferrari?

PC "Why should we? It is true that engines like that help the aesthetics, but this combination has produced a number of truly remarkable cars. Just take a look at the Dino Parigi of 1965, what Pinin would call 'my little grand-daughter,' still beautiful today, and stylistically the mother of all modern Ferraris. All of the Lancias by Pininfarina have always pleased me in particular, especially the Aurelia B24 Spider, a formal theme that we see again in the Alfa Romeo Giulietta

Spider, where, however—in a shorter car body—it proved of course less harmonious. Moving from the sports cars to the saloons, I am particularly impressed with the elegant sobriety of the Peugeot 404."

LC These are the strong points. What about the weak points?

PC "Like all independent designers, they too often have an internal consensus and they forget the consensus with the brand with which they have to work. In other words, there are profoundly 'Pininfarina' ideas, which to us sometimes seem not to be sufficiently characteristic of our vision of an Alfa, a Fiat, or a Lancia. From an industrial point of view, we have watched them suffer and grow. When, just after its introduction, production of the Fiat Coupé reached a rate of 100 units a day, their corporate culture, based on more limited production, revealed a number of weak spots, critical flaws. Still, I must honestly say that they overcame these problems quite well and that today the objective situation has changed, as is demonstrated for that matter by sizeable jobs assigned to them by other car makers."

The awarding of a prize to a young student at 'La Salle.'

Pinin at the inauguration of the school 'La Salle' in Grugliasco, with Bishop Bonetti.

The technical school 'La Salle,' a centre for learning and leisure time built by Pinin for the training of young workers.

The cover of an issue of the magazine 'Pininfarina,' 1964.

Pinin with Bill Mitchell and his staff, in Detroit, on 17 April 1964.

Sergio Pininfarina at the General Motors Styling Center, again with Bill Mitchell and his staff.

Right
With Bill Mitchell, vice president of General Motors Design, in a prototype Corvette during a visit to Detroit in April 1964.

On the preceding page
Pininfarina with a Ferrari 275 GTB in the Parco del Valentino (1965).

The Ferrari 250 LM owned by the English importer for the Casa di Maranello (1963).

Pinin in St Moritz with the Flaminia 2800 Speciale and the Florida II.

The first-series Ferrari 330 GT 2+2 at the Automotive Beauty Contest at Cortina d'Ampezzo (1964).

Sergio with a Ferrari 330 GT 2+2, mass-produced by Pininfarina.

The Spider version 330 GTS. This is no. 8899, first of the 100 produced, finished in July 1966.

A second-series Ferrari 330 GT 2+2, recognisable by its single front headlights, its elongated parking lights/turn indicators, and the beaks on the bumpers (1965).

A Ferrari 330 GTC, two-seater car on a chassis with wheelbase shortened to 2,400 mm, presented at Geneva in 1966.

What impresses me most is the longevity of the collaboration between Peugeot and Pininfarina. It began at the turn of the Fifties with the 403 and it continues today. By now, it has been nearly fifty years, and that is quite a long time. Pininfarina was already working for Italian car builders, but strangely the longest-lasting relationship was with a foreign company," points out Jean Boillot, director of Peugeot until 1990.

LC What memories do you have of Pinin?

JB "Only faded ones. At the time of his most frequent presence in Peugeot I was not yet working on product. I saw him later, when I had become the commercial director, even though my closest working relationships were, from 1965 on, with Sergio and his brother-in-law Renzo Carli".

LC How could you describe Pininfarina's influence on Peugeot?

JB "He helped us to grow up, to become great. We began to work together immediately after the war, we were starting from nothing, with bombed-out plants. Until the Second World War, our production was made up of mass-production and limited-production vehicles, and after the war a more mass-market product prevailed, whereupon design—until then an almost exclusive province of the coachbuilder—made its way into the plant. And so we were obliged to create an in-house Styling Centre, but in any case we needed an external adviser. From our meeting

with Pininfarina we succeeded in obtaining both things, while still focusing on a single result: in any case to create a superior product."

LC In Italy, there is an old proverb that says that you can't have the barrel full and your wife drunk, roughly equivalent to having your cake and eating it too. From what you are saying it would seem that Peugeot, with Pininfarina, has succeeded in having things both ways.

JB "I would say so. Being able to rely on the external shock of Pininfarina has been an enormous advantage for us. Over time, we have managed to balance two competing Styling Centres, without one prevailing over the other. For a corporation it is extremely important to have a strong in-house style, but it is equally fundamental to enjoy the contribution of a great outside adviser. To soothe the rivalries between the in-house centre and the external creatives is a problem for management, and in any case less troublesome than the situation of having one's own Styling Centre that, without competition, winds up stagnating. Decades of competition have forced both to grow and to improve continually, with unquestioned benefits on the quality of the design. For years now, it has not mattered for us whether the basic idea comes from Pininfarina or the in-house Styling Centre: the important thing is that the vehicle should be the right Peugeot for the moment."

LC Competition sharpens the facilities of the creative, and yet in the last 50 years there have been some Peugeots that were, shall we say, unattractive.

JB "True, but it has not always been the designers' fault. The 204 had the gearbox under the engine, and so the bonnet was unusually high and the aesthetic outcome could not be much to brag about. In order to make the 205 a pretty vehicle, we designed a new engine and a new gearbox that would not create any more problems for the designers."

LC Who is 'truly' responsible for the style of the 205?

JB "More Peugeot than Pininfarina, even though I must say that I rejected the initial models from each. It was only after a long joint effort that we came up with the 205 that we all know. The 405 was the reverse: much more Pininfarina than Peugeot. Yet another situation obtained with the 306: we built the saloon, they built the convertible. In reality, the question of 'who won' is something that only journalists seem to care about, what I am most interested in is that the best model emerges from the competition. And that model may not be the most beautiful one in absolute terms, as much as the one that best corresponds to the image of the brand and the expectations of the market."

LC Among the many research prototypes developed by Pininfarina on a Peugeot platform, which would you most have liked to see go into production?

JB "Without a doubt the Peugette. A very interesting vehicle, with the added detail of the symmetry linking bonnet, engine, and boot. Unfortunately, at the time, we did not have the mechanical structure suited to put it into production."

189

The Dino Berlinetta Speciale of 1965, presented at the Paris Motor Show: a concept car whose stylistic approach served as a foundation for all the successive Ferrari-Pininfarinas with centrally mounted engine, as well as a source of inspiration for sports cars made by other manufacturers.

The Dino at the Parco del Valentino.

un'impronta unica: linea pininfarina

At the Parco del Valentino, the Dino was placed on a platform for a photo shoot.

An advertisement from 1965, focused on the concept of 'Pininfarina Line.'

Bottom
The Dino 206 S prototype (chassis no. 0840), finished in September 1965 for the Paris Motor Show. The car is now permanently on exhibit at the Museum of Le Mans in Place Pininfarina.

The first company party
for the Gruppo Anziani
Pininfarina, on 3 July 1965;
next to Pinin, the first
president of the Gruppo,
Franco Martinengo, director
of the Styling Centre.

On 7 March 1966, the
President of the Italian
Republic Saragat
inaugurated the new Centre
for Research and
Development in Grugliasco.

Right
The Centre for Research
and Development under
construction. Grugliasco,
1965.

The Centre after the
completion of construction.

194

At the Brussels Motor Show of January 1965, Pininfarina and Ferrari united their stands: in the foreground on the left a Coupé Speciale on a Fiat 2300 S chassis.

The 365 California: the last great custom Ferrari, of which only 11 were built. This was the first (no. 8347), presented in Geneva in March 1966 and later sold to the publisher Dino Fabbri.

Following the inauguration
of the Centre for Research
and Development Pinin,
in his 'Florida II,' left the
factory in Grugliasco
for the last time. The faces
of the onlookers betray
an affectionate concern,
almost a foreshadowing
of his imminent death.

Pinin, with the medal of
the Legion d'Honneur, after
the inauguration, with his
children Gianna and Sergio,
and several friends,
including Carlo Biscaretti
di Ruffia (March 1966).

Pinin died in Lausanne on 3 April of 1966. At his funeral, in the front row his children and grandchildren.

A close-up of Pinin.

Sketches done by Francesco Messina for a bronze bust of Pininfarina, now on display at the main entrance to the company, in Grugliasco.

The Fiat Dino Spider being admired by the French champion skier Jean-Claude Killy.

Enzo Ferrari and Sergio Pininfarina.

Leopold of Belgium with Liliana di Réthy in June of 1966 in Grugliasco.

Left
The Fiat Dino Spider, with a V6 engine derived from Ferrari, presented in Turin in 1966.

At the Automotive Beauty
Contest of Alassio,
the Giulia Sport Speciale.

The Pininfarina family
visiting Pope Paul VI,
in November 1966.

The Peugeot 204 of 1966
designed by Pininfarina.

The classic elegance of the
Peugeot 404 cabriolet,
mass-produced by
Pininfarina.

At the Geneva Motor Show
of 1966, the debut
of the Alfa Romeo Duetto,
'cuttlebone.'

Preceding page
The evolution of the Duetto.
The Alfa Romeo 3500
'Super Flow' (left, top, and
centre), the first
manifestation of several
ideas later made famous by
the Duetto. With the Spider
Super Sport (bottom left,
Geneva Motor Show, 1959)

and the Coupé Speciale (top
right, Geneva Motor Show,
1960) the side groove and
the treatment of the front
wings had come closer to
the ideal form . The
Giulietta SS Spider Speciale
presented at the Turin
Motor Show of 1961(centre
right) and a later version,

the Giulietta SS Coupé
Speciale (bottom right,
Geneva Motor Show, 1962)
further refined the formal
solution, which became
definitive.

The bodyshells of the Alfa Romeo Duetto were built along the same lines as the Fiat 1500 and the Peugeot 404.

Sergio Pininfarina and Renzo Carli with a prototype of the Duetto.

Poster for the movie 'The Graduate' (1967). The 'Duetto' was the graduation gift for the main character, played by Dustin Hoffman, and the car appeared in many scenes in the film.

Princess Grace of Monaco with a Duetto.

Vittorio Gassman at the presentation of the Duetto in the United States.

A sketch of the 1750 dated 1967 with the characteristic 'truncated tail.'

The year was 1969:
The 'truncated tail' of the 1750.

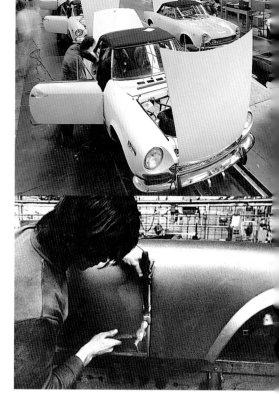

The 'Rondine' Coupé Speciale of 1963, built on the mechanical components of the Chevrolet Corvette; this version was a forerunner, in the treatment of the rear, of the Fiat 124 Spider of 1966.

Right
The manual operations in the finishing of several 124s destined for the American market.

Phases of mass-production of the 124 Spider in Grugliasco.

The Fiat 124 Sport Spider 2+2 of 1966, one of the most successful models mass-produced by Pininfarina: more than 200,000 built between 1966 and 1985, when the last 'Spidereuropa' version actually bore the name of, and was directly marketed by Pininfarina. Exported in considerable quantity to the United States, this Spider has Fiat 124 Sport mechanical components and an innovative system for raising and lowering the convertible top: when the top was lowered the side windows automatically dropped into their housings.

Following the race cars derived from production models, Pininfarina proposed a limited series of Fiat 124 Sport Rally previously prepared and lightened, meant for private racers (1972).

At the starting line of the first Giro d'Italia (1973), the 124s of Pianta-Pica and Pinto-Bernacchini.

The Fiat 124 Sport Rally, thanks to the loving care offered by Abarth, enjoyed considerable success in competition. Here we see it in 1970 being driven by the racer Alcide Paganelli, an Italian Rally champion.

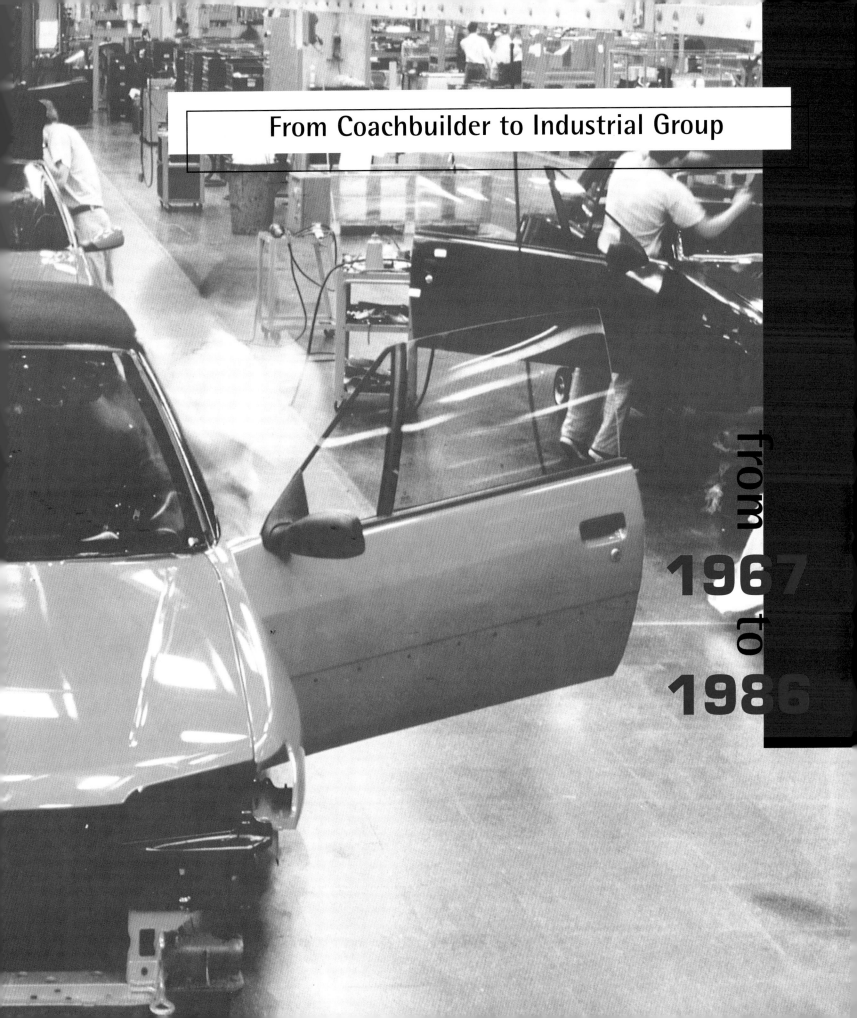

From Coachbuilder to Industrial Group

from 1967 to 1986

On the preceding pages
Assembly lines dedicated to the Peugeot.

Gianni Agnelli, with his cousin Giovanni Nasi, and the racer Mike Parkes, examining with interest his 365P Speciale, in the presence of Sergio Pininfarina and Renzo Carli.

On the following page
At the Brussels Motor Show of January 1967, the adjoining stands of Ferrari and Pininfarina.

Bottom
The Ferrari Speciale for Gianni Agnelli: it was built in 1966 on a 365P chassis (no. 8971): this unusual Berlinetta—inspired by a car shown at the Paris Motor Show that same year—has a distribution of volumes reminiscent of the Dino, and a side sleeve groove reminiscent of the Daytona, while the central driver's seat was the result of a sophisticated technical innovation made possible by the rear-central mounting of the power plant.

The Ferrari 365 GT 2+2 of 1967, presented at the Paris Motor Show; 801 of these cars were then built.

FERRARI

PININFARINA

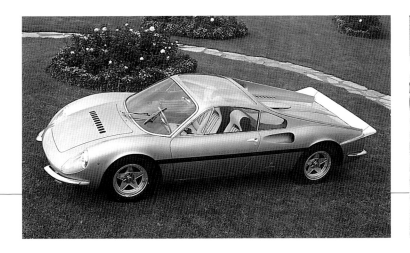

The Dino 206 GT seen from
above.

The church of Grazzano
Badoglio, before and after
the restoration financed by
Pininfarina, at the behest
of Pinin.

The 'Enciclopedia dell'Automobile', published by Fabbri Editori in 1967, on a plan by Pininfarina.

The Oratory of Cortanze d'Asti, birthplace of Pinin, dedicated by him to his mother Giacinta.

The Carli and Pininfarina families on the occasion of the presentation to the press of the technical school 'La Salle' at Grugliasco in June 1967.

Prototype BMC 1.8 of a two-volume sedan, which nowadays appears perfectly normal, but which in 1967 was revolutionary and violated all of the current technical and stylistic standards.

Graphic representation of the stylistic and architectural heritage of the innovative aerodynamic sedan built by Pininfarina on BMC 1800 mechanical components.

The silhouette shows how advanced the aerodynamic approach was.

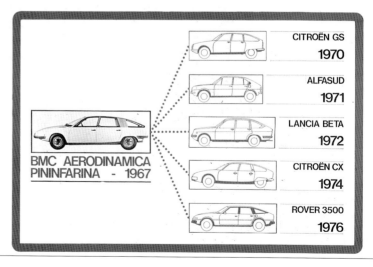

CITROËN GS 1970

ALFASUD 1971

LANCIA BETA 1972

CITROËN CX 1974

ROVER 3500 1976

BMC AERODINAMICA PININFARINA - 1967

A nice image of the Dino 246 GT.

A theme that was later to be developed on an Alfa Romeo chassis, here treated masterfully on Ferrari P5 mechanical components. The time was June 1968, outside of the Los Angeles Motor Show.

An example of advertising
with the Dino from the late
Sixties.

Right
Same car, the Dino
Competizione, at the
Los Angeles Motor Show
of 1968.

214

LIGNE
PININFARINA

The Dino Competizione
presented in 1967 at
Frankfurt. Presently the car
is in the Pininfarina
Collection.

At the Turin Motor Show
of 1968, Sergio Pininfarina
and Renzo Carli show
Giulio Andreotti the
prototype of the Alfa
Romeo P33.

215

The Piaggio-Douglas
PD808 'executive' jet,
designed in collaboration
with Pininfarina Research
and Development, 1968.

The interior of the Piaggio-
Douglas PD808.

The Peugeot 504, designed by Pininfarina, 'Car of the Year,' 1968.

The bodyshell of a Peugeot 504 Coupé emerges from the Body Department at Grugliasco.

The painting facilities in the factory of Grugliasco in the early Seventies.

Finishing: you can recognise the Peugeot 504 and the Alfa Romeo Spider.

The Peugeot 504 Coupé,
presented at Geneva in
1969.

The Cabriolet version,
presented at the same time
and place, and also mass-
produced by Pininfarina.

The 504 Coupé in 1974,
in a V6 rally version, during
preparations for the East
African Safari of 1975, from
which it emerged victorious.

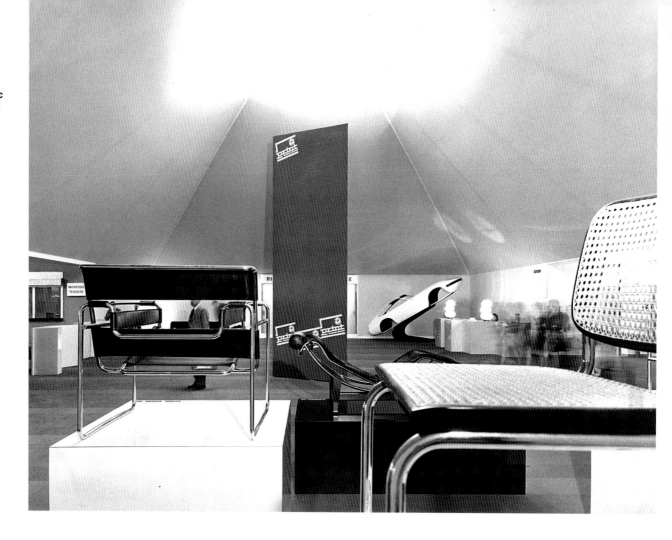

At the Salon of Domestic Arts in 1971, a Daytona bodyshell.

One of the first official photographs of the Ferrari 365 GTB/4 Daytona, taken at the presentation in Paris in 1968. A completely new line, with great expressive power, the last great Berlinetta with a front-mounted engine until the Ferrari 456 GT of 1992.

1969 - SIGMA GRAND PRIX

Equipement mis à notre disposition:

- Double circuit indépendant de freinage,
  (Ate-Teves, Frankfurt)
- Système anti-incendie automatique,
  (Graviner, Colnbrook)
- Réservoirs de carburant de sécurité,
  (Pirelli, Milan)
- Ceintures de sécurité,
  (Repa, Berlin)
- Conseils techniques de Fiat,
  de Mercedes-Benz et de Ferrari

Parts supplied by:

- Ate-Teves, for the braking system
- Graviner Ltd., for the fire - extinguishing system
- Pirelli, for the fuel tanks
- Repa, for the safety belts
- Technical advice of the Fiat,
  Mercedes-Benz Co. and Ferrari

pininfarina

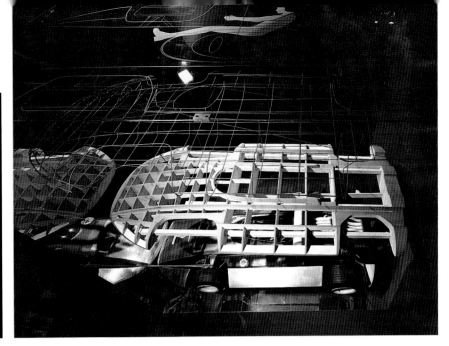

Pininfarina gives credit to
the partners in the Sigma
Grand Prix research project.

At the Paris exhibition
'Bolide Design' of 1970,
Pininfarina showed the
wooden model of the Sigma,
as well as the Alfa Romeo
P 33 and the Fiat Abarth
750.

Centre
The Sigma Grand Prix,
prototype for research into
innovative solutions for
safety in Formula 1:
undertaken with the Swiss
magazine 'Automobile
Revue,' it was presented
at Geneva in 1969.

At the presentation
of the Sigma; a group photo
of all those who worked
on its design. From left:
Robert Braunschweig of
'Automobile Revue,' Sergio
Pininfarina, Ernest Fiala,
Paul Frère, and Renzo Carli.
In the car, Michael
Henderson.

The Fiat Abarth 2000 prototype on display at the Brussels Motor Show of 1969.

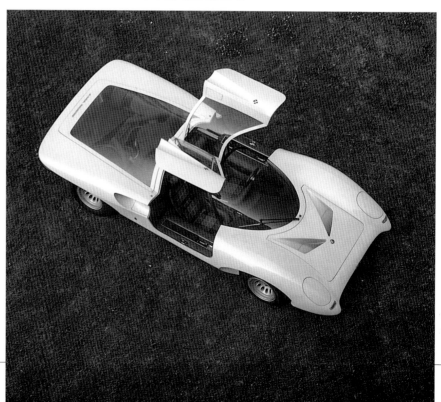

The prototype built on Alfa Romeo 33, presented at the Paris Motor Show of 1969.

Sergio Pininfarina showing
Gianni Agnelli the
Ferrari 512 S presented
at the Turin Motor Show
in October 1969.

The same car, owned by
a collector in Provence,
on display at the New York
Motor Show of April 1970.

In Montreal, in 1971,
the 512 S with its original
method of opening.

During work on the Modulo, Sergio Pininfarina, Renzo Carli, and Franco Martinengo, director of the Styling Centre, with Gio Ponti.

The Modulo in 1979, at the Russian exhibition 'Autotechnology Italy.'

The Modulo, envoy of Italian design, in Mexico City in 1971.

The Modulo marked an era. An extreme, single-volume Berlinetta, it ended a period of research into pure form, and was presented at Geneva in 1970.

'Escorted' by two helmeted and armed soldiers, the Modulo represented fine Italian coachbuilding at the Expo of Osaka in 1970.

In 1971 the Centro di Calcolo and Disegno Automatico was built, to complement the Centro DEA of 1967 equiped with measuring machines, tracing machine, three-dimensional machines, equipment for designing point to point and to scan designs.

The Centro DEA, built in Grugliasco in 1967, made it possible to determine sizes in three dimensions with total precision. A fundamental step forward in the design of car bodies.

Technical progress continued: one of the new automatic devices of the Centro DEA was this numerically controlled milling machine.

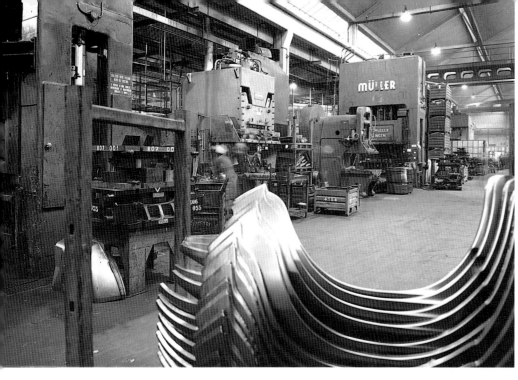

The painting, in 1970, of the bodyshells of the Fiat 124 Spider, the Lancia 2000 Coupé 2+2, and the Peugeot 504 Coupé and Cabriolet.

The Stamping Department of the factory of Grugliasco in 1970.

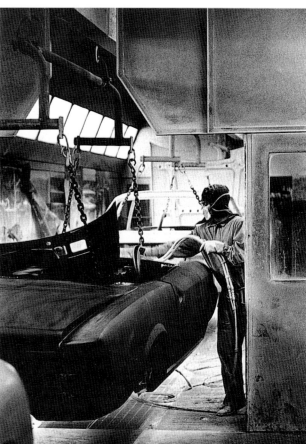

Thus began production of the Fiat 124 Sport Spider.

The Painting Department at Grugliasco.

The new Assembly Department, which showed considerable versatility, since both the Fiat 124 Sport Spyder and the Peugeot 504 Coupé could be treated on the same line.

The water test, at the end of the assembly phase.

At the London Motor Show of 1970, the Ferrari 365 GTB/4 and one of the rare Mercedes Benzes with body by Pininfarina: the 300 SEL 6.3 prototype.

In 1971 Pininfarina built the Ferrari 365 GT BB prototype, meant for production from 1973 on. This study for a sporty, high-performance vehicle with a central rear-mounted engine, presents a streamlined, avant-garde line, characterised by a sleeve groove running the length of its form, creating the perception of two clamshell configured halves, with the lower half in black resin.

The BB would also have a racing career. Here, one of the first models to be run in competition in America by Luigi Chinetti's North American Racing Team.

At the Paris Motor Show in October 1971, the formal research prototype Peugeot Riviera estate, along with the Fiat 130 Coupé, the Lancia 2000 Coupé, and the Alfa Romeo Spider.

The Lancia 2000 Coupé, designed and produced by Pininfarina (1971).

The Riviera estate (1971), a new project on a Peugeot 504 base, on the theme of sporty and luxurious estate cars, which later evolved with the Fiat 130 Maremma and the Lancia Gamma Olgiata.

"When I was a boy, Pininfarina was synonymous with an extremely Italian way of interpreting cars in terms of design, and quite frankly, closely identified with Ferraris. I remember my extreme mental confusion when I first saw a beautiful Maserati by Pininfarina: I could not quite grasp the idea of a coachbuilder working for different car makers. In this confusion, however, there was also an internal contradiction of my own: when I thought of Pininfarina, the first thing I though of was a Ferrari, but the second thing was a Lancia," recalls Luca Cordero di Montezemolo, now the president and managing director of both Ferrari and Maserati.

LC When did you begin to become familiar with the 'inside' of Pininfarina?

LdM "My first encounters dated back to 1973, when I was working in the field of Formula 1 racing. I had no direct professional contacts with Pininfarina, and for racing we only used their wind tunnel on occasion, but in various public relations-related events, especially at the various motor shows, I began to become acquainted with Sergio. He was the first to fall in love with Ferrari, but he was also the first to understand just how important Ferrari was for the image of Pininfarina around the world. Ever since I went back to Ferrari in December of 1991 to run the whole company, we worked together quite a bit, really a lot. Those were difficult years, with the market in crisis, the project drawers empty, and a certain arrogance that it was enough to be called Ferrari to be successful. At times like those, I found that Sergio was a great and determined proponent of the necessity to change, and that was precisely what I wanted to bring to Ferrari."

LC The 'new' Ferrari under Montezemolo passes via Pininfarina. And yet it was precisely under Montezemolo that Pininfarina found itself facing systematic competition in terms of design...

LdM "A little good competition helps everyone to bring out the best in themselves, not only in

terms of exterior design, but also for the in-house staff, a chapter that has historically been somewhat overlooked in the long partnership of Ferrari and Pininfarina. First the 456, then the 355, the return to the front-mounted engine with the 550 Maranello, the advanced streamlining of the 360 Modena: all excellent results, all signed Pininfarina."

LC Does tradition or innovation bulk larger in the design of Ferraris in the new millennium?

LdM "They each need to be there. In this area, Sergio's contribution has been fundamental: he is a great connoisseur of our world, our clients, our stereotypes. Together we have found ways of reconciling tradition and innovation: with citations of the 250 GTO in the 550 Maranello, of the Dino and the 250 LM in the 360 Modena. And, above all, a comfort and convenience on the interior and an accessibility that would have been unthinkable in the Ferraris of the old days, but obtained here without taking anything away from the good design."

LC What more could you ask of Pininfarina?

LdM "Not much. Perhaps, because of the way I work, I would like a bit more of a 'summit-meeting' approach in the work teams with Ferrari. I would also like to find more young designers working in the front line, not only on the models but also in operative meetings, so as to bring more freshness of ideas,

more various views. I always say: it is much easier to 'normalise' a very advanced idea than it is to make a traditional solution fresher and more captivating."

LC When you were a boy, a Maserati designed by Pininfarina confused you. As president of Maserati you chosed the design by Pininfarina for the upcoming Quattroporte. Historical nemesis?

LdM "If one day there could be a four-door Ferrari, I would never have involved Pininfarina in such a project. Since there will never be such a Ferrari, the idea occurred to us to develop a future Maserati Quattroporte, or four door, with all of the class, the style, and the Italian spirit of Pininfarina. Above all, a splendid automobile."

LC The three best Ferraris of all time, and the three least successful Ferraris of all time?

LdM "Daytona, 250 GTO, and Dino are the three best. The Dino GT/4 by Bertone never really convinced me entirely, it certainly demonstrated a new approach, but it lacked that mental training, that culture of the brand that are needed to make a real Ferrari. Then there was the Mondial 8 of 1980, another interpretation on the same theme, the 2+2 with a rear-mounted engine which, even though it was by Pininfarina, also lacked the allure of a great Ferrari. In a certain sense the Testarossa of 1984 also had something that didn't ring quite true: last heir to a generation of great Ferraris, it was stupendous to drive, while the extremely powerful and high-impact style might make it look today like the lowest-class vehicle in our history."

The Ferrari 365 GTC/4, presented at the Geneva Motor Show of 1971.

In March 1972 'Style Auto,' the respected design magazine edited by Fulvio Cinti, later the founder of 'Auto and Design,' awarded this plaque to Pininfarina.

On the same occasion (Geneva 1971), the splendid Fiat 130 Coupé.

The 130 Coupé was built with the Lancia 2000 Coupé.

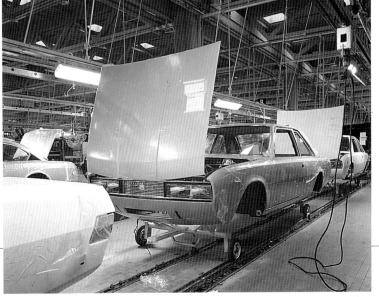

At Geneva in 1972,
the Dino 246 GTS was
presented; more than 1,200
were produced, until 1974.

At the Paris Motor Show
of 1972, the 365 BB was
at the centre of attention.

A demonstration of the
attention turned by
Pininfarina to sectors other
than that of cars, the
'Cigarette 37 S' speedboat
by Intermarine, presented in
1972 at the Boat Show of
Genoa.

The Ferrari 365 GT 4,
introduced in Paris in 1972,
was to be produced in
various versions right
until 1989.

An even more refined
evolution of the 'three-
volume grand coupé' theme,
the 365 GT 4—with
successive versions—would
remain perfectly up-to-date
for almost twenty years.

One of the first sketches, dating back to 1965, of the Wind Tunnel, inaugurated in 1972.

The project dates back to 1967, construction to 1970.

Architectural model of the Wind Tunnel.

Work on the construction
of the Wind Tunnel, the first
in Italy.

The main structure was
completed in 1972.

On the occasion of the
inauguration, there was a
visit from—among others—
Bill Mitchell, vice president
of General Mortors.

Sergio Pininfarina
and Renzo Carli, in front
of the new Wind Tunnel with
the Fiat 130 Coupé.

In 1973, this inexpensive and sporty little car was designed: the Autobianchi A112 Giovani.

The Pininfarina stand at the Frankfurt Motor Show of September 1973.

A month later, in Paris, the Jaguar XJ12 PF, a proposal for a sporty and modern sedan.

The 2 doors Peugeot 104 C designed by Pininfarina was quite successful.

The Ferrari CR 25 research
prototype of 1975.

235

At Geneva in 1974
Pininfarina displayed this
Abarth 2000 SE 027.

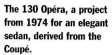

The 130 Opéra, a project from 1974 for an elegant sedan, derived from the Coupé.

Another one-off on a 130 Coupé base was this splendid estate car ('giardinetta'), the 130 Maremma, used by Gianni Agnelli.

At the Brussels Motor Show of 1974, Sergio Pininfarina talked with the Prince of Lieges, later King Albert, on the right, and with Jacques Swaters, in the middle.

At the Paris Motor Show of 1974, Pininfarina with President Giscard D'Estaing.

"Pininfarina is my second family and also my second home. I don't say it in a rhetorical manner, like a character in a kid's book, but with the rational analysis of an engineer. In the last thirty years I have spent much more time in Pininfarina than with my family. And for three years I oversaw every detail of the construction of Pininfarina Studi & Ricerche, and I know every corner of the place, better than I know my own home." Lorenzo Ramaciotti, general manager of Pininfarina Studi & Ricerche, took a degree in mechanical engineering at the Polytechnic of Turin. With Colin Chapman as his idol, he ought perhaps to have been—if not a pure engine man, as his birth in Modena would have seem to dictate—at least a chassis and frame man. Instead he wound up working on the more frivolous side of the automobile: design.

"We coachbuilders are to the world of cars as special effects are to the movies. We are supposed to give people dreams, not only with esoteric dream cars, but also with more workaday ideas such as the Metrocubo: five passenger in little more than two-and-a-half metres of length. I experienced that research project as a personal challenge, an homage to Sir Alec Issigonis: with the technologies of today, what could the new Mini be like? We obtained the same inhabitability while 'saving' a half-metre in length! We creatives, for that matter, are the least codified aspect of the world of cars. Every time that a designer begins with a blank sheet of paper, it is in fact a voyage into the unknown. A little war that we wage against ourselves. Against banality, mediocrity, and ugliness."

LC Can we speak of a 'calling' to become a designer?

LR "Perhaps that is too high-flown a term, but certainly I had cars in my blood, and I was already designing them when I was a little boy, using the tissue paper from our Christmas presents as tracing paper. And then there are those chance events that may actually be the true signposts of destiny: I saw Pinin Farina for the first time when I was twelve years old. I was at the Monte Carlo Grand Prix with my father, where he was tearing along in his black Florida II, a car that he had designed for himself, and therefore a perfect expression of his taste and personality."

LC Designers like to talk about their successes, and skip over their failures. Be honest: what still rankles with you today?

LR "A competition in 1967, the Grifo d'Oro, organised by the Carrozzeria Bertone. The year before, Enrico Fumia had won, a guy who later worked with me here in Pininfarina for many years. The next year, a German won, Neumeister; now he designs trains. The year that I competed, the prize was not awarded at all because 'the quality of the submissions had not been judged to be sufficiently high,' even though I still think that my project actually deserved to win."

LC The outside world perceives only a tiny sliver of what goes on in a think-tank like Pininfarina Studi & Ricerche. If you could raise a veil, what would you show us?

LR "The importance of Sergio Pininfarina in our work as creatives. He is a genuine president, not just for show. He loves drawings, he especially loves models. In terms of design, he plays a much more active role than people imagine.

Even when he does not decide directly, he has a very precise influence on the directions we pursue, he does not impose his will with the weight of authority, but he does know how to give the proper importance to his own observations. It is a process of mutual respect that is developed over time. I myself, after a decision has been made to pursue a solution, which may not be the one that I prefer personally, never try to sway the creatives, on the contrary I try to defend the original idea to the bitter end. To me, it seems that this spirit of true and sincere partnership is a special characteristic of Pininfarina; perhaps it can be found everywhere, because to do this kind of work, you have to love it, with a passion."

The London Motor Show of 1975, in the foreground the Alfa Romeo 'Eagle' Spider 1800.

The Alfa Romeo 'Eagle' Spider 1800, shown by Pininfarina to Niki Lauda.

In the meantime, technological evolution continued with the purchase of more numerically controlled machinery for scanning surfaces.

The Peugeot 604 of 1975: an unmistakable Pininfarina line.

In 1975 a rather unusual collaboration took form: Rolls-Royce began production of the Camargue Coupé, designed by Pininfarina and built by the British car maker, with 529 made over ten years.

In 1975 the Ferrari 308 GTB, heir to the Dino, was built.

The Ferrari 308 GTB was followed in 1977 by the 308 GTS.

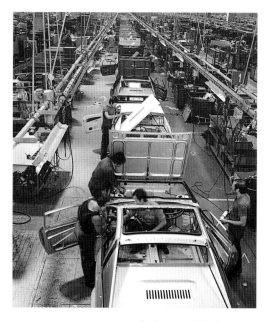

In the case of the Lancia
Beta Montecarlo,
Pininfarina built the entire
car, including the chassis,
with a new conception.

The Lancia Beta
Montecarlo, introduced in
1975.

The Lancia Gamma Coupé,
produced in Grugliasco.

At the Geneva Motor Show
of 1976 the Lancia Gamma
saloon was presented.

At the same time as the
saloon, the Coupé was
presented.

On the same occasion (Geneva
1976), a visit from Bill
Mitchell, shown here with
Sergio Pininfarina.

A new design for an inexpensive and sporty car for young people, the Peugette 104, characterised by its symmetrical front and rear sections and two doors.

In June of 1976 Sergio Pininfarina was honoured by the prestigious award of the title of Cavaliere del Lavoro, or knight of labour.

Pinin, in 1953, had received the same honour.

IL PRESIDENTE DELLA REPUBBLICA

IL PRESIDENTE DELLA REPUBBLICA

Along with the Frankfurt Motor Show of 1977, the 'European Motor Conference' was held by the specialty magazine 'Automotive News' and the London daily 'Financial Times.'

The Peugeot 305 of 1977.

At the exhibition of Italian coachbuilders, held in Tokyo in July 1977, Pininfarina showed several of his most advanced prototypes.

"In the mid 1970s, when I was director at Honda R&D, we decided to look for an external design consultant. We came across several valid opportunities but in the end we chose Pininfarina, as we were impressed with its consistency and validity in advanced research" recalls Nabuhiko Kawamoto, who went on to become chairman of Honda Motor Company and who is to date a senior counsellor.

LC What exactly did you ask Pininfarina during your first meeting?

NK "I asked them to design a sports car but was rather surprised at their remark. They said they would be pleased to collaborate with us but not with sports cars, as they had a close relationship with Ferrari and did not intend damaging this in any way. I thoroughly appreciated their honesty and loyalty to their clients. These two qualities determined the lengthy duration of the relationship Honda-Pininfarina".

LC Honda and Pininfarina secretly began working together in 1978. The world 'discovered' their relationship only in 1984 when the HP-X was launched at the Turin Motor Show. What did this proposal represent for Honda?

NK "It was intended to be a simple concept car, a static model. Its futuristic design, however, appealed to us so much that we decided to 'test' it as though it were a real car. Therefore we gave it a 2-

litre engine which, at the time, was being used in Formula 2. We were prevented from going ahead with this project by the marketing team: they thought that the HP-X model could have been considered a true 'status symbol'. This status, however, was at the time unrealistic for Honda".

LC Eleven years on from the HP-X, the Argento Vivo was created. This time getting closer to the production stage...

NK "We studied at length to build this model. At that time we were developing two projects: the SSM, now known as the S-2000, which was to be produced in Japan. This car was produced with a specific layout: front engine and rear-wheel drive. This was our opportunity to try out a technical experience that was new to us.

Argento Vivo was based on the Integra platform, hence front-wheel drive, and was intended for Europe, not as a true 'sports car' but more like a 'sporty car'.
Unfortunately the change in the Japanese economical situation forced us to carry out only one of these two projects and for the technical reason of having to look into a new mechanical layout for Honda, reluctantly Argento Vivo had to be surrendered. The problem was quite simple: there was no certainty that we would reach the necessary quantities in Europe. We even contemplated importing it to Japan but even then the accounts didn't balance.
I personally apologised to Sergio Pininfarina: 'We were unable to find the necessary quantities for such an attractive idea. Let's hope there will be other occasions in the future' I told him. With the second plant in Europe which is now fully operative, our total quantities will rise, thus increasing the possibility to maintain our promise".

A view in 1978 of the factory at Grugliasco: Fiat 124s, Alfa Romeo Spiders, and Peugeot 504s shared the same assembly lines.

The Assembly Department, in 1978.

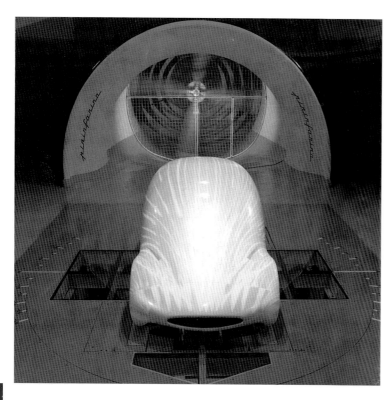

A life-size model of the CNR prototype of 1978, part of a quest for an ideal aerodynamic form. This was the beginning of an intense collaboration with the Consiglio Nazionale delle Ricerche Italiano, Italy's national research council, on various projects meant to optimise means of transportation.

The model of the CNR at the International Energy Expo in Knoxville, in 1982.

At the Birmingham Motor Show of October 1978, the Jaguar XJ Spider, in its first dark green hue.

In 1979 the car was painted metallic silver.

JAGUAR XJ SPIDER *pininfarina* presented with *Autocar*

Succede ad Alberto Benadì, rimarrà in carica per due anni

Sergio Pininfarina, nuovo presidente dell'Unione industriale di Torino

L'uomo che disegna le auto

Sergio Pininfarina

E questi sono i vice

Renzo Villare

Andreatta vuole un

Su Liquigas il governo d

Ferruccio Bernabò

In July of 1978 Sergio Pininfarina was elected President of the Industrial Union of Turin.

Pininfarina, in a photo from the Eighties, in front of the headquarters of the Industrial Union.

247

Interior of the Ecos.

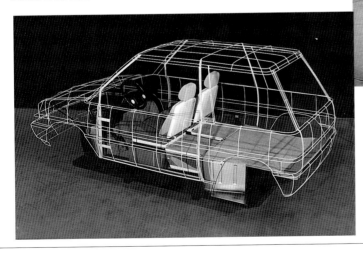

The Ecos of 1978, a project for a small electric sedan, developed in conjunction with the Fiat Research Centre.

At the Singapore Motor
Show of 1978, the role
of envoy fell to the Abarth
2000.

Again, at the Singapore
Motor Show, the Ferrari
512 S.

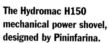

The Hydromac H150
mechanical power shovel,
designed by Pininfarina.

The Fiat Agri Series 80
tractor, designed by
Pininfarina.

At the exhibition of Italian
coachbuilders, 'Carrozzeria
Italiana Cultura and
Progetto' held in 1978:
Cesare Romiti, Sergio
Pininfarina, and Gianni
Agnelli.

The Peugeot 505 of 1979.

Sergio Pininfarina was elected member of the European Parliament in June of 1979 with 268,000 votes.

In 1980 at the European Parliament.

In 1979 Pininfarina took part in updating the model range of the Autobianchi A112.

The Lancia Beta saloon, after the 'face-lifting' done by Pininfarina.

At the exhibition of Italian coachbuilders in Tokyo, in 1979.

In October 1979, in Helsinki, the exhibition 'Italia Presenta' was held: the CR25 on the Pininfarina stand.

At 'Autotechnology Italy,' Moscow 1979. Sergio Pininfarina with the mayor of Moscow, the Italian ambassador, and Sigma Grand Prix.

In 1979 in Belgrade, the Pininfarina stand at the Motor Show presented the Ferrari 308 GTS, the Lancia Gamma Coupé, and the Abarth 2000.

The Pininfarina stand at the Geneva Motor Show of 1980: the introduction of the Ferrari Mondial 8.

The Ferrari Mondial

On 19 April 1980 at the Industrial Union of Turin the fiftieth anniversary of Pininfarina was celebrated.

Sergio Pininfarina with Ferrari Pinin, research prototype for a four-door Ferrari.

At the Motor Show, the stand featured a review of the most important creations and the unprecedented Ferrari Pinin.

The Ferrari Pinin seen
in front of the Renaissance
Center in Detroit.

Dating back to the same
year is the cable car
system designed for
Agudio and still functioning
at La Thuile.

The year was 1980: the
Lancia Montecarlo Turbo,
with body by Pininfarina,
won the World Endurance
Championship in its class.

A Montecarlo Turbo official
in the box at Brands Hatch
in the 1980 season.

At the Paris Motor Show of
1980 Pininfarina met once
again with the French
President Giscard d'Estaing.

"When I think of Pininfarina, I think of one of the most famous coachbuilders and design houses on Earth. The name itself is a compendium of design excellence in the field of automotive design. Of course, I also think of Ferrari, because Pininfarina is universally associated with that legendary name," explains Jack F. Smith, president and managing director of the General Motors Corporation.

LC No patriotism? In effect, there has been more than one episode with Pininfarina in the long and complex history of General Motors...

JS "It is true, GM has a 'history' all its own with Pininfarina. Certainly our best known collaboration has been on the two-seater Cadillac Allanté in the Eighties: an elegant and sumptuous roadster in those days. All the same, GM and Pininfarina began to work together in the early Thirties, with the Cadillac V16 and then the Cadillac Eldorado Brougham, built in limited series in 1959 and 1960."

LC Even though it has been quoted on the stock market since 1986 and it is endowed with a complex managerial structure, Pininfarina is still a company with a strong family identity. In an increasingly globalised automotive marketplace, is this an advantage or a disadvantage?

JACK SMITH

JS "I have had lots of opportunities to meet with Sergio, especially when I was working in Europe and during the collaboration on the Cadillac Allanté. I found him to be a cordial and fascinating person, with a great love of cars, and proud to work with General Motors on a number of projects. Personally, I admire the way in which Sergio has carried on the great design tradition begun by his father, the way he grew the company and expanded its business. He was also able to involve his children in the family business and so help continue that tradition over time. He is proud of that, as he well should be."

LC For you too Pininfarina is synonymous with Ferrari. What then would be the handsomest vehicle you could think of to put on display in a museum in order to express the work these two companies have done together?

JS "If I were asked to select a single Pininfarina for some hypothetical Automobile Hall of Fame, I would really have some problems. In fact, there are lots of 12-cylinder Ferraris that are famous

around the world, cars whose design has made Pininfarina well known to one and all."

LC From Detroit, on the bridge of the most globalised car manufacturer on Earth, how do you see the future of a "small Italian company" like Pininfarina?

JS "Nowadays the panorama of the world of automobiles has changed... and it is continuing to change rapidly and substantially as we enter the twenty-first century. There is no company that can count on all the good things it has done in the past to guarantee an assured success in the future as well. In an increasingly competitive and global automotive marketplace, the only ones who will prosper are those who know how to perceive and respond to the wishes of the clientele by offering innovative high-value products. In this new world that stretches out before us, the 'house' quality of Pininfarina will allow them to prosper and create in the future cars with a memorable design."

In 1981 Pininfarina also
designed a line of watches
for Orfina.

Sergio Pininfarina at
a Ferrari meet in Pasadena,
in California, observing
a Ferrari 250 Europa GT.

The Quartz, built on Audi
Quattro mechanical
components:
a technological and formal
study with the use
of innovative materials.

The Fiat 124 Sport Spider
had become the 2000 IE.

Pininfarina with Jean Boillot, general manager of Peugeot, in 1982.

The Peugeot 505 estate of 1982.

The Lancia Rally won the World Rally Championship in 1983.

The Talbot Samba Cabriolet, produced at Grugliasco.

In 1982, the first car actually bearing the Pininfarina name, the Spidereuropa was produced, heir to the Fiat 124 Spider.

The magazine advertising conveyed the joy of living in the open air exemplified by the Azzurra, the first Italian yacht to challenge the America's Cup.

CON LO SPIRITO DI AZZURRA. SPIDEREUROPA PININFARINA

The director Mario Monicelli with the Spidereuropa during shooting of 'Amici Miei Atto II.'

Gastone Moschin, one of the stars of the film, with the car called for by the script.

Right
This advertisement for daily newspapers noting the specifications of the car and its price.

Nuovo Spidereuropa
Pininfarina

Spidereuropa Moderno nei concetti base, elegante per la sua linea classica e compatta, raffinato per l'impiego di materiali di qualità e per l'alto grado di finitura. 2 litri, 105 cavalli. 4 freni a disco e oltre 180 Km/h. E poi ruote in lega, pneumatici P6, iniezione elettronica, vetri atermici, alzacristalli elettrici, apertura elettrica del baule, tutto compreso nel prezzo: lire 14.000.000 chiavi in mano.

Proprio come pensavate
sarebbe stata un'auto tutta Pininfarina.

pininfarina f

In 1982 the Centre for Research and Development, inaugurated in Grugliasco in 1966, changed location and became Pininfarina Studi and Ricerche SpA. The new building stood in Cambiano, near Turin, on a surface area of 51,000 square metres, of which 8,796 square metres were roofed and 13,780 square metres were developed. It was officially inaugurated on 20 April.

The Style Office at Cambiano.

One of the areas destined for the construction of models.

The Collezione Pininfarina, an integral part of the complex of Cambiano, in an image from 1985.

Left
The 63-foot Magnum
Marine at the Boat Show
of Genoa in 1982.

Top
In September 1982 the
Gruppo Anziani Pininfarina
visiting the Pope
at Castelgandolfo.

Bottom
Cambiano, 1982: the Lancia
Gamma Coupé with the
research prototypes
developed on the same
mechanical components:
from left, the Berlina
'Scala,' the Spider 'T-Roof,'
and the Giardinetta
'Olgiata,' an estate car.

The new Peugeot 205,
presented at Geneva Motor
Show in 1983.

LA GRINTA DEL VOLUMEX,
IL PIACERE DI UN GRANDE SPIDER.

NUOVO
SPIDEREUROPA VOLUMEX
PININFARINA

The actress Eleonora Vallone picking up her Spidereuropa.

The advertising for the new 'Volumex' version of the Spidereuropa.

Roger Moore, talking with Jackie Stewart, is about to run a demonstration lap before the 41st Grand Prix of Montecarlo, in 1983, with the Spidereuropa.

The Bredabus 5001,
designed by Pininfarina.

The Fiat forklift, a work
tool in which looks and
function are combined.

264

The Shergar, a fast motor-
boat driven by two
turbojets, designed
by Pininfarina for the Aga
Khan Karim.

An executive of the Italian-American consortium Fiat Allis with Sergio Pininfarina, on the occasion of the presentation of a new earth-moving machine.

The Pope, during a visit to the 'Cottolengo' hospital of Turin in 1983, used the Gamma Spider 'T-Roof.'

In November 1983 the Royal Society of Arts conferred upon Sergio Pininfarina the title of 'Royal Designer for Industry.'

The same award had been given to Pinin Farina in 1954.

To Sergio Pininfarina
GREETING

THE ROYAL SOCIETY OF ARTS
acting through the Council under an Ordinance made at the Society's House in the Adelphi, London, the eleventh day of October one thousand nine hundred and thirty-seven and subsequently amended, hereby confers upon you the Title of Royal Designer for Industry (Designer for Industry of the Royal Society of Arts) in consideration of your eminence & efficiency in creative design, believing that you will on every occasion exert yourself in support of the honour, interest and dignity of the Society and faithfully discharge the duties required of you under the said Ordinance.

Given at the Society's House the seventeenth day of November 1983.

President

Martin Moss   Chairman

Attested   Master of the Faculty & Member of Council

Member of Council

Counter-signed Christopher Lucas   Secretary

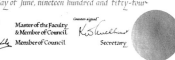

PININ FARINA

Greeting:
THE ROYAL SOCIETY OF ARTS, acting through the Council, under an Ordinance made at the Society's House in the Adelphi, London, the eleventh day of October, one thousand nine hundred & thirty-seven, do hereby, in consideration of your high eminence & efficiency in creative design for Industry, confer upon you the Title of Designer for Industry of the Royal Society of Arts, believing that you will on every occasion exert yourself in support of the honour, interest & dignity of the Society & faithfully discharge the duties required of you under the said Ordinance.

Given at the Society's House the fourteenth day of June, nineteen hundred and fifty-four

President   Master of the Faculty & Member of Council

Chairman of Council   Member of Council   Secretary

At the Turin Motor Show of 1982, Pininfarina presented a project for integral-traction mechanics for the Alfa Romeo 33.

The 33 4x4 was later produced by Pininfarina at Grugliasco.

The production version of the Alfa Romeo 33, presented at the Frankfurt Motor Show of 1983.

"It seemed too wonderful to be true. Lean production, seen in operation (and it was almost like spying) at the end of the Eighties, before 'the machine that changed the world' celebrated it far and wide, really seemed like something out of a dream. I would rub my eyes and wonder: if this way of organising labour works for a large factory, it means that even a small manufacturing operation like Pininfarina could have a future." Renato Bertrandi, at the time quality director for the Cadillac Allanté assembly line, currently general manager of Industrie Pininfarina, was not mincing words.

LC What was the value of this revelation?

RB "At the end of the Eighties with Andrea Pininfarina we were wondering how we were ever going to survive. It seemed that the only way to offer quality was to invest in technology. Pininfarina had always offered quality, but with the added value of the specialised worker. If were only going to produce limited series then we could not count on the resources to keep up with western industry in an unbridled technological race, which in those years looked endless and unlimited in terms of expense. Had we small-scale coachbuilders really entered a blind alley? I was beginning to think so, until I visited NUMMI, the Californian joint-venture of General Motors and Toyota. The Americans had ensured themselves for ten years an office inside the plant to study the Toyota Production System directly."

LC What ideas could you derive from a plant with a production capacity of 200,000 units a year for your assembly lines, generally producing only about a tenth of that volume?

RB "The organisation of labour in terms of interfunctional teams with very few hierarchic levels. Limited automation and, above all, automation that is decided by the line workers, not by management. Open stock management. Bonuses for ideas, almost a marketing of suggestions."

LC When and how did the ideas of modern lean production come to Pininfarina?

RB "With the Fiat Coupé, which we began building in 1993. On paper it was a very simple process to apply, but in practice we encountered considerable resistance. With the passage of years, the hierarchic relationship in the factory had become one of sanctions, now we were trying to return to the origins, to the model of

participation. It was difficult for everyone. On the one hand for the factory worker, who now felt he had become nothing more than manpower, no longer a source of useful new ideas. On the other hand, for management, which was obliged to continually modify the model of participation, something that is very difficult to maintain, especially when one is obliged to offer guaranteed jobs in the face of the uncertainties of the marketplace. Assisted by our size and by circumstances—a gap in production between the completion of certain commissions and the beginning of work on others—we were in any case the first in Italy to apply modern lean production. And we did the training ourselves: you can hardly summon outside consultants to explain a new organisational model, instead you have to work hard in person to demonstrate that this is not some abstruse formula, but something in which you really believe. In this we were helped by the fact that it is a family company, that we are not obsessed with short-term results, but that we focus on obtaining advantages over the medium-to-long term."

LC Before coming to Pininfarina, you changed jobs and even sectors repeatedly. What convinced you to stay in the same company for 14 years now?

RB "In effect, I always promised myself that I would get a new job every five years, because it is only in this first period that you really give a company your best contribution. And vice versa. In reality, however, I have completely changed jobs at Pininfarina a number of times, which always set my 'five-year odometer' back to zero."

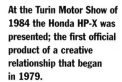

At the Turin Motor Show of 1984 the Honda HP-X was presented; the first official product of a creative relationship that began in 1979.

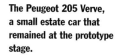

The Peugeot 205 Verve, a small estate car that remained at the prototype stage.

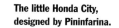

The little Honda City, designed by Pininfarina.

At the Brussels Motor Show, in January of 1984, the Audi Quartz, the Ferrari Mondial Cabriolet, the Spidereuropa Volumex, the Alfa Romeo 33 4x4, and the Talbot Samba.

Francesco Moser prepared for the hour record in the Pininfarina Wind Tunnel.

Reinhold Messner tested his equipment in the same facility.

The Alfa Romeo 33 4x4 estate car, designed and produced by Pininfarina as a complete vehicle beginning in 1984.

March 1984, Geneva: Pininfarina with the president of Alfa Romeo Massacesi, during the presentation of the 33 4x4.

The Ferrari 288 GTO in
1984.

The Ferrari Testarossa was presented by Ferrari at the 'Lido' of Paris. The Testarossa marked a sharp turning point in the design of Ferraris: this radical new car was packed with unprecedented aesthetic content, an exciting new design: new technical demands, such as the shift of the radiators from the front to the middle of the car, meant the addition of large new air intake vents on the side, a distinctive feature of the style. The car won prestigious design awards (Auto Expo of Los Angeles and Car Design Award in 1985) and with more than 7,000 built, and bodies manufactured by Pininfarina itself, it is the best-selling Ferrari ever built.

At Grugliasco the body of the Testarossa was taking shape; the mechanical components were then manufactured in Maranello.

Sergio Pininfarina. Membre depuis 1973.

Ne sortez pas sans elle.

This photograph was taken by Annie Liebowitz for an advertising campaign in 1990 for American Express.

At the Turin Motor Show Pininfarina showed the new Ferrari to Italian President Sandro Pertini.

In 1987 this one-off
Testarossa Spider was built
for Gianni Agnelli.

Pininfarina with the
President of France,
Mitterand, at the Paris
Motor Show of 1984.

At the Auto Expo of Los
Angeles, Pininfarina
received a prestigious prize
for his design of the
Testarossa.

At the Turin Motor Show in the same year, Sergio Pininfarina shown with his sons Andrea and Paolo.

The 200,000th Fiat 124 Sport Spider produced in the Spidereuropa version.

The Breda E 454 locomotive, designed by Pininfarina.

The Ferrari 412 of 1985, evolution of the Ferrari 400.

The Griffe 4, a study for an innovative coupé that celebrated the 30 years of collaboration between Peugeot and Pininfarina.

The Griffe 4 at the Geneva Motor Show of 1985, where it was displayed alongside a Peugeot 403 sedan of 1955, the first Peugeot to develop from the collaboration with Pininfarina.

"Pininfarina is one of the great design houses in Italy and renowned throughout the automotive world. Pininfarina started the era of fine coach design houses that became known for building very creative, charismatic vehicles. The design legacy started by Battista (Pinin) Farina and carried on by his son Sergio has withstood the test of time and maintained its prestige" explains Wayne Cherry, director of the Design and Portfolio Development Centre of General Motors Corporation.

LC The value and importance of a trademark are increasingly important. In your opinion, who do you think has benefited more from this longstanding collaboration between Ferrari and Pininfarina?

WC "The alliance that Sergio and Pininfarina formed in designing the Ferrari added enormous prestige to the Pininfarina signature. Ferrari is one of the most exotic sports car platforms...indeed one of the most prestigious sporting labels on Earth. Ferrari and Pininfarina have a truly synergistic relationship and it's a superb example of where one plus one is definitely more than two!"

LC All over the world the number of independent car manufacturers is decreasing while the big are getting even bigger and have a remarkable line-up of experienced style centres distributed in every corner of the planet. Do you believe there will be space and a position for a design house such as Pininfarina?

WC "With increased emphasis on design and technology in our rapidly changing and highly competitive global industry, the enduring excellence of Pininfarina should help it to stay at the forefront of style and creativity".

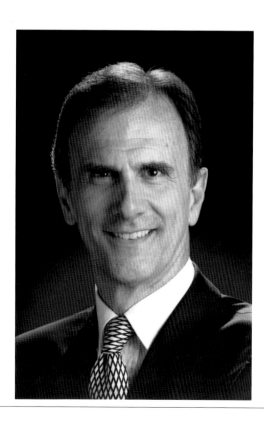

The Ferrari 328GTS and,
bottom, the 328GTB both
heirs to the Ferrari 308.

Sergio Pininfarina with
Cesare Romiti in 1985.

The Peugeot 205 Cabriolet, designed and produced by Pininfarina, with more than 70,000 cars built.

Sergio Pininfarina at the wheel of a Peugeot 205 'Roland Garros.'

At the Geneva Motor Show of 1986, Roland Peugeot with Sergio Pininfarina and Renzo Carli.

The assembly line of the Peugeot 205 Cabriolet.

At Cambiano in April 1986, the Peugeot 205 Cabriolet was presented, the fruit of a design process that went on for more than two years, and which brought great satisfaction to both companies.

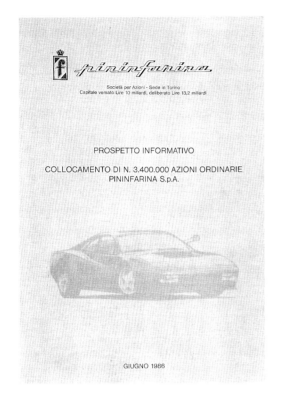

In 1986 the Pininfarina Group was officially quoted in the Italian Borsa with 25.76 per cent of its own capital. The operation was run by Mediobanca, which took a 3.41 per cent share.

The Lancia Thema estate car, designed and produced by Pininfarina.

An advertisement published in 'Fortune,' May 1986.

The panoramic 'MOB' train, for Breda.

The factory of Industrie Pininfarina in San Giorgio Canavese, inaugurated in September 1986: the new industrial site stands on an area of more than 200,000 square metres, 30,000 square metres of which one roofed, and was at first meant for use in the assembly of the Cadillac Allanté, as well as for track testing of cars with Pininfarina mechanical components.

Bottom left
The start of production of the Cadillac Allanté: Sergio, Andrea, and Paolo Pininfarina with Roger Smith, president of General Motors.

Bottom right
The Cadillac Allanté (1986). For this GT, a luxury convertible of compact dimensions, Cadillac availed itself of the design and manufacturing capacity of Pininfarina, which supplied Detroit with completely finished bodies via an airlift flown by Alitalia, from Caselle Airport near Turin. From 1986 until 1993 more than 22,000 Allantés were flown in to the United States, where they are still cars sought after by collectors' and enthusiasts' clubs. One Allanté is in the Collezione Pininfarina.

Sergio Pininfarina with the Cadillac Allanté.

Pininfarina and the president of Cadillac, John Grettenberger.

The Allanté on its world debut at the Paris Motor Show of 1986.

The headquarters
of Pininfarina Extra
in Cambiano; the company,
founded in 1986, was run
by Paolo Pininfarina.

The Style Office of
Pininfarina Extra.

Pininfarina in 1990. Behind
him, style models,
the Coupé and the Spider
Vivace, on Alfa Romeo
mechanical components,
of 1986.

Sergio Pininfarina with
Lalla Romano and Luigi
Firpo at the Premio del
Circolo della Stampa, the
Italian press club,
in 1986.

"I always dreamed of designing, hovering between my love of art, especially the avant-gardes of the turn of the century, from the Italian Futurists to the Russian Suprematists, and my imagination of a real future, i.e., industrial design. I got my first electroshock at the age of 14: I was watching the spaceships of '2001—A Space Odyssey,' and I became convinced that I needed to design the future. The real revelation came at the end of the Seventies, with the exhibition: 'Carrozzeria Italiana. Cultura e Progetto' (Italian Coachbuilders: Culture and Design). I stood amazed before the Carabo by Bertone: a continuous solid with vanishing air intakes and windows. A marvellous object. The sense of the modern." For Giuseppe Randazzo, director of the Centre for Modelling and Computerised Animation at Pininfarina Studi & Ricerche, the automobile is not an end, but a means, to which one must apply not only creativity but also new technologies.

"I have closely followed the development of computing in automobile design, to some extent simply implementing market standards, and to some extent constructing original solutions on my own in the spirit of the experimental craftsman. My advantage has always been that of being—remaining—a designer. Therefore, in the digitalisation of a little model developed on paper, I feel as if I am a link in the chain joining style and design. It is not a negligible role, because one has to find the way of preserving an idea's freshness while continuing to place it within the context of the client's input in terms of technology and production costs."

LC You design automobiles, but you do not see yourself as an 'automobilaro,' or car guy, as they would say in America. What is the automobile for you?

GR "A terrible object, a curse. The best designers on Earth tremble when they face the challenge of an automobile. It is truly something that is constantly in motion, not only intrinsically, but also in terms of technologies, which in turn are constantly changing the object itself. In this perennial transition that has become crazier and crazier, I increasingly appreciate time as a measure of the validity of a project. If an idea has truly left behind something important, you understand that only fifty years later."

LC Pininfarina has been around for 70 years. Therefore we can look back only at its first twenty years of activity: what do you like best?

GR "I really loved the Cisitalia, its purity, its naturalness. It

seems like a seashell found on the beach. When the energy is properly put together, it endures over time, it doesn't have those conflicts and tensions that sometimes emerge with the passing of the years. What remains is freshness, the natural object, never forced and therefore elegant. Another much more recent car that has the same effect on me is Giugiaro's Medusa: a sculpture, a pure form with a constant cross section that runs through the entire car. It is a research prototype that has greatly influenced many production cars. Again, in terms of experimentation, I would like to mention the design of the Eta Beta. A project in which I actively participated, trying to employ compostional criteria that were close to those of 'product design': functional break-down, unpainted surfaces in view, attention to symmetry in order to reduce the number of components."

LC The development of automotive design is not constant, it moves by leaps and bounds. Why?

GR "Progress is made up especially by strong, courageous actions. There are times of greater openness, like the Seventies, when we all hit a lot of high notes, perhaps because there was not yet any such a thing as an Italian school of design, everyone was learning design on their own, and therefore there were lots of much more personal solutions. In these days, on the other hand, there is much more of a sense of fashion and little true innovation. I like the classical, that which lasts over time and so I really don't know what to make of many of the retromobiles of today, which bring no real innovation but only a harking back to the past."

LC Divided between pure creativity and virtual technologies, how do you see the future?

GR "Without a doubt the nature of the new millennium is digital."

Toward the Future

from 1987 to 2000

The presentation of the
Ferrari F40 at the
Frankfurt Motor Show
of 1987.

On the preceding pages
The Ethos project.

Conceived to celebrate the
40th anniversary of Ferrari,
the F40 was enormously
successful: it offered the
best of automotive
technology, with a chassis
with a mixed structure,
in steel and composite
materials, a body made
of composite materials,
and advanced streamlined
design. With a coefficient of
0.34 and practically no lift
at all, without aerodynamic
appendages, it offered the
excitement of the track on
ordinary streets and roads.

A handsome photograph of Sergio Pininfarina by the photographer Jean Loup Sieff, on the occasion of the exhibition 'Hommage à Ferrari' at the Cartier Foundation in Paris.

289

"Blue Ribbon," the Atlantic Challenger, built by the Azimut shipyards, goes for the record for an Atlantic crossing. The super structure was designed by Pininfarina.

The articulated bus, the Dual Bus Seattle, designed by Pininfarina for Breda in 1987.

Bredabus 2001, an urban and suburban bus, 1986.

The first ETR X 500, a high-speed train for the Italian railways, whose interior and exterior design was done by Pininfarina, as well as the aerodynamic research, receiving the salute of the Frecce Tricolori, in 1987.

A scale model of the ETR X 500 on display at the Porta Nuova railway station in Turin, for the exhibition, 'Vivere il Treno,' February 1988.

The scale model of the Breda ETR X 500 in the Pininfarina Wind Tunnel.

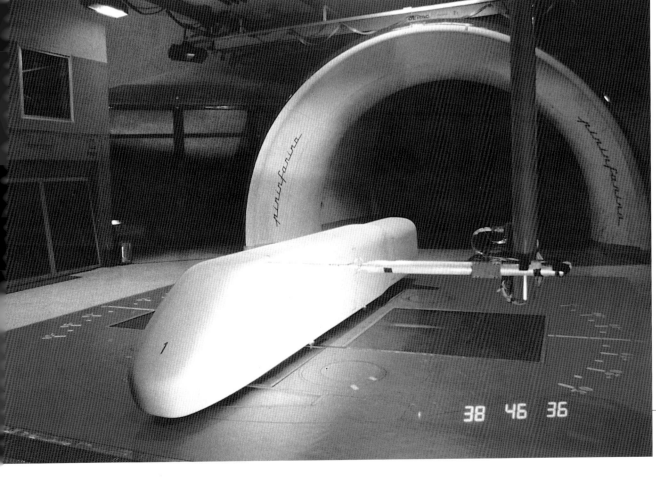

The Peugeot 405, born of the collaboration between Pininfarina and Peugeot in 1987.

A model of the Peugeot 405 sedan in the Pininfarina Wind Tunnel.

The Alfa Romeo 164
of 1987, designed
by Pininfarina, marked the
revival of the Alfa Romeo
name on the markets of
the world. In 1988 the Alfa
Romeo 164 took the Car
Design Award as the best
production car of 1987.

Premio Agrodolce 1988
(literally, Sweet-and-Sour
Prize). Sergio Pininfarina
with the actress Sandra Milo
and the comedian Walter
Chiari.

The Peugeot 405 estate,
designed by Pininfarina.

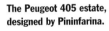

"When I think of Pininfarina, what comes instinctively to mind is the 406 Coupé, the car that I launched together with them when I was first made product director at Peugeot. As soon as I saw the model, all discussion ended: 'that' was the car we would make. The decision, then, was immediate and unanimous, even though concerning certain details, such as the headlights and the overall width, we had very long talks," explains Frédéric Sant-Geours, director of Peugeot since 1997. "Getting past my love for the 406 Coupé, in second place what emerges inside me is also the sense of 'historic partnership' between our two companies. This is a relationship consolidated on the basis of mutual trust and capacity to face problems together, something which always develops in a long-term relationship."

294

LC What is Pininfarina today for Peugeot?

FSG "The fundamental, systematic contribution, is the consultation on style, in house and externally. The industrial part, on the other hand, is more episodic, and it depends on many factors, which are often outside of the relationship between Peugeot and Pininfarina. In more general terms, one thing that we have always appreciated in Pininfarina is the willingness to approach any problem with confidence and to find a solution together. Over time, we have gone beyond the pure relationship of client and supplier: there is now a reciprocal respect and understanding. Our spirit of partnership continues even though there has been a generational shift. There was this sort of special relationship between Peugeot and

Pininfarina in the time of Boillot, it still exists now with me at the helm."

LC Often, in design competitions, the in-house styling centres start off with a certain 'advantage' over outside consultants. Is this true at Peugeot?

FSG "In the second phase, when we select the stylistic theme, we issue an identical briefing to everyone, and so the competition is absolutely balanced. We want things to stay this way, not only out of respect for the work of outside contractors, but also to keep in-house workers from feeling that they are working in monopoly conditions. Phase 1, which is when we establish the architectural principles, the customer profile, and the understructure to be used, is an entirely in-house process, as is for that matter phase 3, when we determine how to manufacture the model selected at the lowest possible cost."

LC From time to time Pininfarina presents 'freely interpreted' prototypes on Peugeot themes. For the company, are these exercises only stimulating surprises or are they perhaps occasionally even unwished for suggestions?

FSG "I would say that the problem does not even arise. We talk about it in advance, because among other things Pininfarina shows us in advance models of the project, giving us approval and asking permission to use our trademark. And so there have never been conflicts. For instance, when they decided to build the Nautilus, we approved it with the greatest tranquility because the design of the 607 was already locked in."

LC What does Peugeot expect from Pininfarina in the third millennium?

FSG "I want ideas for our phase 1, the phase in which we invent new types of vehicles."

LC Objects like Metrocubo, you mean?

FSG "No. Metrocubo is an interpretation of an existing theme, urban mobility. From Pininfarina instead I would like an idea for something that does not yet exist."

Bottom
The research prototype Hit on display at the Turin Motor Show was a global study, which included the design of the chassis in composite materials on Lancia Delta Integrale mechanical components. In the photo from left:

Lorenza, Sergio, Paolo, and Andrea Pininfarina during the presentation to the press in April 1988.

Right
Sergio Pininfarina presents the Hit to Gianni Agnelli at the Turin Motor Show.

The Hit being road-tested.

INGENJÖRS
VETENSKAPS
AKADEMIEN

HAR HARMED ARAN KALLA

MR SERGIO PININFARINA

TILL
UTLANDSK LEDAMOT

Stockholm den 26 maj 1988

On 26 May 1988,
in Stockholm, Sergio
Pininfarina was named
a Foreign Member of the
IVA, the Royal Swedish
Academy of Engineering
Sciences.

The election of Sergio
Pininfarina as president
of Confindustria, the Italian
association of industrialists,
on 26 May 1988.

On the same occasion,
Paolo, Lorenza, Sergio,
Giorgia, and Andrea
Pininfarina.

On 13 December 1988,
Paris, meeting of the
fourteen presidents of the
European associations
of industrialists.

The light rail cars designed for Breda, in service in Lille in 1988.

Il Benéteau First 45 F5 of 1989, a yacht mass-produced by the French company and designed by Pininfarina.

In the Wind Tunnel, railway cars for lorry transport are tested, before use in Le Shuttle trains under the English Channel (1989).

Designed by Pininfarina, Breda built in 1989; panoramic railcars for Swiss railways.

Top
The Ferrari Mythos, compact and sporty. The Mythos, presented at the Tokyo Motor Show of 1989, was a research prototype that harked back to the tradition of the dream cars that had made Pininfarina famous in the Sixties. It is not an abstract sculpture, even though the relationship among the volumes is provocative and in a certain sense, extreme; on the contrary, it manifests all its aggressive bite in the way it moves and hugs the road. It features Ferrari Testarossa mechanical components and has the allure of the two-seater Ferrari Barchetta.

Bottom left
In 1989 the Japanese magazine 'Car Styling' gave the Mythos its Golden Marker Trophy.

Bottom
The Ferrari Mythos photographed at Palazzo Te in Mantua.

1989
Golden Marker Trophy
Assegnato alla Mythos giudicato il più bel prototipo presente al Salone di Tokyo.

The Mythos and
the Cadillac Allanté
at the Detroit Motor Show of
January 1990. In March
1990 the Mythos took
the prestigious Car Design
Award for the finest and
most innovative concept
of 1989 in the world.

Lorenzo Ramaciotti, general
manager of Pininfarina Studi
and Ricerche, with the
Ferrari Mythos in Tokyo.

Next to Alboreto, Lorenza
Pininfarina.

Testing the Mythos with
Michele Alboreto.

Top Executives of G.M. Sergio and Lorenza Pininfarina with Chuck Jordan, vice president of General Motors.

At the Tokyo Motor Show, Amintore Fanfani with Sergio Pininfarina.

Sergio Pininfarina with the President of Portugal Mario Soares.

On the occasion of his state visit in December of 1989, the Russian President, Gorbachev, delivered a speech in the Castello Sforzesco of Milan. On his right, Gianni De Michelis and Sergio Pininfarina; on his left, Giulio Andreotti and Eduard Shevarnadze.

In 1983, the three MPVs from General Motors made their debut in the United States, their technical development had been conducted by Pininfarina as had been their prototype production right up to the pre-mass-production. Here is the Oldsmobile Silhouette, the Chevrolet Lumina APV, and the Chevrolet sold as a Pontiac Trans Sport.

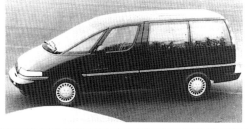

The Ferrari 348 TB and
the 348 TS of 1989. Both
models, presented at the
Frankfurt Motor Show, were
distinguished by
a longitudinal centrally
mounted engine,
and replaced the Ferrari
328 with equal success.

"It was one thing to be 'subjected' to a factory, it is quite another thing to create one of your own. To decide how to organise an entire line of production is in fact a fascinating and alluring challenge. Along with three other individuals, I was fortunate enough to be able to 'create' Bairo Canavese. The space was one binding consideration, because we had to make use of an existing structure and could do little to expand it, and that is why we developed the 'serpentine' assembly line," explained Paola Mensa, mechanical engineer specialising in the automotive field, who joined Pininfarina as a body designer and is now in charge of the plant at Bairo Canavese that produces the Mitsubishi Pajero Pinin.

LC How can you reconcile 'just-in-time' production for a vehicle whose entire mechanical structure is shipped from Japan?

PM "The easiest thing would have been to have a hopperful of parts and components, but these days such a thing is no longer conceivable. And so it became necessarily to work very carefully in terms of logistics, since we had to place orders three months in advance in Japan, considering that in any case we had to allow 45 days for shipping by sea. In technical jargon, here is what I would say: try to maintain a sufficiently taut workflow so as not to create gaps in production."

LC What is it like to produce in Italy for a Japanese client?

PM "You need to get used to working with them, but it is much less traumatic than many people think. The Japanese are very sincere, much more straightforward. Unlike many Europeans, they really don't know how to lie. In the factory right now, we have eight out of a staff of over 350."

LC Pininfarina hired 120 new workers for Bairo: how did that go?

PM "Well, though there was a relatively high turnover, about 30 per cent, a fairly typical rate in the Canavese area, and one which we had already seen with the plant at San Giorgio. In the Canavese area, as opposed to the greater Turin area, for instance, even though there is a greater supply of workers, I would say that there is a lesser degree of 'mental' flexibility. There are lots of young men and women looking for jobs, but after you hire them, they make their decisions: they don't want just any job, they are looking for a certain kind of job."

LC When you were a girl, did you think that you would become the supervisor of a car factory?

PM "Absolutely not. My basic nature is that of a wild creature, I love absolute freedom. But when you decide to go to work, you have to give your best. On my own, I would never have thought that a company could understand you and make the best use of you. Moreover, I really liked designing car bodies, which is a complicated but enjoyable job, while I was absolutely indifferent to manufacturing per se. Nowadays, with experience, I have discovered that I really love manufacturing. To be a boss takes the right stuff, but when things are well made, it is a result of

cooperation. With Bairo we started from scratch and what we created, first and foremost, was the daily pleasure of working together as one big team."

LC You 'build' automobiles but you love motorcycles, to the point that you often travel from home to factory—a distance of 112 kilometres—on one of your three motorcycles. What would a motorcycle 'by Pininfarina' be like?

PM "It would be very technological, and therefore with a really great frame, which is the real heart of a motorcycle. And then, since it would be by Pininfarina, with a first-class design."

LC And would you prefer to supervise the design or the production of this motorcycle?

PM "Neither one nor the other. I would transfer over to the testing division, so that I could ride it all day."

LC Plans for the future?

PM "A range of things: from rebuilding yachts in the Caribbean to farming in the Tuscan hills. Or maybe just go on building cars."

Articulated Breda trams, designed by Pininfarina, in service in San Francisco since 1990.

In 1990 Pininfarina Deutschland was founded in Renningen: the company works in the sector of models, equipment, and prototypes for the German automotive industry.

Jean Boillot, general manager of Peugeot, Sergio Pininfarina and Jacques Calvet, president of Peugeot, at the Geneva Motor Show of 1990.

Paolo and Sergio Pininfarina, also in Geneva in 1990.

Giorgia and Sergio
Pininfarina in an audience
with Pope John Paul II
in December 1990.

San Giorgio Canavese:
the assembly lines for the
Rover and MG convertible
top.

On the spectacular terrace
of Forte Belvedere,
overlooking Florence, the
remarkable exhibition 'Idea
Ferrari,' which celebrated
the creativity of the
Modena-born car maker
who died in August 1988,
also offered a concrete and
visible tribute to Pininfarina
and to his technical
and visual contribution to
the creation, from 1952 on,
of the Ferrari legend.

The 60th anniversary of Pininfarina at the Turin Motor Show in April 1990.

The latest version of the Alfa Romeo Spider, an evolution of the Duetto of 1966, presented at Detroit in 1990.

The CNR E2, a prototype derived from the joint research with the Centro Nazionale delle Ricerche, or Italian National Research Council. Eleven years after the formal design done for the CNR, this new exercise on the theme of energy saving was focused on the construction of a mid-sized European five-seater sedan with body in plastics and with Fiat mechanical components: it was hoped to reconcile in practical terms the demands of production, comfort, and safety without exceeding the coefficient of 0.19. An ambitious objective, attained without sacrifice of appearance or style.

Right
The Cisitalia 202 on the occasion of the exhibition 'Grafie Pininfarina' held in Spoleto in May 1990.

Top
On the same occasion, Cesare Romiti with Lorenza Pininfarina, the president of Frau, Franco Moschini, and Fredi Valentini.

Pininfarina converses with Agnelli during a conference organised in May of 1991 by the Associazione dei Cavalieri del Lavoro at the Museo dell'Automobile of Turin.

In the summer of 1991, in a joint initiative of the Department of Architecture of the Polytechnic of Milan and Pininfarina, and with the official patronage of the City of Milan, the exhibition 'Pininfarina, Progetto e Prodotto' was held, exploring in depth Pininfarina's design methods, and examining the entire creative and technical process that leads from an idea to a new product, whether research or for production.

At the Detroit Motor Show in January 1991, Sergio Pininfarina and Lorenzo Ramaciotti presented to the press the research prototype, the General Motors 'Chronos' based on GM mechanical components, in particular from the Opel Lotus Omega, which was then the fastest sedan on Earth. The idea was to pay a concrete homage to collaboration with GM by building an extreme coupé-roadster, capable of synthesizing exceptional performance and excellence of design: a concept well in line with the Pininfarina tradition in the design of high-end sports cars from major manufacturers.

Andrea Pininfarina in Detroit with Mr Macdonald, President of General Motors.

Sergio Pininfarina with the GM Chronos, in a photograph by Peter Vann.

In Detroit in June 1991, at the event 'Eyes on the Classics,' an exhibition was presented on Pininfarina. Sergio Pininfarina was given the 'Lifetime Achievement Award,' established by Chrysler, Ford, and General Motors in 1988. He was the first Italian to receive it. Chuck Jordan of General Motors presented him the prize.

Part of the retrospective organised for that occasion.

In October of 1991 Pininfarina took part in a mission to China organised by Confindustria.

During the mission he had an opportunity to meet the Premier Li Peng.

In December Boris Yeltsin took part in a Confindustria conference.

"To me, Pininfarina represents a successful union between excitement and the aesthetics of the automobile. And there are very few 'car designers' on Earth who manage to obtain this result in their work. It is clear that the first thing that one associates with the name Pininfarina is automobiles, because in this field they were able to create both interesting concept cars and successful production cars. The most recent projects in terms of design are in any case a logical extension of previous work. Pinin Farina understood, in his turn, the importance of keeping faith with his own personal line and to produce it, and this represents a fundamental value as well for the designers of toay," explained Ferdinand Piëch, president of the Volkswagen Group.

LC What car by Pininfarina do you admire most, and why?

FP "It would be wrong to limit the answer to a single car. Certainly, the designs of sports cars that Pininfarina did in the Sixties and the early Seventies had a grandeur all their own."

LC Do you see Pininfarina more as a designer or a limited-edition car maker?

FP "Pininfarina is both those things, and that is the exact reason for such great success. There are certain models produced in small volumes that major manufactures might not always be willing to make in their own plants. Now if the major manufacturer also needs a hand on the design of this niche vehicles, then Pininfarina is one of the first to compete for the job."

LC The Volkswagen Group today has more brands than ever. Why is it that Pininfarina does not work for any of them?

FP "What Pininfarina does for other car makers is truly remarkable. All the same, we at Volkswagen have decided to follow a different path. The design is managed and developed within each of our brand names: since this is a crucial matter, we think it is best to manage it in-house. The reaction of our customer base shows us that we are taking the correct approach."

LC Are there cars designed by Pininfarina for other car makers that you wish you could have had for one of your brands?

FP "Without a doubt, Pininfarina has created cars that have become classics. The nine brands of the Volkswagen Group, in their turn, can of course continue to develop and improve. All the same I believe that, as far as the models are concerned, the individual brands are nicely set up, and in fact I cannot imagine now as we speak a car that is lacking in the Group. Certainly, there are details in the vehicles by Pininfarina that I look on very favourably, and I am sure that they will do well on the general market, enriching the overall heritage of the world of automobiles."

In 1992, Pininfarina Extra developed golf clubs for the Japanese company Mizuno; they possessed excellent aerodynamic characteristics, tested and refined in the Wind Tunnel.

'Egomeeting': a series of easy chairs developed for Poltrona Frau.

A scale model of the Swiss Schindler LOK 2000 locomotive in the Wind Tunnel in the late Eighties.

The locomotive, 20 of which were produced by Schindler, beginning in 1991.

Lorenzo Ramaciotti with a model of the Azimut 65, in 1992, at the Genoa Boat Show.

The Peugeot 106, developed
in 1991 in collaboration
between Peugeot and
Pininfarina.

Top right
The Fiat 500 pickup,
a formal-research prototype
presented at the Turin
Motor Show of 1992.

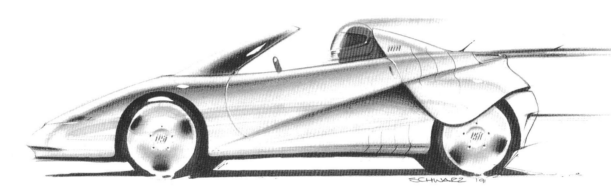

Sketch for the Ethos.

The Ethos 1992: research
prototype, the first in a
series of ecocompatible
concept cars, the Ethos
is a sporty and ecological
Spider, ultralight and
entirely recyclable, full
of innovations beginning
with the Australian Orbital
2-cycle, 3-cylinder, 95hp
engine which made it
possible to approach the
fateful threshold of 'zero
emissions.' Also important
were the new-conception
platform made of extruded
aluminum and the
bodywork, made entirely
of thermoplastic materials.

Grugliasco, 1992:
the assembly lines
of the 512 TR, evolution
of the Ferrari Testarossa
of 1984.

Bottom
Sergio Pininfarina in 1992
at the Club Europe
Argentine in Brussels with
Carlos Menem, President
of Argentina.

At Geneva, in 1992, with
Jacques Calvet, President of
Peugeot.

The same year, with the
Spanish royal family.

Left
Luca di Montezemolo, President of Ferrari, with Sergio Pininfarina, at the presentation of the 456 GT in September 1992 at Brussels.

Right
Press preview for the new Ferrari 456 GT in Brussels in September 1992: in the front row, from left, Lorenzo Ramaciotti, Andrea Pininfarina, Piero Ferrari, Sergio Pininfarina, and Luca di Montezemolo.

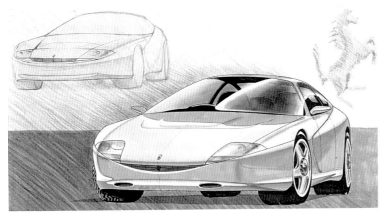

The 456 GT 2+2 Ferrari, heir to a great tradition, returned to the earlier engine, which had been absent since the time of the Daytona. It is a car of timeless beauty, and was named the 'Most Beautiful Car in the World 1993.' The 456 GT joined the Ferrari power with the elegance of a coupé, the spaciousness of the interior and boot with the extreme compactness of the typical volumes of a sporty Berlinetta.

Sergio Pininfarina with his 456 GT in front of the Museo dell'Automobile in Turin in 1993.

"At times, I felt like I was the last surviving Indian, defending the fort from a concentric attack from all the cavalry. And then, looking out of the window, the drifting snow would jerk me back into touch with reality: this wasn't the Wild West, this was Sochaux, the Centre for Research and Development at Peugeot where I was the 'resident engineer' from Pininfarina for the 406 Coupé," recalls Giorgio Astesano, now director of Experimentation and Prototypes at Industrie Pininfarina. "And yet it had been no one but me who wanted to venture into the lion's den. As soon as I took my degree in mechanical engineering at the Polytechnic of Turin, I had received five job offers: from the paper mills Cartiere Burgo, from the Fiat research centre or Centro Ricerche Fiat, from FATA Automation, from Prima Industrie, and from Pininfarina; I opted for Pininfarina because they were offering to send me abroad immediately. At first, I got beat up pretty badly, and then I learned to tailor and edit, to go back to headquarters only with truly important issues. I have to say that, once I got over my initial bewilderment, it was a really interesting experience: from Monday to Thursday, the engineers at Peugeot would bring up problems, and then on Friday I would rush back to Turin to find a way to solve those problems with a truly close-knit and helpful team. They were three very tough years, but it was worth it. The assembly-line 'debut' of the 406 Coupé clearly showed that all of us, every last man jack, had worked our hardest and best."

LC And once you went back to Turin?

GA "I immediately left again, this time heading for Polynesia because I had got married and it was time for our honeymoon. In a routine phone call home to my mother, I discovered that a certain Engineer Bertrandi had called to announce that I had become the director of 'something' that she couldn't exactly remember. On the one hand, I wanted to call the company immediately to find out exactly what I had 'become,' but on the other hand I was far away and on my honeymoon. So I forgot about it, I didn't call Pininfarina, and I enjoyed my honeymoon without thinking too much about what was to come next."

LC And what had changed back at the factory?

GA "An internal reorganisation, The existing division of Standards and Testing had been split in two: Standards became independent, and testing was joined with the division of Prototype Construction. And so, at the age of 29, I found that I had become the chief of the newly founded division of Experimentation and Prototypes, with 30 or 35 people working under me."

LC After Peugeot, you had extensive contact with Honda. What differences are there between French and Japanese engineers?

GA "I would have to say no real differences at all: you are always working with extremely high-level technicians who can teach you a great deal, and that is what I like best about it. The approach has nothing to do with nationality or race, but quite simply the approach. It is important to understand one's own limitations and the limitations of the structures available. To be straightforward and clear always pays off in the end. The rest changes in every case, because there are differences in the client's mindset, the general method and approach, and the manufacturing target for the specific model of car."

LC What does Pininfarina mean to you?

GA "A 'reality-based' company, that not only designs beautiful cars, but also builds beautiful pieces of machinery, often in turn-key projects: exactly what I had been looking for ever since my university days, not just theory, but also a close and continuous contact with everyday reality."

At the ceremony for the awarding of the degree, Italian President Scalfaro spoke.

In January 1993 in Rome, Sergio Pininfarina being awarded an honorary degree in Business and Economics from the LUISS (Libera Università Internazionale degli Studi Sociali).

On 29 October 1993, at the Museo dell'Automobile in Turin, a commemoration of the centenary of Pinin Farina's birth. Among the speakers, from left to right: Amedeo Peyron, President of the Museo dell'Automobile, the architect Vittorio Gregotti, the journalist Paul Frère,

Gianni Agnelli, Sergio Pininfarina, Alessandro Colombo, President of the Associazione Italiana per la Storia dell'Automobile, the journalist Gino Rancati, and Ernesto Caballo, author of the book, 'Pinin Farina, nato con l'automobile.'

315

In the audience, Nuccio Bertone, Cesare Romiti, and Luca di Montezemolo.

In Grugliasco, in 1993, the assembly of the bodyshell for the Peugeot 306 Cabriolet.

Assembly Department

On 31 August 1998 the 50,000th Peugeot 306 Cabriolet was produced.

The awarding of the prize 'Cabrio of the Year' for the 306 Cabriolet, at the Geneva Motor Show of 1998.

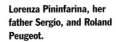

Lorenza Pininfarina, her father Sergio, and Roland Peugeot.

At the Geneva Motor Show of 1995, the third generation, all present and accounted for: Lorenza, Andrea, and Paolo.

The Peugeot 306 Cabriolet, presented at Frankfurt in 1993, won the title of 'Best-Looking Cabriolet of the Year' in 1994.

Ethos and Ethos 2
at the Geneva Motor Show
of 1993.

The streamlined coupé
Ethos 2, second prototype
of the Ethos project,
achieved the excellent
coefficient of 0.19.

The Fiat Coupé at its debut at the Bologna Motor Show of 1993. The collaboration between Pininfarina and Fiat for the construction of this model focused on the design of the interior, the technical development, and the production of the complete car.

Top and centre
The interior of the Fiat Coupé, designed by Pininfarina.

At San Giorgio Canavese in 1999 the remarkable figure of 70,000 cars produced was attained. Thanks to its performance, along with its excellent comfort, high standards of safety, cutting-edge technology, and attractive appearance, the Fiat Coupé won the titles of 'Sportiva dell'Anno 1994' and 'Best Car of 1996.'

In 1994, the Ethos and the Ethos 2 were joined by the Ethos 3, an entirely recyclable sedan, with a low-emission Orbital engine, ideal for use in the city, but not limited to city use, seating six and three driving positions in just 3.24 metres of length.

The year was 1995: on the Pininfarina stand at the Los Angeles Motor Show, Ethos 3 EV made its debut, the latest diversification of the Ethos project. This was the advanced electric version of the Ethos 3, meant for urban and extraurban use, and designed especially for California and its anti-pollution programmes which called for the progressive introduction of zero-emission vehicles (ZEV) beginning in 1998.

The Ethos 3 completed the first research cycle in the 'Ethos Project,' focusing on the optimisation of a family of vehicles with thermal engines.

The Alfa Romeo Spider
and the Alfa Romeo GTV,
at the Paris Motor Show of
1994. They were produced
directly by Pininfarina
beginning in the autumn
of 2000.

The journalist Paolo Frajese
in an Alfa Romeo Spider.

The Fiat 'Spunto,' at the
Turin Motor Show of 1994.
The stylistic research by
Pininfarina on the theme of
the new Fiat Punto resulted
in the construction of this
model, which interpreted
the concept of a hatchback
car for leisure time.

"In effect, for nearly half a century there have been privileged relations between Pininfarina and the car maker Peugeot. The 403, in fact, made its appearance in 1955, and represented the first fruit of an exemplary collaboration that still continues today," explains Jean Martin Folz, president of the PSA Group, Peugeot-Citroën.

LC After the great success of the 403 Berlina, of which more than 1.2 million units were sold, a considerable number for the time, how did relations between Pininfarina and Peugeot—which had in the meanwhile created its own Styling Centre—evolve?

JMF "Beginning with that success, the history of the Peugeot brand was marked by the success of the cabriolets and the coupés, whose design was a product of the genius of the stylists at Pininfarina. The most recent fruit of this collaboration is the Peugeot 406 Coupé which, unquestionably, represents a masterpiece of the art of the automobile."

LC A history of reciprocal satisfaction, then. What should we expect from the new millennium?

JMF "Pininfarina can be proud of the contribution to Peugeot's success, and the company is well aware of how much it owes to its 'Turinese friends.' We shall continue in the future as well to rely on the talent and creativity of their designers in the hope that the upcoming projects that we work on together may generate new triumphs."

On the Ferrari track of Fiorano, the F355 was presented in 1994, the heir to a dynasty that began with the Dino, one of the finest Ferraris ever built. Its performance was even better than its looks: aerodynamics taken to an extreme, leading for the first time to an optimization of the car's 'sixth face,' the bottom of the bodyshell.

The 'Drago' forklift, designed for CESAB, in 1994 won the Golden Compass award from the ADI.

Pininfarina Extra worked on a project for a residential and tourism development on the island of Malta.

At the presentation of the F355, Niki Lauda, Luca di Montezemolo, Sergio Pininfarina, and Antonio Ghini.

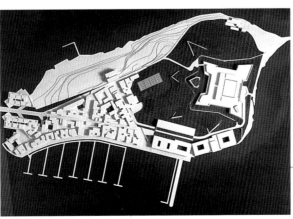

In May of 1995 Renzo Carli died, who with his brother-in-law Sergio Pininfarina had taken the mantle of Pinin and converted a company doing crafts work into an industrial group, excelling in creativity, technical development, and production.

324

The year was 1994: Sergio Pininfarina received from the AISM (Associazione Italiana per gli Studi di Marketing) the 'Guglielmo Tagliacarne' award for the role he played in promoting and sustaining the worldwide prestige of Italian creativity and production. The awards ceremony took place in Milan at the Palazzo dei Giureconsulti.

A sketch of the Ferrari F50
signed by Sergio Pininfarina.

Maranello, spring of 1995:
the Ferrari F50, heir to the
F40, was presented,
a genuine street-legal
Formula One machine, of
which 349 were produced.

Sergio Pininfarina at the
Geneva Motor Show with
the F50, a vehicle that was
radically innovative and
technologically advanced—
in its mechanical,
structural, and functional
solutions. The design of the
F50 emphasised its
technical contents and
underscored Ferrari's
competitive tradition
without betraying the forms
and styling born of the well-
consolidated collaboration
between Ferrari and
Pininfarina.

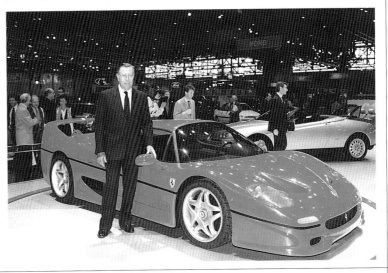

XVII
Premio Compasso d'Oro
ADI

Sergio Pininfarina

**Premio Compasso d'Oro
ADI 1994 alla Carriera**

Comitato Direttivo ADI
Il Presidente:
Augusto Morello

The 'Golden Compass',
another award that Sergio
and Pinin had in common.

premio *la*Rinascente compasso d'oro

per l'estetica del prodotto

Villa d'Este, 28 Settembre 1957

milano via san raffaele 2 telefono 8852

ASSEGNAZIONE GRAN PREMIO NAZIONALE
LA RINASCENTE COMPASSO D'ORO

La Commissione costituita per l'assegnazione
del Gran Premio Nazionale La Rinascente Compasso d'oro,
ha esaminato e discusso le proposte dei singoli Commissari
e, tenuto presente i concetti informatori e le finalità del
premio, ha deciso all'unanimità :

Gran Premio Nazionale La Rinascente Compasso d'oro da
attribuirsi a quella persona o Ente tecnico-industriale le cui
benemerenze nel campo dell'Industrial design sono partico-
larmente riconosciute

assegnato a :

Cavaliere del Lavoro PININ FARINA

LA COMMISSIONE

Aldo Borletti

Giulio Carlo Argan

Misha Black

Tommaso Gallarati Scotti

Johannes Itten

Mario Labò

Ivan Matteo Lombardo

Almost forty years passed
between the award received
by the father, who was
particularly proud of it, and
that of the son.

The Bentley Azure, presented at the Geneva Motor Show of March 1995, was the fruit of a joint effort on the part of Rolls-Royce Motor Cars and Pininfarina.

In particular Pininfarina was entrusted with the job of styling, design, and actually manufacturing the convertible roof: its automatic mechanism, which completely concealed the top under a rigid roof-cover flush with the body, was of particular aesthetic and technical value. Moreover, Pininfarina handled the assembly and painting of the bodywork, as well as the construction and the installation of the convertible top system.

At the Tokyo Motor Show of 1995, alongside the Fiat Coupé, Bentley Azure and the Ferrari F50, the surprising Honda Argento Vivo, a world premiere.

The interior of the formal
and technological research
prototype Argento Vivo:
in this case Pininfarina
focused on wood, which
it used to cover the interior.
Wood is seen as a
fundamental architectural
and design element. There
is a sort of kinship with the
most refined sports boats. A
warm, living material, joined
with other natural
materials, such as leather.

The Argento Vivo was
presented to the
international press at the
Tokyo Motor Show of 1995
by Sergio Pininfarina and

Nabuhiko Kawamoto,
President of Honda. At the
important Japanese event,
Argento Vivo encored the
success enjoyed by the

Ferrari Mythos in 1989,
winning the 'Golden Marker
Trophy' awarded by the
Japanese magazine 'Car
Styling' and the 'Best in

Show' from the American
magazine 'AutoWeek.'

In Turin too the Argento Vivo
aroused great interest.

The Argento Vivo, design for an 'open top' vehicle, represents a significant progress in the Pininfarina culture in this area. Conceived in a year (the first designs date back to September 1994), Argento Vivo represents a refined exercise in style, an image-car that projects its personality into the world of automobiles. With innovative solutions, like that developed for the convertible hardtop, which can slide back automatically and then be housed in a space behind the two seats, leaving the luggage compartment unencumbered. Argento Vivo is an automobile that marries hot Latin passion, a love for sporty aggressive cars, so typical of the Italian tradition, with the rationality of a sophisticated brand like the Honda. All contained in a middle-to-high-class car, with an engine ranging in displacement from two to three litres (the use of aluminium limits weight and avoids reliance on powerful, large-displacement engines) and reduced size (the length is just slightly over 4.2 metres).

Argento Vivo immediately evokes the concept of sporty and technological elegance. There are a few outstanding points of interest, including the return to the two-tone colour scheme, undertaken with a skilful blend of cutting edge fine materials. Aluminium, which with the basic structure constitutes the heart and spine of the new Spider Pininfarina, becomes a fundamental component in the two-tone interplay and in the enlivening of the car's surfaces. The engine and luggage compartments, the roof structure, the air intakes, and the exhaust vents are all made of this material, which calls to mind sporty and competition vehicles of extreme class and, at the same time, offers a sense of solidity, protection, and functional refinement. The rest of of the bodywork, on the other hand, is made of resin painted dark blue, a sort of support into which the aluminium parts are inset.

"The Fiat 1500 Cabriolet by Pininfarina, an automobile of rare beauty, was my dream as a boy. But for my first car I had to settle for a second-hand 1500 Berlina. Even though as a youngster I had to remain 'far' from the cars of Pininfarina, I was much closer to their family: Sergio was a friend of my father, and later a friend of mine, just like Andrea and Lorenza, with whom we were almost the same age. The chances of life later brought us together professionally as well," explained Roberto Testore, managing director of Fiat Auto.

LC In your opinion, is Pininfarina more of a designer or a coachbuilder?

RT "Instinctively, he is first and foremost a designer. When I think of the work of the company, I almost automatically think of the Lancia Beta Montecarlo, a legend for my generation. Then there was the Fiat 124 Spider. Obviously all of the Ferraris, a great family with a strong stylistic identity. Going further back in time, the Fiat 525, the first car built by Pinin as an independent contractor on a Fiat frame, a lively two-tone sport coupé that was to win the Beauty Contest of Rome in 1931. Only later did I encounter Pininfarina as a manufacturer as well, where he carved out a prominent position. In any case, to me Pininfarina means above all, style. Looking at what they have done in the last 70 years, they are by now a name that represents Italy throughout the world, like Gucci, like Ferrari."

LC Many talk of a 'Pininfarina style' that lasts over time and which characterises their design

independently of the manufacturers for whom they were working.

RT "It's true, because Pininfarina is a certain type of taste, a measured aesthetic, very Piedmontese. In their creative production, you will always find a great consistency. There are various cars that represent the different eras in which they were developed, but they never abandon this measured elegance, never anything garish."

LC When you commission Pininfarina to design something, what do you ask for?

RT "I would like them to interpret the product briefing by offering an aesthetic solution that is not obvious. When a manufacturer brings in an outside designer, it must know exactly what it wants. In certain ways, the

creatives, both in-house and external, in the car industry today are a sort of software: their output is in any case a function of the input that the manufacturer has provided. The advantage of Pininfarina as compared to other independent designers is that, having a manufacturing structure as they do, they are always keenly aware of feasibility and production costs.

Good designers are in fact those who present feasible cars, not just ideas that are aesthetically attractive but complicated to industrialise. Moreover, in a market that is increasingly fragmented, it is increasingly difficult to 'invent' something completely new, while the winning solutions are often the product of incremental reasoning, since they develop out of a lengthy confrontation among various and diverse professions and corporate cultures."

LC Let's climb up the tower and toss out two recent cars by Pininfarina: one for the Fiat Group, and one for the competition.

RT "Tossing nice cars from a tower would be a crime. So let's name the cars that I would not like to see falling from the tower. From our company, the Ferrari 360 Modena, because it is diverse but still the product of a certain evolution: the more I see it, the more I like it. From the competition, the Peugeot 406 Coupé, which I like almost as much as the Fiat Coupé."

The Schindler tram went into service in Zurich in 1995 and was designed by Pininfarina.

The Breda tram in service in Boston, also designed by Pininfarina in 1995.

Bottom
At the Geneva Motor Show, the traditional visit of the actor Peter Ustinov.

On the same occasion, Paul Frère, racer and journalist, with Lorenzo Ramaciotti and Christian Philippsen, Belgian journalist.

Pininfarina continued working with Breda for this BMB 321 bus, of 1996.

Twin-current locomotive E402 for the Ferrovie dello Stato Italiane, or Italian Railways, designed in 1996 by Pininfarina for Breda.

'Modulo' briefcase (1996), limited production for Ruspa Leather Goods, design by Pininfarina Extra.

In April 1996 Gianni Agnelli received from the Italian President Scalfaro the 'Leonardo' prize, established by Leonardo, Italian Quality Committee, headed by Sergio Pininfarina from 1993 to 1996.

The Bentley Azure and the Alfa Romeo GTV both received the 'Most Beautiful Car on Earth'. Piero Dorazio delivered the prize, one of his works, to Sergio Pininfarina during the ceremony held at the Milan Triennale in 1996.

332

In 1996 a major exhibition was held in Korea, dedicated to Pininfarina design. The exhibition 'Civilization, City and Car. Pininfarina: from Leonardo to the Future' was housed in two exhibition structures, the Seoul Art Centre and the Sung-kok Art Museum. The exhibition, which explored five themes linked to the world of Pininfarina—the company's history, its present, its research, its diversification, and its legend, in a setting expressly dedicated to the creations of Ferrari and Pininfarina—was intended to acquaint visitors with the work of Pininfarina, its methods and achievements and, at the same time, overcoming the well-known dialectic between the figurative arts and industrial production, demonstrate the complexity of 'automobile design' and its fallout in other sectors of industrial design. The Sung-kok Art Museum set aside 1,200 square metres of exhibition space in a large room dedicated to the English painter Dexter Brown (in the photograph) who painted the most important vehicles by Pininfarina and who has become famous for his distinctive painting technique, which gives its subjects a particular light, colour, and dynamism.

One of the five themes developed by the exhibition: research.

Reproductions of the models for machines by Leonardo da Vinci, from the bicycle to the helicopter, the gearbox, the transmission chain, and the ball bearing—the exhibition in the Arts Centre occupied roughly 5,000 square metres and offered an opportunity to bring the public into contact with an ancient Italian culture and tradition that sank its roots into the model offered by the Renaissance atelier and the aesthetic and scientific research of Leonardo da Vinci.

Leonardo's 'Man,' symbol of the exhibition.

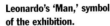

Left
Scale model of the Eta Beta
at the exhibition
'Pininfarina: from Leonardo
to the Future.'

Bottom
The 'concept car' Eta Beta,
further fruit of a joint study
with CNR, in several images
done with CAS (Computer
Aided Styling).

Facing page
Lorenzo Ramaciotti presents
Eta Beta at the Centro
Congressi of the Lingotto,
during the press days of the
Turin Motor Show in 1996.

Giorgetto Giugiaro observes
the new 'concept car,' Eta
Beta, on the Pininfarina
stand at the Turin Motor
Show.

Bottom

Eta Beta is the result of a research project undertaken on behalf of the Italian National Research Council, in the context of the Applied Research Project 'Trasporti 2' and aimed at the creation of a prototype with modulated interior, equipped with a low-emissions dual-power plant, constructed with entirely recyclable light materials and ideally suited for urban use and for medium-range out-of-city travel. The goal of the flexible and modular interior led to an atypical definition of the architecture of Eta Beta. It is possible to extend the rear section of the car telescopically by 200 mm, configuring the car in three versions: urban minicar (2+2 short tail), car for travel outside the city (four-seater, long tail), and long-distance car with luggage compartment (two-seater, long tail). With Eta Beta the tendency to break away from the monolithic concept of the automobile was accentuated: it was through the diversity of form and the surface treatment of the components, the aluminum of the doors, roof, and structure, the mass-dyed thermoplastic resins of the other panels, that we 'read' the car.

In the summer of 1996 the new two-seater 12-cylinder Ferrari GT was presented at Nürburgring: the 550 Maranello. The progress of technology eliminated the need for the centrally mounted engine. The 550 Maranello therefore has a front-mounted engine, an intentional return by Ferrari to a solution that is nowadays capable of offering unquestionable advantages in terms of comfort without any sacrifice in terms of performance.

The mock-up of the interior of the 550 Maranello, in one of the presentation rooms at the Pininfarina Studi and Ricerche in Cambiano.

A prototype, not yet definitive, subjected to aerodynamic testing in the Pininfarina Wind Tunnel.

One of the first sketches of the Maranello. The 550 possesses a capacious and comfortable passenger compartment, as well as ample space for luggage, all factors that allow a broader use of the vehicle. Even getting in and out of the vehicle is incomparably easier than with the Berlinettas it replaced. It enjoyed unprecedented international success precisely because it was a vehicle that blended innovation, functionality, comfort, and exciting performance: a major step forward.

Sergio Pininfarina at the Geneva Motor Show of 1997 with the Ferrari 550 Maranello.

Bottom
Pininfarina approached, with great interest in conceptual and stylistic terms, the theme proposed in 1996 by Fiat Auto for the Turin Motor Show; after the designs for the Cinquecento in 1992 and the Punto in 1994, the stylistic interpretations of Italian designers and coachbuilders were directed toward the Bravo and the Brava. With the goal of being able to treat this theme in broader terms, Pininfarina produced two similar versions of the same concept, the compact minivan (a vehicle type that has proven increasingly popular), but with diverse characterisations: the Sing, presented on the Pininfarina stand, and the Song, displayed on the collective coachbuilders' stand (ANFIA), designed expressly for off-road use.

Beginning from the base of the Lancia K saloon, Pininfarina derived, in collaboration with the Lancia Style Centre, the definition of the style of the estate car version, and then going on to handle the industrialization and complete production in its own factory. The result is an elegant and dynamic vehicle, at the top of the sector of luxury estates, thanks to the engines and mechanical components, the painstaking solutions on the interior and in the luggage compartment, and the aero-acoustic comfort at speed.

Facing page
Sketches of the Peugeot 406 Coupé.

The bodyshell of a prototype of the Peugeot 406 Coupé is subjected to modal analysis in the metrological laboratory of the Industrie Pininfarina.

The thermal chamber, in the experimentation laboratories, makes it possible to simulate the most extreme climatic conditions, to analyse and optimise the behaviour of the vehicle at temperatures ranging from 40 degrees C below zero to 100 degress C above zero, with humidity ranging from 30 per cent to 95 per cent.

338

At the inauguration of the Turin Motor Show of 1996, the presentation of the Lancia K Estate in the presence of the Prime Minister of Italy, Lamberto Dini.

The Peugeot 406 Coupé of 1996: pure elegance. Fruit of the consolidated collaboration between Peugeot and Pininfarina, this model blends the class of a high-end car with stylistic innovation, aesthetic personality, and extreme quality of construction. Designed, developed, and produced by Pininfarina, the 406 Coupé offers excellent performance, safety, comfort, and real driving pleasure. The Peugeot 406 Coupé received many important prizes, for the excellence and quality of its design: 'The Most Beautiful Coupé on Earth 1997,' Milan Triennale, 'Car Design Award 1997,' Turin, 'The Most Beautiful Car of the Year 1998,' Festival of Chamonix.

Sergio Pininfarina with the 406 Coupé, during the road test organised by Peugeot at Aqaba in Jordan in 1997.

In the case of the 406 for the first time since its collaboration with Peugeot began, Pininfarina was asked to take care of the entire construction of the vehicle which, after static and dynamic testing, was sent directly to the sales network of the French car maker.

Pininfarina in October 1997, with his 406 Coupé.

Andrea and Sergio Pininfarina with Jacques Calvet, President of the PSA, at the Paris Motor Show.

In 1998, Pininfarina received the 'Car Design Award' for the Peugeot 406 Coupé. At his side, Fulvio Cinti, editor of 'Auto and Design,' which organized the international award conferred by the specialist publications of the world.

November 1999: the general manager of the PA, Frédéric Saint-Geours, with Sergio Pininfarina celebrating the 50,000th 406 Coupé.

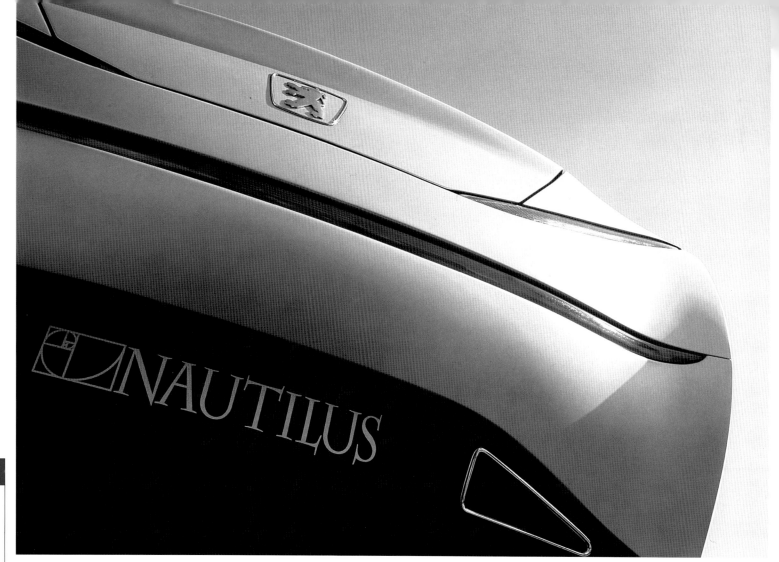

The Nautilus at Geneva in 1997. The car is an exciting study of form that was not to have any further industrial development, but which was meant to interpret in purely stylistic terms the theme of large and high-class sporty sedans.

The basic concept of the cockpit was inspired by the idea of two possible uses: a sports car driven by its owner, or a businessman driven by a chauffeur. For that reason, the ambience enjoyed by the passengers in the front seats is different from that of the passengers in the rear seats. The front area has a sporty connotation and layout, while the rear area tends to emphasise the appearance of the drawing room. The instrument panel too was designed for a dual use: digital for a relaxing drive, analogue for a sportier drive.

Preceding page
In homage to the collaboration with Peugeot, Pininfarina presented at Geneva in 1997 the formal research prototype Nautilus on mechanical components from the French car maker. The Nautilus is a stylistic prototype, a creative interpretation of a large four-seater notchback sedan, which rejected the rigidity of certain models in this class in favour of a dynamic and streamlined silhouette. Sportiness, luxury, and innovation coexist in a car with a lively personality that blended a passion for the Gran Turismo with the natural 'importance' of a status symbol model. This is a design that emphasises lively shapes, with soft features but pronounced corners, so as to endow the whole with force and character: the extended bonnet impresses the car with a sense of power while the front assembly, with the very low air intake, underscores the sportiness of the vehicle, suggested also by the design of the fenders, the small size of the roof, the elongated window surfaces, and the reduced height of the top (just 1.35 metres).

On 28 January 1997 an agreement was signed in Tokyo with Mitsubishi Motors for the production of the Pajero Pinin: Sergio Pininfarina and Hirokazu Nakamura, Andrea Pininfarina and Katsuhisa Sato, Mario Trinchieri and Takemune Kimura all shake hands.

On 18 December 1997 Sergio Pininfarina received in Paris the 'France-Italie' award from the Italian Chamber of Commerce for France: the justification was the long and production collaboration with the French automotive industry, as well as his work as chairman of the Committee

Promoting the Construction of the High-Capacity Rail Link between Paris-Lyons-Turin-Milan-Venice and Trieste. In this picture, Sergio Pininfarina with the Italian ambassador Sergio Vento and the chairman of the Italian Chamber of Commerce for France, Antonio La Gumina.

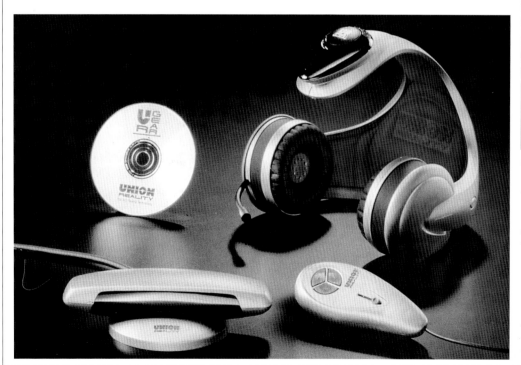

The Urgear designed in 1997 by Pininfarina Extra for Computer Union is a revolutionary product, an interactive helmet transmitter system. The absolutely innovative characteristic is the possibility of operation in a point in three-dimensional space on four axes with extremely high precision; the first application of this technology is in the videogame sector.

The coffee maker designed for Lavazza.

Paolo Pininfarina (1997) with a golf club designed for Mizuno in 1992.

An other project by Pininfarina Extra: the Sirio 2000 telephone for Telecom Italia.

The Ola kitchen designed for Snaidero in 1997.

The 71-foot Magnum Marine, designed in 1997.

Pinin's Légion d'Honneur, 1966.

Sergio Pininfarina, 'Chevalier de la Légion d'Honneur,' in 1978.

Again Sergio Pininfarina, 'Officier de la Légion d'Honneur,' in 1997.

At the awards ceremony in the French Embassy, Sergio Pininfarina with Romano Prodi and Guido Carli.

Pinin Farina received the Légion d'Honneur on 7 March 1966. In the photo, from left, the ambassador Armand Max Berard, Ernesto Carbonato, Franco Martinengo, Pinin, Giorgio Guillaume, and Sergio Pininfarina.

"If you stripped the threads on a bolt, you were in trouble: we had the exact number of pieces—no more, no less—for assembling the factory of the Mitsubishi Pajero Pinin. And even the factory at Bairo Canavese was itself still partly under construction. We were just eight young men, all new hires, with three Group Leaders, and we would build one Pinin every 7-10 days, making do with photo copies of exploded views sent from Japan, assembly plans we had put together ourselves, limited experience because none of us had ever seen the vehicle in question, basic instincts, and often a bit of good luck," Mauro Barbierato remembers with a touch of nostalgia; he was born in 1975, and is now a Team Leader at Bairo Canavese.

LC What does it mean to be a factory worker in the year 2000 and a team leader at the age of 25?

MB "If you experience the eight hours of work every day as nothing more than a way to earn a living, you will certainly feel unstimulated, and you will be bored and listless. If, on the other hand, if—like me—you are excited and passionate about your work, and you think of it not only as work but also as creating 'pieces', then you will also look for solutions, you will dream up the right little tool to do your job in a simpler, easier way. The result is that you feel more relaxed, you work better, and the days goes by in a flash.
Being a 'boss' means that you overcome the difficulties of individual production to move on to a more overall role, a job involving organisation and oversight. In any case, I like to stay in close contact with the assembly line. If I happen to have nothing in particular to do, I like to 'spell' a worker from his cycle and for 6-8 minutes I go back to assembling pieces on the line, so that I do not forget what manual labour is, and to 'break up' the day."

LC How did you happen to wind up at Pininfarina?

MB "When I think about it, I almost feel like laughing: it was my mother's idea! In 1997 I had a permanent job in a machine tool shop just 200 metres from home and, all things considered, I liked my job. My mother, however, would criticise me every time I came home: 'Look at you, you're filthy, find a cleaner job that pays a little more.' I would just let her talk and then one day—on the local television news—I noticed that Pininfarina was about to open a new factory in Bairo Canavese and I decided to apply for a position. Myself, I wasn't too sure about the idea, but I did it so she wouldn't criticise me. And here I am."

LC And yet you decided to leave an open-ended contract in exchange for a contract that ended after just eight months...

MB "That's true, not having a secure job worried me considerably. On the one hand, I would say to myself: 'I am really going to do my best, and so they will want to keep me on,' and on the other hand I wondered if I hadn't been a fool to leave a safe—maybe not wonderful, but safe—job for a job that might have been more interesting but also much riskier. At the end of the second eight-month contract, we decided—along with Ivan Dettore, who was hired on the same day as we had been—to

bring a tray of pastries to the factory to celebrate. We actually hoped that we might be celebrating permanent jobs, but we were also ready to celebrate the end of sixteen wonderful months.... and we all got our wish, including six other 'pioneers' at Bairo, all of us joined in a close-knit group."

LC And so your mother was right to pressure you to go to Pininfarina. Now what does she say?

MB "She continues to consider me the 'baby' of the family. It wasn't until, once the Pinin was on the market, I opened the bonnet and showed her all the mechanical components, faced with that complex welter of parts, wires, and tubes that in those days I was putting together on a daily basis, she changed her mind a little bit, using a typical Piedmontese expression, 'Te nen propi pastisun cume che la pensu mi' (so you're not so clumsy as I used to think).

347

Sergio Pinifarina with Walter Veltroni on the occasion of the 50th anniversary of Ferrari.

In May of 1997 the 50th anniversary of Ferrari was celebrated in Rome. Sergio Pininfarina, with the Italian President Scalfaro, Luca di Montezemolo, and Paolo Cantarella.

In July of 1997 Andrea Pininfarina was elected president of Federmeccanica; in July 2000 he was to become president of the Unione Industriale di Torino.

The 'Grand Princess,' 1998, for the construction of which Pininfarina worked with Fincantieri.

The Derecktor Shipyards catamaran, designed by Pininfarina in 1998.

In Geneva in 1998:
Bernard Cahier, Lorenza
Pininfarina, Peter Ustinov,
and Andrea Pininfarina.

In July 1998 in Paris
the exhibition 'Extradesign.
Pininfarina Design in 20
Objects for Everyday Use'
was inaugurated at the
Italian Chamber of
Commerce in France. In
the photograph, from left
to right, the president of
the Chamber of Commerce
Antonio la Gumina, Sergio
Pininfarina, and Paolo
Pininfarina, managing
director of Pininfarina
Extra.

In June 1998 Andrea
Pininfarina was elected
president of the ITP, Agenzia
per gli Investimenti a Torino
e in Piemonte.

At the Turin Motor Show
of 1998, Sergio Pininfarina
with Michael Schumacher.

Andrea and Sergio
Pininfarina with Rosario
Alessi, president of the ACI.

Sergio Pininfarina with
Norberto Bobbio, at the
inauguration of the State
Archives in Turin in May
1998.

Turin Motor Show, 1998:
the mayor of Turin
Castellani, the Minister
for Industry Pier Luigi
Bersani, the president
of the Piedmont Region
Ghigo and Paolo Cantarella
at the presentation of the
Dardo.

The Alfa Romeo Dardo,
admired by fans.

Left
The corporate advertising
image in 1998.

Tutto è cambiato
ma non il nostro modo di pensare l'automobile.

Fabbrica di idee. Fabbrica di automobili.

Andrea, Lorenza, Paolo, and
Sergio Pininfarina with the
research model of the Alfa
Romeo Dardo.

The Alfa Romeo Dardo on the Lingotto track. A pure formal design, without any prospect of production, the Dardo is a Spider with a powerful impact. The source of inspiration was the Alfa Romeo 156, the new saloon from Alfa Romeo, 'Car of the Year of 1998,' an extremely successful car with an extremely incisive image: the Dardo still represented once again Pininfarina passion's for the automobile as object, a quest for innovative formal expressions, a project that, presented at the 67th International Turin Motor Show, '3rd World Revue of Style,' was an homage to a trademark, Alfa Romeo, that incarnated several of the finest qualities of Italian cars: sportiness, imagination, technology, and performance.

Also in the spirit of the trademark of Alfa Romeo, based on values of competition and technology, the interior of the Dardo was rigorously redesigned, using special fabrics and materials for the dashboard and seats and upholstery in 'metallizzata' leather.

The Everest snowcat, designed by Pininfarina for Prinoth.

The railway sector has become an important one over the years for Pininfarina: here, an Adtranz train.

The watch designed by Pininfarina Extra in 1999 for the G-Shock line of the Japanese Casio company.

The Peugeot 406 saloon, presented at the Geneva Motor Show of 1999: Pininfarina was responsible for its restyling, and worked diligently to preserve the original character of the vehicle.

Ivan Gotti doing tests in the Pininfarina Wind Tunnel.

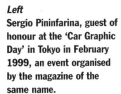

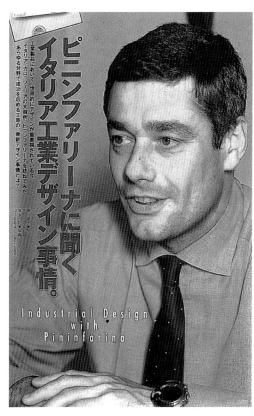

ピニンファリーナに聞くイタリア工業デザイン事情。

Industrial Design
with
Pininfarina

Left
Sergio Pininfarina, guest of honour at the 'Car Graphic Day' in Tokyo in February 1999, an event organised by the magazine of the same name.

Sergio Pininfarina with Paolo Cantarella, managing director of Fiat and Paolo Fresco, president, at the Geneva Motor Show of 1999.

Paolo Pininfarina, on the cover of a major Japanese magazine.

March 1999: the 'Leonardo' prize, awarded by Italian President Scalfaro.

Right
In March 1999, Sergio Pininfarina with Lorenza accepted the 'Leonardo' awarded, conferred by Italian President Oscar Luigi Scalfaro. The Leonardo Committee saw in Sergio Pininfarina an emblem of the finest characteristics of 'Made in Italy,' taken as a harmonious fusion of creativity, tenacity, and high quality.

Ferrari

Style sketches for the Ferrari 360 Modena. The Ferrari 360 Modena marked another major step forward in technological and aesthetic terms. It is significant that the two radiators were positioned in front of the front wheels with the two air intakes separated on either side of the front assembly.

As far as the rear assembly is concerned, an innovative solution was adopted, with the inclined rear window merging directly with the surfaces of the bodywork, allowing an aerodynamic improvement. Of particular importance was the decision to make the engine visible from the exterior through the rear window, highlighting its aesthetic content and enhancing its importance in a car with such extreme performance.

Aside from the improvements in aerodynamic efficiency and the increase in the capacity of the trunk, notable in a car with a centrally mounted engine technical and functional progress had translated into a shape that was innovative when compared to the classic shape of the Ferrari with a central air intake: the two separate air intakes had been seen on Formula One 1500 Ferraris and on the sports cars of the Sixties, and nowadays this layout was being adopted once again as a result of significant progress in aerodynamics.

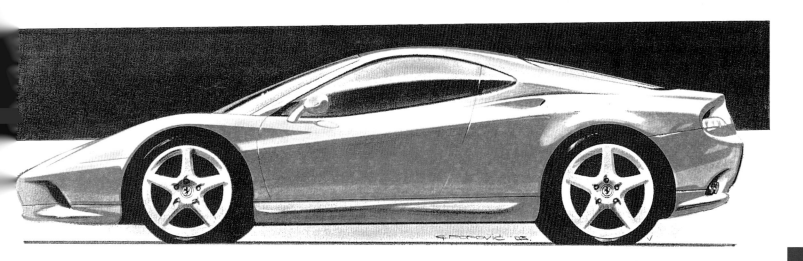

Sergio Pininfarina with the Ferrari 360 Modena at the Geneva Motor Show 1999. The Pininfarina company has been designing since 1952 for Ferrari: with the 360 Modena, there have been 163 models developed from this collaboration, ranging from cars initially built for individual customers and for racing, to later models for mass-production, to research prototypes built from the Sixties on.

The Ferrari 360 Modena, presented to the public in Geneva in 1999, heir to the F355, was the outcome of innovative technical foundations that immediately communicate through the car's appearance, qualities of performance and power, lightness, compactness, and safety, in the tradition of pure Ferrari personality.

Special attention was devoted to the construction of the interior with innovation in the sporty Ferrari tradition, but also with a level of comfort and ergonomics never before seen.

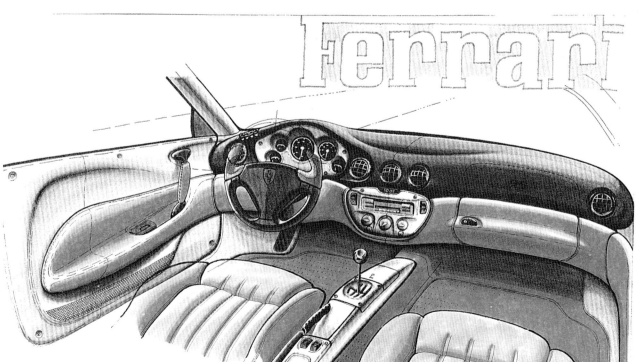

At the Frankfurt Motor Show of 1999, alongside the Ferrari 360 Modena and the Pajero Pinin the Fiat research prototype Wish was also presented. Built by Pininfarina to commemorate the Centenary of Fiat, the Wish was a study for a 2+2-convertible capable of being transformed in a few seconds from Cabriolet to Coupé and back through a refined electro-hydraulic system that tucked the roof away into the upper section of the boot.

The Wish was built on the mechanical components of the Fiat Punto, a 'young' and charming car that unites technological content, innovation, and technical quality.

At the Frankfurt Motor Show, Lorenza Pininfarina operating the electric/hydraulic mechanism of the Wish that automatically and in a few seconds allows the car to be transformed from Coupé to Cabriolet and vice versa.

"It would have been easy for us to simply import the Japanese version of the Pajero Pinin to Europe. Instead, we decided to team up with Pininfarina, recognising their ability and competence in industrialisation and production. The outcome is to have achieved an innovative product combining the background of the Pajero with a touch of Pininfarina in design and production" explains *Katsuhiko Kawasoe, chairman of Mitsubishi Motors Corporation in 1999.*

358

LC What made you choose Pininfarina as your production partner?

KK "Jokingly I could say that it is like asking a husband what made him choose his wife: he simply fell in love with her. More precisely, Pininfarina's business discussions fascinated us: this is not a typical supplier-client approach, rather a true partnership relationship aiming to create an advantageous situation on both sides, or what the Americans would call a 'win-win.'"

LC What does producing in Italy mean for Mitsubushi?

KK "The new plant in Bairo Canavese strengthens our presence in Europe along with the Carisma and Space Star which we produce in Holland. With the Pajero Pinin we become the first company to introduce the GDI direct injection petrol engine technology to Europe even among the Sport Utility Vehicles, making it our third victory after having introduced this new technology with the Carisma in the automobile category and with the Space Star in the MPV category. By manufacturing in Italy, apart from a wider range of products on offer, we have extended our group of traders by using 60 European component suppliers who guarantee three quarters of this new vehicle. Finally, a touch of luck would not go amiss: by using the name Pinin, which is so important to Italy, we are hoping it will help us be successful all over Europe".

LC Pininfarina is renowned worldwide for his talent in design. Mitsubishi seems only to be attracted to the productive aspects...

KK "I am very pleased with the industrial relationship with Pininfarina. Sergio-san is an extremely dedicated man and is enthusiastic about the collaboration with Mitsubishi. We have started getting to know each other for the production aspects and the rest will surely follow, including design. At present, there are no definite ideas although we are already thinking about and discussing what design could be used for Europe. Moreover, as we have several new categories of innovative vehicles in mind, which we call the 'past-sedan', or rather the future 'beyond' the sedan, we are certain that Pininfarina's contrast, support and experience can only help us take the route, among the many, which will lead us in the right direction".

The three Mitsubishi Pajero Pinins shown at Geneva—two on the Mitsubishi stand (left) and one on the Pininfarina stand (bottom)—were stylistic interpretations by Pininfarina of the new compact Sport Utility Vehicle from Mitsubishi Motors, and they develop different elaborations on this type of vehicle, with particular emphasis on sportiness and comfort. The three vehicles are bellwethers of the agreement to collaborate signed by Mitsubishi and Pininfarina in Tokyo in January 1997, calling for the industrialisation and production by Pininfarina of the new compact SUV destined for the European market, with commercialisation on the European markets beginning in Autumn 1999.

Sergio Pininfarina with Tatsuhiko Yokoyama, president of Mitsubishi Sales Europe in 1999, at the press presentation on the Mitsubishi stand at the Geneva Motor Show.

Pininfarina with the president of the Mitsubishi Motors Corporation, Katsuhiko Kawasoe, and of Mitsubishi Sales Europe Tatsuhiko Yokoyama in July 1999, at the inauguration of the factory at Bairo.

Top left and bottom
The factory at Bairo, dedicated to the production of the Mitsubishi Pajero Pinin. In particular, the SUV was assembled and painted in the plant of the Industrie Pininfarina at Grugliasco while the operations of assembly, finishing, and testing were undertaken in the new plant at Bairo Canavese, specially built. Then the vehicles were sent by Pininfarina directly to the European distribution network of Mitsubishi. The vehicle's mechanical components were built in Japan while the body components—exterior, interior, and hardware— were built entirely by Italian suppliers. Beginning in Autumn 2000 Pininfarina would also build the five-door version of the Pinin.

With the decision by Mitsubishi Motors Corporation to produce in Italy the new car in the popular Pajero series meant for the European market, a clear reward was given to Pininfarina's commitment both as a global partner for car makers and as a supplier of specific knowledge services through each individual phase in the process of developing and producing a new product, from design to technological development and industrialisation, right up to production. The role that Pininfarina was asked to play in the context of the industrial agreement with Mitsubishi confirmed the company's excellence in the ratio of quality-costs-service offered both in the context of production and in the areas of design and creativity.

Showgirl Ellen Hidding, was godmother to the first Mitsubishi Pajero Pinin to come off the assembly lines of the factory at Bairo. Present, from left to right, were Hirokazu Nakamura, Katsuhiko Kawasoe, and Sergio and Andrea Pininfarina.

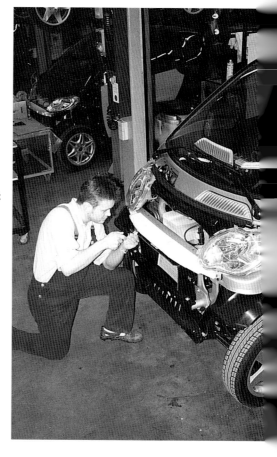

The factory of Pininfarina Deutschland in Renningen, near Stuttgart.

A chapter all its own, the Smart: Pininfarina Deutschland, a company of the Pininfarina group operating since 1990 in Germany in the sector of modelling, prototypes, and equipment, built the prototypes for the Smart in 1994 (right) and in 1999 the prototypes for the Smart Cabriolet (left).

Visiting Beijing, with the Chinese deputy premier Wu Bang Guo, in June of 1999. The visit to China was linked to the project of the Minivan Songhuajiang

Zhongyi, designed and developed by Pininfarina for the Chinese company Hafei Industrial Group Corporation.

The top executives of the Chinese company Hafei Industrial Group Corporation with Giorgia and Sergio Pininfarina.

松花江中意

SONGHUAJIANG the van to my liking

Italian/Chinese collaboration gave origin, as a first step, to the new Songhuajiang Zhongyi Minivan, with a task force made up of engineers and technicians from Pininfarina in China assisting in the industrialisation phase for the vehicle. The fruit of this joint effort made its debut on 3 June at the Beijing Motor Show during a press conference on the Hafei stand; the vehicle was a new Minivan, or better, an MPV, with Suzuki chassis and mechanical components and equipped with one of two types of engine (970 cc and 1051 cc, gas-powered, 4 cylinders) installed beneath the front seats. The car was produced in China, where it went on sale beginning in August 1999, with roughly 100,000 units a year. Pininfarina contributed to the birth of the new vehicle, offering its own know-how in terms of style, design, construction of master model and prototypes, and industrialisation.

For the centenary of the Fiat company, the coachbuilders' group of ANFIA (Associazione Nazionale fra Industrie Automobilistiche) organised the exhibition '70 Capolavori per la Fiat' or 'Seventy Masterpieces for Fiat' in Piazza Carignano (right) and Piazza Carlo Alberto. At the inauguration (top) on 10 July 1999, Piero Fusaro, president of ANFIA, Franco Mantegazza, president of the Gruppo Carrozzieri, and Lorenza Pininfarina, vice president of the taskforce that organized the exhibition. Also present were the top executives of Fiat—Agnelli, Cantarella and Testore, among others—and representatives of the most important local institutions (top right): the mayor of Turin Castellani, the deputy mayor Carpanini, the president of the Region of Piedmont Ghigo, and leading officers of the police department Moscatelli and Izzo, and the provincial commander of the Carabinieri Del Sette.

Bottom
Sergio Pininfarina with the general manager of Cadillac John Smith, at the 'Concorso Italiano' in Carmel, California, where in August 1999 the collaboration between Cadillac and Pininfarina was celebrated.

At the 'Concorso Italiano' many research and production vehicles were shown, fruit of the collaboration with General Motors and Cadillac, beginning in 1931. Among them, the Cadillac 'Jacqueline' of 1961.

One of the scale models developed for the 'Antarctica Project,' developed by Pininfarina Extra, during testing in the Wind Tunnel. The architectural module will be placed in Antarctica during the course of the year 2000, in Livingstone, where it will remain as an integral part of the Spanish scientific base.

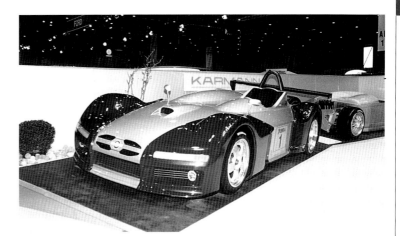

At the 69th Geneva Motor Show EUROC was presented, the project for racing cars undertaken at the behest of the company of the same name (European Roadster Championship). The new single-seater Barchetta developed out of the idea of creating a championship for cars with front-mounted 8-cylinder engines, open to all those who wished to privately race their cars with equivalent chassis. The car was presented in Geneva with a neutral front assembly that could be personalised according to the engine selected by the individual driver. Pininfarina was responsible for the car's exterior style and collaborated on its production with various technical partners: BBS (wheels), Bosch (electronics), Dallara (design and production), Dekra Automobil (overhauls), Karmann—in whose stand the car was displayed—(chassis technology) and Michelin (tyres).

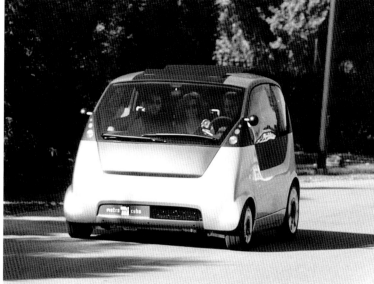

Metrocubo represents a different and up-to-date response—as compared with the Ethos and Eta Beta projects—to the theme of eco-compatible urban cars. The challenge to be met here was to increase the compactness and intelligence of the architecture, reducing the bulk and increasing interior volume. The opportunity was offered by a technology developed by Michelin, the Pax System tyre: a new development with so much potential that it might make it possible to revolutionise the very architecture of cars.

The possibility of eliminating the spare tyre, to use different diameter wheels front and back, capable of housing mechanical parts, made it possible to obtain a totally flat chassis, which could be used in an optimal exploitation of spaces. The mode of access was differentiated: a sliding door on the driver's side which offered no lateral bulk, a large rotating door on the passenger side, a large rear hatch with parallelogram aperture and limited bulk which, given the flat configuration of the platform, could be used effectively also as a third entry door.

From the sketch of the Metrocubo it is evident that, with a length of just 2.58 metres (and a width of 1.78 metres), maximum comfort and flexibility were obtained. At first, a line of three seats had been planned, the driver's seat with the other two set slightly back. The possibility of adding a fourth and fifth rear seat in a transverse position made it possible to attain a complete modularity.

Sergio Pininfarina presenting Metrocubo to the international press, invited on 7 October 1999 to Pininfarina Studi and Ricerche for a dynamic test of the vehicle, equipped with hybrid parallel engines.

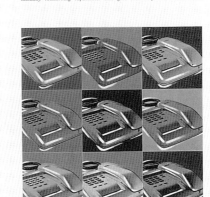

Artist Objects.

The new advertising campaign showed, for the first time, items extraneous to the world of cars.

The Metrocubo prototype in the new advertising campaign.

Artist Autos.

At the Tokyo Motor Show, Metrocubo was presented, not just by Pininfarina, but also on the Michelin stand.

Presented in a world premiere at the Frankfurt Motor Show, the Metrocubo is the fruit of the joint efforts of a team of technical partners: beginning with Michelin, and including Lombardini, which supplied the compact motor-and-generator assembly, set in the front in a block with the alternator built by Vickers. The energy is stored in a group of absorbed lead batteries supplied by Exide Europe, which also oversaw the packaging and management of the batteries themselves. The electric traction system mounted longitudinally in the centre of the car was developed and

manufactured by Siemens AG. The cockpit was enclosed within large glazed-in surfaces—the polycarbonate for the windows was supplied by Isoclima Aerospace—while the lamellar sunroof built by Webasto (which also supplied the heater for the cockpit) is largely transparent. The light-alloy wheels, arranged at the four corners, were built by BBS. Valeo contributed the elliptical technology headlights, and lastly Technogel ensured, in the construction of the seats, optimal seating comfort.

On 27 January 2000, in the presence of the mayors of Turin, Valentino Castellani, and Grugliasco, Mariano Turigliatto, the Via Lesna in Grugliasco (where the Industria Pininfarina has its offices, the Technical Centre, and the assembly and painting lines for all of its products) changed its name, and was dedicated to the founder of the company, Battista Pininfarina, just 42 years after the move of the historic headquarters of Pininfarina from Turin to Grugliasco.

On the following page, middle and bottom
The Ferrari 360 Spider on the Pininfarina stand: this advanced Spider combined the refined technological functionality of the convertible roof mechanism, along with the comfort and superior ergonomics of the interior, with the sportiness, power, and lightness peculiar to the purest personality of the Ferrari brand. In terms of the design, note the soft lines enlivened by the dihedral silhouette of the flank; the two rear fairings with rollbars fit onto two barely hinted fins that serve to support the convertible roof, creating a central volume that joins with the rear wings, a further element of dynamism along the side. The interior features in the rear a series of modifications due to the presence of the rollbars. Moreover, with the decision to obtain continuity of treatment in terms of both colour and materials between engine compartment and interior of the vehicle, it was decided to hark back to an element once typical of the Barchetta.

Niki Lauda, Sergio Pininfarina and Luca di Montezemolo with the Ferrari 360 Spider at the world debut in Geneva on the Ferrari stand.

The 360 Spider on the Pinifarina stand in Geneva.

In March, at Geneva, Luca di Montezemolo and Sergio Pininfarina presented the Ferrari 360 Spider.

The Ferrari 360 Spider designed by Pininfarina arrives exactly one year after the Berlinetta 360 Modena, a model that enjoyed enormous acclaim from the press and media and popularity with the consuming public, both because of its design and its advanced technical characteristics. The 360 Spider was presented as the fastest and most powerful open-top vehicle ever produced by Ferrari, a two-seater Gran Turismo with elevated technological contents. Made entirely of aluminum, it is the first convertible with a rear/centrally-mounted engine, equipped with an automatic roof that vanished completely into a space integrated flush into the bodywork. Of particular importance was the decision to make the motor visible from the exterior on the Spider as well, thus enhancing the aesthetic content and emphasising its essential importance in such an extremely high-performance car.

At the 70th International Geneva Motor Show Pininfarina celebrated its 70 years in business and presented vehicles that testified to its ability to collaborate with car makers in an articulated manner. From left: the Songhuajiang Zhongyi by the Chinese company Hafei Industrial Group Corporation: the van is currently being built in China at the rate of about 100,000 units per year. Next is the Daewoo Tacuma, designed by Pininfarina, and then the Peugeot 406 Coupé 'Pininfarina 70 Years,' a one-off, a creative interpretation built especially for the occasion.

Sergio and Andrea Pininfarina with Roberto Testore, managing director of Fiat Auto, at the Geneva Motor Show 2000.

The relationship with Breda-Menarinibus produced in 2000 the Zeus-M200 E, presented on 3 February 2000: the first bus with wholly electric traction, and small in size. Its name came from the initials of the four words that described the engineering solution: Zero Emissions Urban System.

Another view of the
Pininfarina stand at the
Geneva Motor Show, the
Mitsubishi Pajero Pinin, the
Fiat Coupé, and the Peugeot
306 Cabriolet represented
the various forms of
collaboration in the field of
design and production with
car makers, while

Metrocubo represented
Pininfarina's vocation for
research.

Geneva 2000: Sergio
Pininfarina with the
President of Hafei, Xuewen
Cui, in front of the
Songhuajiang Zhongyi.

The Tacuma, designed by
Pininfarina for the Korean
car maker Daewoo.

Pininfarina officially celebrated its 70 years in business at the Turin Motor Show of 2000. The company history was presented with seven iconographic canvases, one per decade, and seven historic vehicles. The present and the future were represented with research, design, and production vehicles and the formal research prototype, the Ferrari 'Rossa,' making its worldwide debut.

Three moments in the Pininfarina press conference at the Conference Centre of Lingotto: Sergio and Andrea Pininfarina presenting the 'Rossa,' with Lorenzo Ramaciotti.

Following page, top
The front assembly of the 'Rossa' integrates the classic Ferrari radiator grille, with its rounded trapezoid shape, with two pronounced side air intakes which conduct air to the brakes and the engine compartment. Although they have entirely different functions and forms, we find three elements of the latest generation of Ferrari with the same general layout. However, the surfaces in which these apertures appear have a strong character: the central part of the front assembly extends forward, while the air intakes are set further back, inscribed within the natural perimeter of the vehicle.

Sergio Pininfarina and Luca di Montezemolo unveil the 'Rossa' before the international press. Great excitement for a prototype that interprets and develops several of the outstanding themes of the working relationship between Ferrari and Pininfarina, a prototype which constitutes proof of how a homogeneous and innovative vision of an old theme—the two-seater Spider with a front-mounted engine—might evolve in the third millennium.

Lorenzo Ramaciotti, general manager of Pininfarina Studi e Ricerche, in the 'Rossa.'

During the inauguration of the Turin Motor Show, the press collects around the 'Rossa.'

Sergio Pininfarina presents the 'Rossa' to the Minister for Public Works, Nerio Nesi, the mayor of Turin Valentino Castellani, and the president of the Province of Turin, Mercedes Bresso.

The 'Rossa' left the upper part of the engine uncovered to keep the length of the engine compartment from draining tension from the whole. The engine, thus emphasised, was not mere decoration: it made it possible to keep the line of the bonnet much lower and to obtain that magical equilibrium of those sports cars with much higher wings, which wind up framing the bonnet.

The interior of the 'Rossa,' a cockpit carved out of the flow of the lines that characterise the body of the vehicle, does not interrupt the dynamic quality of the exterior. The engine compartment, bent by the windscreen, drops down to become the dashboard, accommodating in its climb back up the backrests which then harmoniously

transform it into the boot. The door panel is also largely the colour of the car, padded only in the passenger area. The gear stick stands on the central console in contrast with the dominant red.

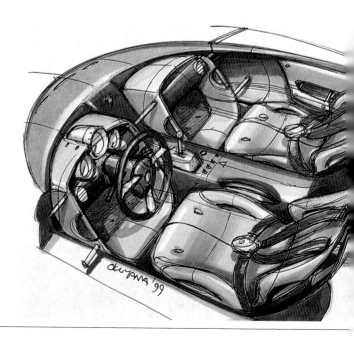

The ridge of the wing tapers toward the cockpit generating the base of the small side window. A solid and fluid cross-section, which is counterbalanced by the hollow of the front wing, so inset that it is little more than an external sheath for the engine compartment. This subtle equilibrium between empty and solid is broken by the rib that rises from the sill to crown the front wheel: a quotation in contemporary terms of one of the outstanding features of the 1958 Testarossa.

In the side of the 'Rossa' we find, once again, the theme of soft surfaces bounded by sharp corners. The glasswork is an element that completes the whole, where the only break is represented by the two rollbars.

An equilibrium of solids and voids in the tail of the 'Rossa,' which repeats the dominant graphic themes of the front assembly. The mouth of the radiator grille here becomes a bas-relief housing the registration plate; the two lateral air intakes are transformed into housings from which the dual exhaust pipes emerge. There is, instead, a sharp counterpoint in the running lights: in the front, a mere stroke on the ridge of the wing, in the back, a double inset. The two pronounced rollbars are linked by a transverse wing with a dual function: one is a matter of visible impact, since it contains the LED lights of the third brake light, the other purely of service, since it houses two TV cameras. One of these cameras takes the place of the rear view mirrors, the other, which focuses on the interior of the cockpit, transmits an image of the driver.

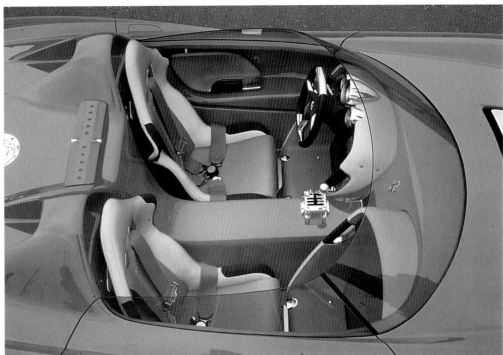

A two-seater Spider with Ferrari mechanical components is a perfect foundation on which to link with an imaginary thread the past of Pininfarina to its future. The 'Rossa,' in fact, interprets and evolves several of the more powerful themes of the long collaboration between Ferrari and Pininfarina: in particular, the racing Spiders of the Fifties and the concept car Mythos of 1989. The mechanical components are those of the 550 Maranello, unchanged in wheelbase and wheel span as well. The formal interpretation, on the other hand, is entirely free, in the best tradition of that pure Pininfarina research that has produced many concept cars on a Ferrari base that time has recognised as masterpieces: the Dino Berlinetta Speciale, the P5, the 512S, the Modulo, and the Pinin, to name only five.

The Peugeot 406 Coupé 'Pininfarina 70 anni,' presented in March at the Geneva Motor Show, as a special creative interpretation, became a manufacturing reality at the Turin Motor Show. The version was to be marketed beginning in October of 2000 in a limited and numbered series which will be equipped with the new V-6, 3-l, 210 hp engine.

Special exterior and interior to underscore the refinement and exclusivity of a vehicle whose original purity and equilibrium of line was intentionally kept unchanged, for a timeless beauty.

The No. 0001 of the special series '70 anni Pininfarina' will be Sergio Pininfarina's personal car.

Pininfarina celebrated its first 70 years with the 'Rossa' and with an international forum entitled 'Sulle Strade del Futuro,' or 'On the Roads of the Future.' The event offered an opportunity to hear analyses and strategies concerning themes of current interest from some of the world's leading experts in the automotive sector: Paolo Cantarella, managing director of Fiat SPA and chairman of Fiat Auto, Luca di Montezemolo, chairman and managing director of Ferrari, Robert Peugeot, director of the sector of Innovation and Quality PSA Peugeot-Citroën, and Max Mosley, president of the FIA (Federazione Internazionale dell'Automobile), with Ernesto Auci, director of the Italian business paper 'Sole 24 Ore,' serving as moderator for the round-table discussion, Derrick de Kerckhove, Canadian futurologist, Massimo Ponzellini, vice president of the BEI, Sergio Pininfarina, and Alfredo Cazzola, president of Promotor International.

...rgio Pininfarina ...ncluding the discussions ...the forum: from left ...right, Robert Peugeot, ...ca di Montezemolo, Paolo ...ntarella, Ernesto Auci, ...fredo Cazzola, Max ...osley, Massimo Ponzellini, ...d Derrick de Kerckhove.

The exhibition dedicated to Pininfarina designs, from the automobile to objects for everyday use, by Pininfarina Extra at the Milan Triennale, June 2000.

Appendices

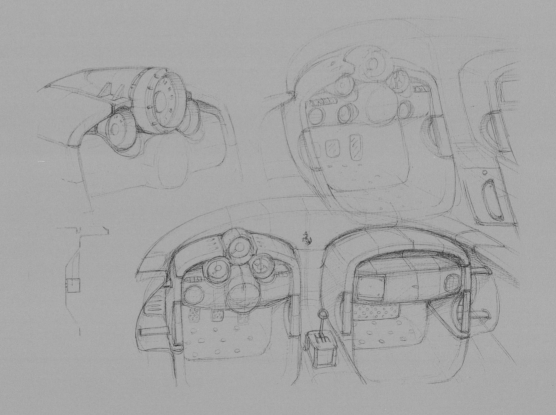

BIBLIOGRAPHY

"L'auto italiana", November 1929, January 1930, June 1930

Balestra N., *Intensamente Cisitalia*, Associazione Italiana per la Storia dell'Automobile, Museo dell'Automobile Carlo Biscaretti di Ruffia, Turin s.d.

Bellucci A., *L'automobile italiana (1918-1943)*, Laterza, Rome 1984

Bernabò F., Rancati G., in Alfieri B. (by), *Catalogue Raisonné Pininfarina*, Automobilia, Milan, 1990

Bessi R., in Morandini M. (by), *L'auto e il cinema*, Edizioni Alfa Romeo, Arese 1985

Bosoni G., Nulli A., *La storia del disegno industriale 1919-1990*, in Castelnuovo E. (by), *Il dominio del design 1919-1990*, vol. III, Electa, Milan 1991

Bossaglia R., *Il Futurismo e l'automobile*, Associazione Italiana per la Storia dell'Automobile, Museo dell'Automobile Carlo Biscaretti di Ruffia, Turin 1998

Branzi A. (by), *Il design italiano 1964-1990*, Electa, Milan 1996

Caballo E., *Pininfarina. Nato con l'automobile*, Palazzi, Milan 1968

Carugati D., in "Intervista", n. 14, July-August 1998

Ciferri L., in Morello A., *Sergio Pininfarina*, ADI, Milan 1985

De Rosa G., *Alfa Romeo Giulietta Spider*, Giorgio Nada, Milan 1994

Felicioli R.P., *Sergio Pininfarina. Car man*, Automobilia, Milan 1998

Felicioli R.P., Ramaciotti L., *Pininfarina Ferrari 50 Figurini/Renderings/Esquisses*, Automobilia, Milan 1997

Grandori L., *Un sogno su quattro ruote*, Rizzoli, Milan 1990

Madaro G., *Alfa Romeo Duetto*, Giorgio Nada, Milan 1990

Morandini M. (by), *L'auto e il cinema*, Edizioni Alfa Romeo, Arese 1985

Morello A., *Sergio Pininfarina*, ADI, Milan 1995

Pininfarina, Sessant'anni, Edizioni Pininfarina, Turin 1990

Ramaciotti L., *Solitaires*, Automobilia, Milan 1989

Ramaciotti L., Alfieri B., *Mythos*, Automobilia, Milan 1989

Rogliatti G., *Ferrari & Pininfarina*, A.T. Anselmi, Turin 1987

Segoni R., *La carrozzeria Pininfarina vista da...*, Associazione Italiana per la Storia dell'Automobile, Museo dell'Automobile Carlo Biscaretti di Ruffia, Turin 1997

Tambini M., *Il look del secolo*, Mondadori, Milan 1997

Thomas P.-Y., *Armonia innovatrice*, in Alfieri B. (by) *Catalogue Raisonné Pininfarina*, Automobilia, Milan, 1990.

INDEX

ACKNOWLEDGEMENTS

The publisher would like to thank the Historical Office of the Communications Division of Pininfarina, Grugliasc

Archives:
Alfa Romeo, Antoine Prunet, Autocar, Bernard Cahier, Bertone, Breda MenariniBus, Cadillac, Daewoo, Dolci Advertising S.r.l., Fantinel, Favìa Del Core, Fiat, Ferrari, Gianni Rogliatti, Lancia, Mazzonis, M.G., Millanta, Mitzubishi, Peugeot, Pininfarina, Rolls Royce, Rover, Sergio Pininfarina, Smart.

Photographers: Alberto Martinez, Paris; Angelo Guerra; Annie Liebowitz; Antinea Press – Cavassi; Antonia Mulas © 1999, Milan; Bertazzini, Turin; Biondo; Bricarelli; Cappello; Cedomir V. Komljenovic; Chiesa Emilio; Fulvio De Luca; Doumic Philippe; Enzo Isaia, Turin; Foto Attualità; Foto Dori; Foto Italia; Foto R6; Foto RG, Turin; Foto Terreni; Foto Torazza, Turin; Foto Valtorta, Montecatini Terme; Fototecnica Amerio; Fumagalli; G Photographic; Garschagen Walter; Giancolombo, Milan; Giorgio Bellia, Turin; Italfoto; Jean Loup Sieff; Jo Bilbao; Julius Weitmann, Stoccarda; La Fotocinetecnica; Lapresse; Light Photofilm; M. Giuliani Marchion; Mauri; Moisio, Turin; Moncalvo fotografie, Turin; Morreau; New Press Service; Novafoto; Olaf; Oteri; P. Lecrêque, Paris; Paolo Pellion di Persano; Paolo Romani ; Peiré; Perini; Peter C. Coltrin; Peter Vann; Publifoto, Turin; Remo Pecorara, Turin; Renzo Muratori, Turin; Riflessi Foto; Rodolfo Mailander, Rome; Rotofoto; Sautelet; Stefano Mu, Turin; Studio cigi 1; Terreni; Torazza; Ugo Mulas © 1999, Milan; Zabban.

Photographic material was also supplied by:
AFE, Archivio Storico del Cinema, Rome; Archivio E. Castruccio, Milan; Farabolafoto, Milan.

Printed and bound in Italy
by Poligrafiche Bolis, Bergamo.